Presented to

_____

By

_____

On the Occasion of

_____

Date

_____

DAILY WISDOM
FOR THE
WORKPLACE

Practical On-the-Job Insight
from Scripture

We work so much of our daily lives that it would be foolish to think God doesn't care about our nine-to-five moments (or whatever hours we spend on the job). No faithful Christian can put work life in one box and spiritual commitment in another. Many of our most challenging faith moments come on the job, when we must choose between what we know is right and what the world expects.

But Christians can be successful in their faith and work. The work world is part of God's world, and He can rule over it—if we allow Him to. To bridge the gap between faith and the world is why this volume came into being.

I have included short prayers, which may be prayed word for word, if desired. But as always in any devotional, these are meant more to give ideas for prayer than to dictate anyone's praying. Speaking to God is a highly personal thing, and every reader should feel free to pray as the Spirit leads, especially on subjects that come to mind during the devotional reading.

May these meditations be a blessing for your entire life, on the job or off.

There is no new thing under the sun.
ECCLESIASTES 1:9

What does this verse mean? Isn't this the *New* Year? Don't we get a fresh start every January 1? Yes, all that is true, but any new year isn't entirely new. It's another 365 days we can fill with good acts or bad plans; but it's still a year, like the last one, made up of days, weeks, and months.

That same-old, same-old quality may be good. What if every year we had to do everything in a new way? What if our old, effective methods had to be tossed out because they were old? Every new year would be a disaster. There's good in some old things.

However, spiritually and emotionally, we often become stuck in nasty, old things we'd like to escape but can't. We have no power to make ourselves over entirely. But God can make us fresh by giving us new life in Jesus. He can do that because He isn't "under the sun," earthbound, He's God! Ask Him to make your life new, and He will. Simply give Him your new year, and let Him show you how you can live it best.

A new year lived in Jesus *is* really new.

Thank You, Lord,
for all the old things in life that work well.
But thanks even more for the new life
that makes them new to me each day.

Therefore I say unto you, Take no thought for your life,
what ye shall eat, or what ye shall drink;
nor yet for your body, what ye shall put on.
Is not the life more than meat, and the body than raiment?

MATTHEW 6:25

It's back to work. You're ready to charge into it, serving Jesus. But where do you start?

As you read this verse, confusion may fill you. *What should I do?* you may wonder. *Does God expect me to sit out on the street begging? Should I refuse to pay the rent and to send my kids to school?*

No, that's not what Jesus was saying. He wasn't trying to create street people. He was telling the disciples they didn't have to worry about their basic physical needs. God knew what they required and was ready to provide. They could depend on Him, while they learned from Jesus and preached the gospel.

You may not stand on a street corner and preach the good news, but God wants to care for you, too. He will *always* provide. So work for your employer as if God really is in control, because, when it comes down to it, you don't have to worry about that next paycheck. God's the boss who pays you. That's job security as you've never seen it before!

Thank You, Lord,
that I can always trust You for every need.

And I have filled him with the spirit of God, in wisdom,
and in understanding, and in knowledge,
and in all manner of workmanship, to devise cunning works,
to work in gold, and in silver, and in brass.

EXODUS 31:3–4

God thinks highly of a good worker. In fact, He gives people the ability to do their work well. This passage shows us that when it describes Bezaleel, the son of Uri, whom God especially gifted so that he could make all the metal things the priests would put in the temple's holy of holies.

Have you ever treated your work as if it were sacred to God? Imagine if every day you were crafting something for God's most holy place. Would that make you think differently about welding together that metal, serving that customer, typing up that report, or balancing those books? Would you feel as if your work was suddenly much more important?

The fact is that each of us *is* working for God. He has given us our abilities, put us in our workplaces, and placed His Spirit in our hearts. When we serve others for Him, no matter what our job titles or pay scales, we are doing the most important labor of all—God's work.

Lord, thank You for giving me this work.
Show me how to do Your works every moment on my job.

And then will I profess unto them, I never knew you:
depart from me, ye that work iniquity.
MATTHEW 7:23

Did you know that there's a bad kind of good works? Not everything well-meaning people do is virtuous—not even those things they mean to do to help others.

In Matthew 7, Jesus talks about people who claimed to do good works in His name. They told others about Jesus, they cast out devils, and they did what they thought were "wonderful works" (Matthew 7:22). But when they reached heaven, Jesus didn't reward them for all these deeds—instead He called their work "iniquity," wickedness. From the rest of the passage, it's not hard to figure these folks felt stunned.

The problem was that Jesus didn't know these "employees." They'd probably done all these "wonderful works" under their own steam, to make themselves look good or feel important. None followed His narrow way (v. 14), because He wasn't their Master.

Today, are you doing good works that will last for eternity, or will even what you mean for good turn to sand because you lack a relationship with God? Realize that no matter how you act, if you're not working for God, at the end it will all be worthless.

Lord, may all my work be good work
as I seek to do Your will.
I do not want to follow my own will, but Yours.

Six days thou shalt labour, and do all thy work:
but the seventh day is the sabbath of the LORD thy God:
in it thou shalt not do any work.

DEUTERONOMY 5:13–14

Workaholics, beware! Don't expect God to sanction your seven-day workweek.

God did not mean our jobs to be everyday things. We wear out emotionally and spiritually if we focus continually on work. Worse than that, it quickly becomes our god. When we become too wrapped up in our careers, the place He is designed for—the center of our lives—becomes filled with thoughts of how we can cram more labor into our days, get things done, and improve our status in the company. Before long, we're empty and tired. We've been grasping at straws, and suddenly we find a hayrack in our hands, not the success we'd looked for.

Life without God is empty. So take a day of rest, worship God, and get your life in focus. Give God His proper place, and life will go more smoothly. You'll find success, even if it's not in the place you expected it.

Lord, I need to keep You in the center of my life.
Help me spend Sunday worshiping You,
not the things I "need" to accomplish.

The righteous cry, and the LORD heareth,
and delivereth them out of all their troubles.
PSALM 34:17

Overwhelming pressure—your boss just handed you a big project and a tight deadline. *No way can I do this!* your mind immediately cries.

Don't give up yet. You haven't even begun to tap into the power that can make it happen: You haven't turned to God.

Coworkers may not be able to solve your problem, but God still has it all in control. The One who created this world and knows just how it is designed bends a listening ear to your troubles when you open your heart to Him. With His help, you may find solutions to your problems that amaze you. What once seemed so hard can flow easily when blessed by His hand.

But whether the job goes smoothly or stumbles to a halt, with God it will all work out. So place your trust in Him. He hasn't forgotten this Bible verse. He promised to get you out of all your troubles, and He'll deliver you from this one, too.

Lord, though I know You want to help when I'm in trouble,
I often look to myself for answers.
Instead, help me turn quickly to You.
Thank You for caring about every little piece of my life.

Fret not thyself because of evildoers,
neither be thou envious against the workers of iniquity.
PSALM 37:1

You'd never do things the way he does. How could you live with yourself—and God—if you did? Yet your dishonest coworker seems to move quickly up the ladder, while your pace is slowed. No one seems to notice his lack of ethics—or care about it.

Don't give in and wander down his quick-success path, because success that comes quickly can also disappear in a moment. Or that fast-track coworker may achieve all his goals, only to find that his hands are empty. All he worked for really meant nothing in the end.

Sometimes God lets evil people be successful because they will never achieve anything but worldly success. Either He can use that empty success to lead them to Himself or use it to close their mouths on complaints against Him when they come to their barren end. Either way, the things God allows the wicked to do will be used to His purposes in the end.

But whatever happens, evil's not the path God has for you. Don't make yourself spiritually empty because you looked only for success. Instead of following evildoers, follow God.

Lord, it's so hard to see wicked people grab so much of the good
things in this world. But remind me that I can expect more
than everything this world has to offer.
Keep my eyes on Jesus and Your eternal reward.

And I have given you a land for which ye did not labour, and cities which ye built not, and ye dwell in them; of the vineyards and oliveyards which ye planted not do ye eat.

JOSHUA 24:13

Sometimes things come easily to us. The work seems to go smoothly, and the rewards seem even larger than we expected. *What, am I on a roll?* we may want to ask ourselves.

No, it's not a roll, it's a time of blessing. Sometimes God just seems to let us have so much, we wonder why He's doing it. Life seems wonderful, and we can enjoy it. But we can't forget that all this blessing has a purpose. God doesn't give a promotion without expecting we'll use our new position wisely. He doesn't give raises that He expects us to spend only on ourselves; we need to remember the work of His church and give accordingly.

Feeling blessed? Have you asked God what you can do to share that blessing? Then, have you done what He commanded?

Thank You, Lord,
for the many blessings You've given me.
Today show me how to use the ones in my hand now.

> *"'Do not use dishonest standards when*
> *measuring length, weight or quantity.'"*
> LEVITICUS 19:35 NIV

Years ago, a company I worked for asked me to do something dishonest. They didn't think it would be a problem—after all, the people they were taking the money from would never know. That company was so big, it would never check the billing. But I felt particularly funny about being dishonest to a company located in the town I lived in.

Because I knew the action they'd asked me to be part of would not honor God, I said no. I lost my job, in part for taking that stand, but it was still the best no I ever said. God honored my honesty. Shortly after leaving the dishonest company, I got the job I'd really been looking for, working in a Christian environment. That new job formed the basis for the rest of my career. I've never been sorry for the stand I took, and I've always been glad I honored God.

When God tells you to be honest, He also supports you in that decision. Whether it means finding a new job or being a testimony in the one you're in, He'll support you to the end.

Help me, Lord,
not to use dishonest standards in any of my workplace dealings.
When I'm faced with hard decisions about
shortchanging someone or being otherwise dishonest,
I want to stand firm.

Because thine heart was tender,
and thou didst humble thyself before God. . .
and weep before me; I have even heard thee also, saith the LORD.
2 CHRONICLES 34:27

God loves to listen to humble people—whether they're CEOs or on the cleanup staff. And when they pray, He acts powerfully to protect them or change their situations. When you have God's ear, it doesn't always matter if you don't have the boss's auditory apparatus.

Josiah was at the top of his organization; he was king of Judah. But when the high priest found the Scriptures Judah had ignored and forgotten, the humble king realized how far his country was from God's Word and the Father's will. Josiah didn't make excuses or avoid the truth. While grieving over that sin, Josiah recognized God's right to judge all Judah. He confessed his country's sin to God, and God heard. God didn't save the country, but He saved the king by bringing him home to Himself before the judgment fell.

Just as God listened to a humble king's prayer, he listens to humble workers today. When your company seems to be going in the wrong direction, maybe He has put you there to be the unobtrusive prayer. He may use you as an agent for change, or He may move you out of that bad spot, as He did Josiah. But He will hear your prayer.

Lord, make me Your agent in my workplace.
I want to serve You every day.

"My Presence will go with you, and I will give you rest."
EXODUS 33:14 NIV

Wouldn't you love to have this promise that God gave Moses before he began to lead all Israel toward the Promised Land? Wouldn't it be grand to know that when you needed rest, it would be there?

Sometimes we get so caught up in work all week and chores all weekend that rest never becomes part of the picture. But did you notice that Moses never took a vacation? He never found a comfy oasis and settled down for a week or two, though he and his people traveled for forty years in the desert.

How did Moses make it, when the pressure was high? Did the Bible forget to tell about the days he simply disappeared for a rest? No, because Moses' rest was in God. Whenever the people frustrated him, Moses turned to Him in supplication. As he drew close to his Lord in prayer, peace settled over the prophet's soul.

God offers you that peace, too. Just spend some quiet time talking with Him. It can feel more restful than a month's vacation.

Thank You, Lord, for the peace and rest I find in You.
When the world starts pushing in on me,
help me trust in Your will and follow Your way.

Six days thou shalt work, but on the seventh day thou shalt rest:
in earing time and in harvest thou shalt rest.

EXODUS 34:21

Your work is important, but fitting in a day of rest is even more significant. God vividly showed that to the Hebrews in this verse. After all, when you're a farmer with a crop to get in, you count every minute in the field. You need to get it safely stored before rain, bugs, or some other natural disaster can affect your crop.

God commanded people who had to live on their crops to take a day of rest, even in their busiest seasons. If they did not get the crop in, they would have a hard winter—perhaps even starve. This was a heavenly message they could hardly miss: They could depend on Him to be sure they could bring in enough of their crop. Even if they lost some, He would provide for them.

Most of us don't face half a year's starvation if we rest on Sundays, but are we more likely than the Hebrew farmers to take a day off for rest and worship? Are we trusting in God less than they?

Lord, help me to spend Sunday with You
in worship and rest.

"But my righteous one will live by faith.
And if he shrinks back, I will not be pleased with him."
HEBREWS 10:38 NIV

Stacy knew Ken hadn't been in charge of the work that had incorrect information that had lost her company an important contract. She wasn't sure who had made the mistake, but because she and Ken had worked so closely on the project, she knew he had done everything thoroughly and was being unfairly blamed. Why, she'd been there when their boss had gone over the work and commended him for a fine job. But Rob had retired last month and could not speak up for Ken.

What should I do? Stacy asked herself. There was a real flap on about this. Her new boss might not like her interfering in it. But the more Stacy prayed, the more certain she was that she had to defend her coworker. It was the right thing to do. A little timidly, she confronted her boss with the information and asked him to pass it on.

When Ken was cleared of all wrongdoing, Stacy was glad she had not held her tongue. If she hadn't stepped forward in faith, what would have happened to her coworker?

Lord, when I need to stand up for You and the truth,
give me the courage I need.

And let us not be weary in well doing:
for in due season we shall reap, if we faint not.
GALATIANS 6:9

Drudgery days. We all have those days when work seems so dull, we wonder if we really like our jobs anymore and why we got into them. Is it all a big mistake? Or has God suddenly changed His mind about where our futures are headed?

When life has just seemed to lose its zip, it's time to take a look at where you are. Is it the dull winter weather that's making you feel bored? Is it a lack of challenge on this job? Do you need to take more time away from work, perhaps going on a vacation or taking a day off? Lots of things contribute to our drudgery days.

But one thing we cannot stop doing—we cannot stop doing good in Jesus' name, on the job and off. No matter what the cause of our drudgery, if we reconnect to God and follow His commands about our situation, He will help us find a way out—one that will not leave us feeling bored and useless.

When we stick with it, we will reap an unexpected harvest. God has promised it.

Lord, when I start to feel tired of work and the world,
fill me with Your Spirit and help me move on in You.

*Those who trust in the LORD are like Mount Zion,
which cannot be shaken but endures forever.*

PSALM 125:1 NIV

Does your job seem secure? Or are you constantly listening to gossip at the water cooler or Coke machine to discover the latest dirt about the corporate finances? Are things looking up for your company, or are they looking mighty grim?

Most of us expect our companies to provide security. We all want good, secure jobs. But when a company starts looking precarious, we worry about the future and may even start looking for another "good, secure job."

Our incomes keep us alive, so of course job security concerns us. We want to pay the rent and grocery bills and can't do it if we don't work. But when we place all our trust in companies, we'll experience disappointment. CEOs can't predict the financial future, hard as they try. Managers can't be certain our positions won't be axed in a corporate downsize.

But when we look to God for security, we will never be shaken. He knows the future. He foresees what jobs we need, long before we find them. Even if we lose our jobs unexpectedly, He helps us pay the rent and feed the kids.

Today, are you trusting in a short-term business or an eternal Father?

*Thank You, Lord, that I can trust in Your eternal care.
I place my future in Your hands.*

If it be possible, as much as lieth in you,
live peaceably with all men.
ROMANS 12:18

"I hate to say it, but I can't stand Vera! She's awful at her job, but none of the bosses know it. She makes them think she's wonderful, even though we have to pick up her slack. And she isn't even nice about it! To top it off, now she's getting a promotion that Janice really earned," Liz fumed to her husband. "How can they promote such a mean, incompetent person?"

There's frequently one person who's impossible to get along with in your work environment. You try and try, but somehow you can't create a relationship that truly works. Whether that person is nasty or conniving, you'd just rather not share your space with her.

God tells you to make every effort. Be nice when she's nasty. Show His love over and over. Don't get involved in the work "gossip pool." But ultimately, if everything you do doesn't work, don't take responsibility for all her issues. If she insists on being nasty, you can't change her attitude. Don't stop loving her as much as you can, but don't let her take complete advantage of you, either. Be a testimony, but not a pushover.

Lord, help me deal lovingly with
that tough person in my job,
but guard me from the hurt that she can also cause.

So then, each of us will give an account of himself to God.
ROMANS 14:12 NIV

Ever felt like playing hooky from work? The day is beautiful, just right for your favorite sport. Who would know if you called in sick and spent the day having some fun?

Your boss might never figure it out. It might not matter to your work, if you weren't too busy. It might not even cost you a raise or promotion. But God would know. In lying about your situation, you would be letting Him down.

So what will it matter to God? you might ask. *If it's okay with my boss, why should it be a problem for Him?*

If you called in and asked for a last-minute vacation day, assuming your company's policy allowed that, it wouldn't be a problem. God isn't a spoilsport. But remember, you are working for Him, too. So if you call in sick and no one catches on that it was really a *slick* day, keep in mind that at the end of time, you'll still be accounting to God for your lack of truthfulness. When you give your final accounting, it won't seem so slick anymore. Instead it will seem like an unnecessary lie. Why face God with any more of them than you have to?

Even when the weather calls me, Lord,
help me to be responsible.
I don't want to hurt You by being less than honest.

A gossip separates close friends.
PROVERBS 16:28 NIV

If you've ever had someone gossip about you, you know why this verse is in the Bible. Put a bunch of people together in the same office or on the same job site, and sooner or later the whispering starts. "Did you hear about. . . ?" "I heard that Mary. . . ." People just can't seem to resist talking about one another.

What may start out as "innocent information" can quickly damage reputations and cause hurt among friends. It can destroy even a close friendship. God warns against gossip because it breaks relationships. He doesn't care if it's "true gossip" or a pack of lies—spreading news of other people is not part of the biblical code.

So when you hear something that you "just have to tell" someone, put one hand over your mouth, bite your tongue, or do whatever you must to keep your mouth shut. Ask God to give you self-control, because you don't want to break up a friendship—especially your friendship with Him.

*Lord, place Your hand over my mouth
when I hear that juicy bit of gossip,
and help me turn away from
the one who's telling that tale.*

Now faith is the substance of things hoped for,
the evidence of things not seen.
HEBREWS 11:1

"Faith is not feelings," a pastor of mine used to say. Over the years, I've discovered the truth of that statement.

Now, what he did *not* mean was that feelings had no place in faith. Without feelings, our faith would be pretty boring or maybe nonexistent. But he was trying to say that our faith should not rely on our feelings.

When I don't "feel" faith, when no spiritual "high" fills my soul, I may still be faithful. While I'm at that spiritual plateau, God may be building my "hoped for" quotient. I'm not seeing exciting evidences of faith, but because I still trust in God, He is quietly increasing my faith each day.

You can relate to this on your job. Every day isn't a thrill, but that doesn't mean that every day isn't important to your work. The exciting days keep you going, and you look forward to them, but if you have too many exciting days in a row, you may just wish for a quiet one to catch up on the chores you haven't gotten to.

On those less-than-exciting faith days, keep hoping and working for God. The job isn't finished yet.

Thank You, Lord,
that even on unexciting days,
You are faithful still. Help me hold on to the evidence
of things I haven't seen while I trust in You.

For the message of the cross is foolishness to those who are perishing,
but to us who are being saved it is the power of God.
1 CORINTHIANS 1:18 NIV

You may work in a rough environment, where people continually take the Lord's name in vain, or your more sophisticated coworkers may act as if believing in Jesus is the ultimate act of foolishness. However they show it, people who don't believe in Jesus live out the first part of this verse. No matter what they *say* about their own religious observances, somehow their actions show where their hearts really are.

Every person's heart shows what's inside by words, actions, and reactions to uncontrollable situations. Often, you don't have to start up a conversation about faith to learn that. How often have you recognized another believer on the job just because of his attitude or her quiet spirit? God's power simply shines through that person.

When people think the cross is foolish, foolishness shows up in their lives, one way or another. When they trust in God's power for salvation, it works within them day by day, working a powerful change in their lives.

Today, is your life foolish or powerful?

Lord, help me understand why
people think You are foolishness,
but help me reach out, too.

*For since in the wisdom of God
the world through its wisdom did not know him,
God was pleased through the foolishness of what was
preached to save those who believe.*

1 CORINTHIANS 1:21 NIV

Speak out about Jesus to enough stubbornly unbelieving coworkers, and you'll understand the wisdom of this verse. Some unbelievers will respond with anger, others with sweet reason, but you'll quickly get the message that what they believe makes all the sense in the world, and what you are preaching is utterly ridiculous.

When you feel frustrated about speaking out for Jesus, don't give in to a desire to go along with the crowd. Don't ignore the faith in your heart and exchange it for worldly "wisdom." In the end, you'll find that's anything but wise, and it will take you to miserable places God's true wisdom doesn't go.

But God's seemingly foolish wisdom not only brings you a peace-filled life with Jesus on earth, it offers a heavenly eternal reward. Though your scoffing coworkers may deny your testimony on earth, eventually they will not deny their eternal options. One day, in judgment, God will make their own foolishness plain.

So don't be a pest, but keep on showing them Jesus. Someday, that scoffing may turn to faith because you weren't foolish enough to give up.

*Lord, keep me as a faithful testimony to You,
wherever I work.*

But God chose the foolish things of the world to shame the wise;
God chose the weak things of the world to shame the strong.
1 CORINTHIANS 1:27 NIV

Maybe you aren't in management, or if you are, you may feel as if you're still on a very low rung of the ladder. If you work for people who have a lot of smarts, it's easy to start feeling as if you have nothing of value to offer. After all, aren't these other folks so much better than you?

Be encouraged. God isn't just looking for the really smart, the really gifted, or the really wealthy to do His work. In fact, He seems to prefer to use the quiet, lowly, but perfectly obedient person.

You may not reach a high position in your job. Perhaps you'll stay pretty much where you are now for as long as you stay with this company. But whatever your place, if your life honors God, your faith can have a powerful impact on your workplace.

You might not get a promotion because someone thinks you're "too honest." You might watch others pass you by because they played some office-politics games you stepped back from. But people will remember you and recognize the things you stood for. A few may even feel shame and wish they'd followed in your footsteps.

Lord, no matter where You want to use me,
I want to be Your servant.
Let my light shine for You today.

"Let him who boasts boast in the Lord."
1 CORINTHIANS 1:31 NIV

Are you on a spiritual high? Is life going well for you at home, at the workplace, and in a ministry? Then you may be in a very dangerous place. You may feel tempted to take credit for all those good things. Perhaps you're starting to feel as if you have some special spiritual knowledge that makes you better than others. Or maybe you've reached out to people on the job, they've responded to Jesus, and you're starting to feel as if you're an outrageous witness for God.

It's great that God is using you so powerfully, but don't forget that He's the One giving you the power to speak those words and that it's His Spirit that's touching the hearts. We are tools in God's hands, and we need to be ready for Him to pick up and use us, but we're not the ones who made the plans and brought them to completion.

Praise God for your successes, but remember that without Him, they are impossible. Boast about what happened, if you want, but boast that Jesus did it, not you.

*Lord, I want to lift up Your name
so others know what's happening and who caused it.
I could never do this on my own.*

I came to you in weakness and fear, and with much trembling.
1 CORINTHIANS 2:3 NIV

Do you know who wrote these words? Paul: That great preacher, the one who almost singlehandedly reached the Western world, came to the Corinthians in fear and trembling. Can you imagine this man, whose signature is on so much of the New Testament, being afraid of telling people about Jesus? It hardly seems possible.

It's not uncommon for Christians to experience fear when they talk about Jesus. Bill Bright, leader of Campus Crusade for many years, admitted that witnessing did not come easily to him. He told his staff that he did it because God had commanded it.

But in the next verse, 1 Corinthians 2:4, Paul tells how he managed to overcome his fear. He spoke not in his own power, but in the power of the Holy Spirit. He explains that he did not want listeners' faith to rest on men's wisdom, but on God's.

Today, are you afraid to share your faith or take a stand for what is right? Don't stand in your own strength, but in God's. Ask the Spirit to guide you, and speak as He directs.

Lord, work in me,
that I might speak Your truths.
May Your Spirit guide my tongue and heart,
and let me share Your truths.

JANUARY 25

"I was sought by those who did not ask for Me;
I was found by those who did not seek Me.
I said, 'Here I am, here I am,'
To a nation that was not called by My name."

ISAIAH 65:1 NKJV

None of us was really searching for God when He found us. Though we may have begun to feel empty inside, we didn't know where to go. Then God brought along someone who told us that He loved us and wanted to share our lives with us. We heard the good news that He wanted to heal and forgive us.

We don't come to God with any status. Everyone who comes, comes as poor, empty sinners. Out of that, God builds new lives. Do we show that truth in our living? Can we accept others, no matter how rich or poor they are, no matter what background they come from? Or are we haughtier than God, requiring financial "perfection" or a certain "acceptable" background of our friends, fellow church members, and acquaintances?

God sought us—unloved, unappealing, seemingly valueless sinners—and gave us all His love. He saw something in us when no one else could. Can't we do the same for all those who touch our lives?

Thank You, Lord,
for accepting me just as I am.
Let me live humbly in Your Spirit, with love for all.

Now the Bereans. . .
received the message with great eagerness and
examined the Scriptures every day to see
if what Paul said was true.

ACTS 17:11 NIV

You hear a lot of "spiritual" talk in church, on your favorite Christian radio station, and from friends. How much of it agrees? Spiritual discussions, at work or church, may get intense. Two friends may each think they have the method for *really* worshiping God. Both seem so sincere, yet they tell you different things. You want to believe correctly. When you've heard a couple of different "truths," how do you *know* which is right?

Don't be afraid to check the Scriptures people quote or to compare ideas against God's Word. After all, Paul applauded the Bereans for doing that when he came into town with his gospel teaching. Christianity isn't a mindless faith. And when you read those Scriptures, read more than that one verse, and you may discover the truth. The paragraph or page around it can change the entire meaning of a sentence.

But don't stop with reading a few Scriptures only when you need an answer. Read your Bible every day. Then when an issue comes up, verses from other parts of the Bible can come to your mind, and God can constantly show you *His* truth.

Lord, spiritual talk sure can be confusing,
and I don't want to be distracted from Your truth.
Help me search and find it in Your Word.

I will praise thee;
for I am fearfully and wonderfully made: marvellous are thy works;
and that my soul knoweth right well.
My substance was not hid from thee, when I was made in secret,
and curiously wrought in the lowest parts of the earth.

PSALM 139:14–15

Hate your job every day? Maybe you're in the wrong one. Perhaps you were never physically and emotionally designed to do this kind of work. After all, God created you with a special purpose and gave you the skills to carry out His plan. If you're not fulfilling His purpose, you're in the wrong place.

Don't let this mistake make you decide you're not suited to any work! God designed you to do something and do it well. He gave you abilities and interests He wants you to use to provide for yourself and your family and glorify Him. You just need to *find* the work you're made for.

Know you're in the wrong job? Don't quit work today. Instead, seek out what you'd be good at. Pick up a book from the library or bookstore that will help you identify your strengths. Pray about it as you read. Then look for the job God made you for. It's out there somewhere. He created a marvelous, incredibly detailed work in you, and He'll help you discover what to do with it.

Thank You, Lord, for creating an amazing me.
Help me use all my abilities as You'd like to have them used.

But I say unto you, Love your enemies,
bless them that curse you,
do good to them that hate you,
and pray for them which despitefully use you,
and persecute you.

MATTHEW 5:44

Hate going into your job every day? Maybe you enjoy the work; it's just that nasty coworker—or even your boss—you can't stand. *If only he weren't here, it'd be better!* you may be tempted to think.

You could respond to your coworker in a lot of ways. You might become so irritated that you quit your job; or you could treat that person like dirt to get even; or you could love him as Jesus does and pray daily for him.

The first response might be giving up too easily; the second is clearly wrong. But following this biblical advice, while more difficult, could make some big changes in your attitude—and your coworker's. Though you may not end up being best of friends, as you pray and love that person, God can begin to work in your relationship to disarm the nastiness. Though it may seem impossible, God can make you at least tolerate each other. Let Him control your feelings and reactions, and you'll be amazed at the work He can do. Prayer really works!

Lord, help me love my enemy today.
Give me the patience and strength,
because I know I can't do it under my own power.

Then Jesus beholding him loved him,
and said unto him, One thing thou lackest:
go thy way, sell whatsoever thou hast,
and give to the poor, and thou shalt have treasure in heaven:
and come, take up the cross, and follow me.
MARK 10:21

Maybe you enjoy your job. It pays you enough to live on and maybe a bit besides. You relish your work, and everything seems to be going well for you. That's great, as long as it hasn't become your love.

This young man who came to Jesus had begun to worship things, perhaps things he'd worked hard for, instead of God. So in an ultimately humbling statement, the Master asked the young man to set all his possessions aside and follow Him. Sadly, the man turned Jesus down because he loved things more than he loved God. He was surely on the wrong track: The Bible never speaks of loving anything but God or other people, because love is appropriately given to someone who can respond.

Jesus didn't hate this young man. His heart reached out to him in love. But because He knew things could never replace Himself, He asked the man to set aside all those distractions and turn to Him alone.

Has work become your love? Is it in God's place? You can't stop working, but you can give your work to Him. He'll love you more than any job.

No matter how I love my work,
let me always love You more, Lord.

Recompense to no man evil for evil.
Provide things honest in the sight of all men.
ROMANS 12:17

"It's not fair!" We've all wanted to cry that at some point in our careers. No matter how dedicated we are to our work, at some point we'll face a situation where we feel we've been treated unfairly, whether we have to give up a vacation week we really wanted or don't get the job transfer we applied for.

When that happens, how do we react? Do we take it out on the company in subtle ways, not working as hard as we used to or taking home a few "extra" pencils for the kids?

It's a natural response to feel hurt when we don't get something we wanted badly. Our hopes are dashed when something enjoyable falls through. But that doesn't mean we have the right to retaliate. Returning evil for evil just puts more evil in the world. But being aboveboard and honest, even when things don't go our way, will return good to the world.

Maybe it's not fair. Maybe you deserved that vacation or transfer. But obeying God will still bring good out of unfairness. All you have to do is give your employer the fairness you never got.

Lord, I know what unfairness is like,
and I hate to be on its receiving end.
But when life is unfair,
help me turn it to Your good as a testimony to right.

"And whoever compels you to go one mile,
go with him two."
MATTHEW 5:41 NKJV

In our independent society, the idea of going an extra mile is completely foreign—as foreign as the ancient Jews who were forced into the Roman army's service on the whim of these pagan leaders. Faced with the same situation, we'd stand on our rights, rights no Jew in Jesus' age had. Things have surely changed in this world, so does that mean we no longer have to go another mile with someone who forces us to divert our lives to a place we'd rather not go?

No, because this verse is still in the Bible. So when your boss asks you to work an extra hour of overtime, if it takes two instead, maybe you shouldn't gripe. If you get moved off one project and onto another, harder one, it doesn't give you complaining rights.

Remember, Jesus went more than an extra mile for us. He set aside His glory, came to earth, and suffered to bring us into heaven with Him. For that, we can go more than an extra couple of miles.

When I'm tempted to complain, Jesus,
remind me of the sacrifice You made for me.
Then help me do what You've asked with a cheerful attitude.

So then, men ought to regard us as servants of Christ.
1 CORINTHIANS 4:1 NIV

Much as we love Jesus, when it comes to being called servants, we may not relish the title. *Servant* seems, well, so lowly. Couldn't we be called something a bit more important? After all, aren't we serving God?

As we're objecting to the title Paul seemed to enjoy and even desire, are we also forgetting the actions that he exemplified as a servant? Are we sacrificially loving our families because we care for them and want them to live for Jesus? Or are we so caught up in what people call us and how we appear that we forget that serving others is the role we've been called to?

Servanthood to Jesus is not degrading. It's a high honor given to those who follow Him wholeheartedly because He has given them so much. Are we sharing the benefits of His gift with our families and friends by showing them His love? Do our children and spouses see love overflowing in our actions?

If not, our eyes are not on the Servant who came so that our sins could be forgiven.

The title servant may not appeal to me, Lord,
but showing Your love is something I always want to practice.
Whatever I'm called, let me always do Your will.

And [Jesus] was transfigured before them:
and his face did shine as the sun,
and his raiment was white as the light.

MATTHEW 17:2

Tell your coworkers you're going to church, and what response will you get? Some may commend you, but others may mock you or even call you a name like Bible Boy or Preacher. When people do that, it's because they don't know Jesus. Their eyes are shut to who He is.

Those coworkers are a little like the disciples the day before the Transfiguration. When Jesus appeared to them in something other than His everyday dress, instead of the ordinary-looking human who roamed Israel, Peter, James, and John saw His glory. Though they'd known Jesus for years, the idea that He was not *just* a person took on a meaning it had not had the day before.

When we accept Jesus, we, too, have a glimpse of His glory. We treat Him differently, and our lives change drastically. But we work with people who haven't yet seen Jesus' glory. Like the disciples, they don't have a clear picture of who He is. If they did, they wouldn't treat you—or Him—like that.

When coworkers mock, understand that they are blind. Pray for them; share as much as you can. And maybe someday, through your life, they *will* see Jesus.

Lord, give me compassion for those who cannot see You.
Touch their lives and show them who You are.

"Suppose one of you wants to build a tower.
Will he not first sit down and estimate the cost to see if
he has enough money to complete it?"
LUKE 14:28 NIV

Sometimes money becomes a job issue when a company is short on cash. As workers, it's easy to complain when we can't easily get supplies that have been plentiful until now. It's natural to complain that our raises weren't larger.

When we do that, we're not seeing things from our employer's point of view. Like the man who prepared to build a tower, the bosses are looking toward the future. They've considered the company's past track record and future prospects, and they may have found their financial cupboard was bare. So they're taking steps to correct that.

We can carp, condemn, and complain. That won't put extra cash in our bosses' hands. It won't sell any more widgets. But it will hurt our spirits and those around us. So maybe it's time to change our attitudes, pitch in, and help.

Lord, I hate it when money is tight.
Help me to understand, have patience,
and depend on You to provide.

*Slaves, obey your earthly masters in everything;
and do it, not only when their eye is on you and to win their favor,
but with sincerity of heart and reverence for the Lord.*

COLOSSIANS 3:22 NIV

Harry really hustled when the boss was standing over him but eased off as soon as he passed by. It didn't take long for Harry to show his true colors and slow down to a crawl. That act might have fooled his boss, but Harry's coworkers quickly caught on. They knew all about his dishonest ways and flattery to the management. Before long Harry was very unpopular with his immediate coworkers, who knew the boss couldn't see through the smoke screen.

As God's employee, can you imagine going to your heavenly reward and trying to put one over on the One who knows all about you, from your first thought to your last action? He doesn't need a heavenful of dishonest workers any more than a corporation does. So He doesn't start creating them here on earth. While we're here, God begins our heavenly training by creating honest, hardworking people He can be proud of. Since we're working for Him now, He should be able to count on our treating our bosses right. After all, aren't we really serving the Ruler of the universe, not the CEO of the company?

*Lord, I don't want to be a pretend person.
Help me to treat my boss as well as I treat You.*

Whatever you do, work at it with all your heart,
as working for the Lord, not for men.
COLOSSIANS 3:23 NIV

Ever wished you were the boss? Perhaps you didn't like the way your boss handled things and thought you knew a better way. Maybe you wished your boss were more up-to-date —or a little less "modern" in thinking. When you feel that way, do you shut down and become as unhelpful as possible? Or do you still do your best work, putting your heart into it and calmly hoping all will work out better than you expected?

However you feel, a shutdown or work slowdown is not what God has in mind. Remember, you are not working just for your boss. God is your ultimate boss, and He says you need to treat your boss with respect. He may not have all the answers, but God placed him in that position, and you are accountable to him.

If your boss's plan doesn't work out, he'll have to report that to his boss and bear the brunt of the criticism. If you've done your work poorly, your boss will take the blame. So do your best job, humbly offer helpful insights, and work as a team. Remember, you're really reporting to God, and you want His "well done" at the end of the day.

Lord, help me remember that I'm really working for You.
Let all that I do be pleasing in Your sight.

Since you know that you will receive an inheritance
from the Lord as a reward.
It is the Lord Christ you are serving.
COLOSSIANS 3:24 NIV

You mean I'm going to get a reward for my work—and it isn't just a paycheck?

Yes, absolutely. You didn't think God would ask you to work for Him without giving you something in return, did you? How unlike our generous God that would be!

This verse directly follows yesterday's, which told us to work for Him. So when we find situations we don't approve of and have a hard time making ourselves do the right thing, we can fix our eyes on God's reward. From our companies, we may never get enough pay to make us do our jobs. The fringe benefits may be small. But the benefits of obeying God make up for every lost dollar and difficult situation. Our eyes are on something much larger, a benefit that will not be destroyed by time or decay.

As we serve Jesus in our workday, He promises that we are earning heavenly benefits. Though we may not name them here on earth, we know the God who offers them and trust that our imaginations will pale beside the reality God holds for us in heaven.

From nine to five—or whatever my hours—
I want to continue to serve You.
Every moment of every day should reflect
Your love in my life.

*Masters, provide your slaves with what is right and fair,
because you know that you also have a Master in heaven.*
COLOSSIANS 4:1 NIV

"I'd never take a job like that again," a manager admitted. He'd come into his company knowing he'd have to let some people go. Though he didn't like the idea, he figured he could handle it—until he, too, was let go after a brief time with the firm. It seemed that what had gone around came around, and he felt he'd done wrong by those workers.

Wronging workers—whether you're at the top of the corporate ladder or many rungs down—has its price. It may cause some people to quit, leaving management in a bind; others simply become angry and hard to manage. But that price is small compared to the spiritual one. For this manager, the job's cost hadn't been worth the spiritual pain.

A cutthroat management attitude is far from a biblical one. And Christians who get caught up in this mentality quickly find their spiritual life suffering. Soon they may be asked to do things they know are wrong. Bound by the need to work, they take steps they'd rather not—and end up feeling guilty.

If your company asks you to do something wrong, stand up for right. It may cost you your job and gain you heaven's reward.

*Whoever does work for me should be treated fairly, Lord.
Help me live up to that commitment every day.*

*Wives, submit to your husbands,
as is fitting in the Lord. Husbands,
love your wives and do not be harsh with them.*
COLOSSIANS 3:18–19 NIV

Just as there's a balance between workers and bosses, there's one in the home. God doesn't encourage tyrants in the workplace or the family. So He evens out authority with a command to live in biblical love. The wife submits "as is fitting in the Lord," not to the point of displeasing God. The husband offers loving and gentle leadership.

Wives and husbands, remember what it's like to have a staff member who always causes trouble, or how difficult it is to work for a harsh boss. Since you'd rather not labor in that kind of environment, don't bring it into the home. Remember, if you treat your spouse harshly or with disrespect, resentment or emotional distance may quickly infiltrate your marriage.

You don't have to bring your work home to build a happy marriage—that could work against it—but learn from the truths that apply on the job. Just as you work out problems in the office or factory and treat others with respect, become a team member with your spouse. When you're going in the same direction, leaning on God for your decisions, the two of you have found His working balance.

*Lord, help my spouse and me to work as a team.
We need Your balance in our marriage.*

> *"I will betroth you to me forever;*
> *I will betroth you in righteousness and justice,*
> *in love and compassion."*
>
> HOSEA 2:19 NIV

How God loved Israel, even when that nation turned away from Him to other gods. Read the Book of Hosea, and you'll see how He drew this country back to Himself by letting it experience all the emptiness that life without Him has. Then He wooed the whole nation back to Himself and gave Israel this promise.

God showed His people a concrete example of how such adultery felt when Hosea, His prophet, married a woman who was unfaithful to him. Through the book, God and His prophet share the pain of unfaithfulness: God with his people and Hosea with his wife, Gomer.

Today an engagement may not mean much. People break them all the time. But in Hosea's age, in order to be free, the one who broke the engagement had to pay the other's family. If a woman was pledged to a man and another slept with her, he was stoned "because he violated another man's wife." God's engagement to His people meant more than a promise to meet at the altar.

Today, are you truly betrothed to God? Have you promised Him your whole life, and are you living for Him? Or are you an unfaithful spouse?

Lord, I want to be faithful to You and my earthly spouse.
Thank You for showing me such powerful love.

"If you love those who love you,
what reward will you get?
Are not even the tax collectors doing that?"
MATTHEW 5:46 NIV

This is the week that love makes the headlines. But it's always romantic love—the ooey-gooey stuff that is so popular in the movies.

It's funny, but the Bible doesn't often mention that kind of love. Though there are some terribly romantic moments in the Bible, they aren't based on pure erotic emotion. That's because love is so much larger than just a male-female romance. The love God speaks of in His Word extends to all people, in all situations, few of them romantic.

Though our romantic lives may be challenging at times, take a look at this verse, and you'll really find a challenge. It's not hard to love people who love you, Jesus points out. Even those who don't know much about God or care for Him can do that. Why should God reward it? But loving your enemy (v. 44) is something worth a reward from God.

So while you're thinking up a Valentine's Day gift or sending a card, also start thinking about how you can love an enemy. The reward God offers for that love tastes better than chocolate and smells better than roses.

Lord, I want to pray for an enemy today.
Help that person who doesn't love me to experience Your love.

But I say unto you which hear, Love your enemies,
do good to them which hate you.
LUKE 6:27

The love Jesus described here is no easy task. On our own, we could barely even start to do it. Before long, we'd get caught up in resentment and anger. Only God can help us love our enemies to the point where we actually do good for them. He gave us a wonderful example of such love in His Son, Jesus, who died for people who didn't care about Him, detested every word out of His mouth, and couldn't stand a thing about Him. We were some of those people before we came to know Him.

Some of the folks we work with may not exactly be enemies, but they may be exasperating. When they expect work in less time than it takes to do it, we could let the resentment burn. Or we could decide that they, too, have pressures on them; and since they don't do our jobs, they can't be realistic about time management. We can love them anyway and do our best. Then we'll be doing good, and God will commend us.

Lord, help me love the people who make me crazy.
I know they often don't do it intentionally.

But woe unto you, Pharisees!
for ye tithe mint and rue and all manner of herbs,
and pass over judgment and the love of God:
these ought ye to have done,
and not to leave the other undone.

LUKE 11:42

As Christians, we may know all the "rules." We avoid doing things that would offend other Christians. To stay pure, we "don't smoke, don't chew, and don't go with girls who do."

Those rules aren't entirely bad. Avoiding questionable things is good, if it doesn't become a "god" in itself. But the Pharisees got so caught up in their legalistic rule keeping, they pushed aside things that were really important to God—they lost track of God's character. They turned a loving God into simply a nitpicky idol, ready to object to any unkept rule.

We, too, can become class-A nitpickers. If we work with someone from another denomination, we can get so caught up in our doctrinal differences that we ruin our testimonies. If our coworkers see nothing but disagreement, they will never be drawn to any church. But if they see love, our Lord will become appealing.

Don't nitpick over every herb in your garden and forget to show God's justice and love—because then you'll be no better than Jesus' enemies, the Pharisees.

Lord, I want to shine brightly with Your love,
not with legalism. Fill me with Your Spirit now.

The Father loveth the Son,
and hath given all things into his hand.
He that believeth on the Son hath everlasting life:
and he that believeth not the Son shall not see life;
but the wrath of God abideth on him.

JOHN 3:35–36

Because God loved Jesus, He gave us to Him, and He gave Him to us. In that act, we became inextricably bound to the love of the Godhead. We can't fathom how God did it or why. Why us and not others? If we're honest, we know we didn't have anything that made us so special that we deserved eternity.

So why did God choose you and maybe not the co-worker next to you? He alone knows. Be glad that He loves you. But don't let it end there. Share the love of Jesus with others around you. Maybe you're not good at preaching, but you can show what God is like by being honest. You can show His caring by lending an ear to a coworker who's going through a personal crisis. You can offer your condo-dwelling coworker some tomatoes from your garden when you have a bumper crop.

You may never hear that person pray to receive Him, but your coworker may just have felt the first touch of Jesus' love.

Use me, Lord, wherever You want to.
Show me how to share Your love today.

I am my beloved's, and my beloved is mine.
SONG OF SOLOMON 6:3

If you've ever had an intense emotional attraction to someone of the opposite sex, you know how this feels. Being in love is fantastic, especially when it's new love. But that heightened awareness changes as your relationship develops. You marry, and things may calm down; yet if you keep your romance alive, that strong undercurrent of belonging remains.

Even when you're at work, you think of your spouse. If you go shopping during lunchtime or after work, you may pick up something your know your husband or wife will enjoy—flowers, a CD by a favorite singer, or just a candy bar.

In this romantic season, don't forget your beloved. God created romance and has called you to love one another. Don't become forgetful or greedy, but show your love through both words and a gift—or if you can't afford a gift, do something wonderful for your love.

I want to show my spouse true love, Lord.
Give me just the right words and gift.

And thou shalt love the Lord thy God with all thy heart,
and with all thy soul, and with all thy mind,
and with all thy strength:
this is the first commandment.

MARK 12:30

This is real love. What value is a small love that only gives a tiny piece of the heart? Especially when the beloved one is God. Many people try to give Him a small portion of their lives. They'll give Him Sunday morning but don't want Him "interfering" with Saturday night. They'll give Him prayer time but don't want to account to Him for their working hours.

What if God gave such halfhearted lovers just what they gave Him? Maybe He'd provide for them for half the year, then ignore them for the other six months. Or He'd help them with family problems every other time—or maybe even less.

We can thank God that He is not so miserly with His love. He cares for us even when we fail Him. He never stops watching over us, even when the situation is really dire and we've brought it on ourselves. Real love doesn't give up on the loved one. It hangs in there through thick and thin—just like God.

Let me love You with all my heart, Lord,
and share that love with everyone I know.

For therefore we both labour and suffer reproach,
because we trust in the living God,
who is the Saviour of all men,
specially of those that believe.
1 TIMOTHY 4:10

When you feel persecuted at work, it's easy to wish that you could share your nine-to-five time with only believers. *How wonderful,* it's tempting to think, *if everyone I worked with was a Christian. There would be no arguments, no problems!*

If you worked solely in the company of Christians, you'd soon discover that they're people just like anyone else. They have different points of view and differences of opinion. Just knowing God doesn't solve every problem.

The apostle Paul knew that. The reproach he talks about in this verse was not only from unbelievers—he also had plenty of trouble from the churches he ministered to.

Whether you work with lots of Christians or are the only one, when work becomes hard and your faith is an issue, take Paul as your example and stand firm. God doesn't promise perfect workplaces, just a relationship with the perfect One.

Lord, the workplace will never be perfect,
but thank You that I can still work for the perfect God.

I planted the seed, Apollos watered it, but God made it grow.
1 CORINTHIANS 3:6 NIV

Did you know you are part of a team—with God? It's true!
You're part of a squad to bring His good news to a hurting
world.

Paul was part of a team, too. He came to Corinth and
preached the gospel. A man named Apollos helped these
new Christians grow. But it wasn't long before Corinthian
Christians started dividing up according to which leader
they thought was best. Some boasted of their connection
with Paul, while others claimed that being ministered to by
Apollos was better. Paul pointed out that God caused spiritual growth, no matter who did the preaching.

Whether it's in church or the workplace, recognize the
importance of what Paul's saying here. No one gets results
alone—everything's a team effort, no matter what your chore
is. So recognize the input others have. Treat your coworkers
as a team and help that team to work at its peak efficiency.

You may have had an idea, but others created it, adver-
tised it, and took it out to the marketplace. Then people
bought it. In the business world, that's growth. None of it
would have happened if God hadn't worked through you.

So recognize your place in the team and give thanks for
those who help you—God especially!

Let me be humble enough, Lord,
to recognize the others on my team and be thankful for them.

Let no debt remain outstanding,
except the continuing debt to love one another,
for he who loves his fellowman has fulfilled the law.
ROMANS 13:8 NIV

On your first job or a new one, someone probably helped you get a start or learn the ropes at a new company. As your career has gone on, people have assisted you in other ways— the new staff person has given you a hand when you were overloaded with work and never complained about the extra hours, or your boss has taken up some slack for you.

Whether or not you feel like admitting it, you are in their debt. But they've already been paid by the company, so what could you do about it? Lots. You may not pay back your boss today, but someday he'll need help. Maybe you can help train a new employee. Your new coworker may need help on how to handle a situation. Or maybe you can offer to double-check something for her.

When you can't repay a debt, you can show your love for the other person by lending a hand. And if you can't give that help to the person who helped you, pass it on to another coworker. If everyone does that, your company will be a great place to work in.

Lord, when someone helps me,
let me repay the debt with love.
I want to work in a great place.

Rejoice with them that do rejoice,
and weep with them that weep.

ROMANS 12:15

Shortly after Sheila began to work for Marvin, he told her that emotions had no place in the workplace. He expected his staff to follow a strict professional code in which no one shared any personal situations. Sheila wasn't surprised that people didn't last long in the department. It wasn't long before she was considering a job change herself.

When you're on the job, you shouldn't spend much time on your personal situation. You're there to work, not solve personal problems or improve your home life. But the wise company will also allow people to share a few personal joys and sorrows. People, after all, are people. They don't drop their humanity at the door of the workplace.

Be careful not to shortchange your boss. Don't spend hours chatting with coworkers. But when someone shares about her new niece, congratulate her. When another's son missed making the team, let him know you're sorry.

When people rejoice with those who are happy and hurt for the sorrowful, they work better together. A team cares about what's on the heart of each member. So care for your team.

Lord, I want to share others' joys and sorrows.
Help me do it in the right way.

Be kindly affectioned one to another with brotherly love;
in honour preferring one another.
ROMANS 12:10

Competition can keep you on your toes—or it can kill an office environment. How you deal with it makes all the difference. In some companies, it's everyone for himself—or herself! The urge to get to the top surpasses everything else, and a cutthroat attitude kills any team spirit that tries to creep in. Other companies learn to foster friendly competition that helps workers do their best without destroying interworker connections.

This verse was addressed to the church. Paul didn't want the Romans putting themselves first and becoming puffed up in their own conceit. But the truth Paul wrote also works on the job. You may not always agree with your coworkers' attitudes or actions, but treat them with love and respect. Give them credit for their good work, and help them when you can. That's the way to "get ahead" and honor God at the same time. If your work environment demands that you do anything else, maybe it's time for a new, God-honoring career.

Getting ahead at any price can be dangerous, Lord.
Help me to honor You at every point in my career.

"Now go out and encourage your men.
I swear by the LORD that if you don't go out,
not a man will be left with you by nightfall.
This will be worse for you than all the calamities
that have come upon you from your youth till now."

2 SAMUEL 19:7 NIV

King David learned the wisdom of putting aside his own
troubles and encouraging the men who fought for him
when he heard this warning from his commander, Joab.
Caught up with mourning the death of his favorite son,
Absalom, David ignored the men who had saved him and
his family from certain destruction by this son, who had
tried to grab the kingdom from his father. When Joab
warned that the soldiers felt unappreciated by the king they
had saved, David spoke the appropriate words.

Does someone work for you? Then it's a wise decision
to offer honest words of praise. Unencouraged people are
not motivated to work hard; all of us like appreciation.
Working for a long time without a "thanks" or "well done"
turns every job into a chore.

As a boss, you may not always feel like giving appreciation, but do it anyway. Make sure the "warriors" on your
team get the encouragement they deserve, or you may find
yourself with no one to "rule"!

Lord, help me to say words of encouragement that
my workers or coworkers need to hear.

"From childhood," he answered.
"It has often thrown him into fire or water to kill him.
But if you can do anything, take pity on us and help us."
MARK 9:21–22 NIV

Without looking at the verses ahead of this one, do you know to whom this man is speaking? Could it be Peter? John? One of the religious leaders of the day?

No, the man whose son was afflicted with a mute spirit that threw him in the fire was talking to Jesus—the God-man who healed the sick and raised the dead. Was there anything He could not do? Surely He could help the suffering boy. But the father didn't quite seem to believe that when he said, "if you can do anything."

The problem didn't lie in what Jesus could do but in what kind of faith the man had. Jesus pointed out to him that anything was possible if he had faith. He was saying that He could heal the boy if the man could believe in Him.

Don't we also suffer from a lack of faith? Though we know Jesus is God, the all-powerful ruler, we still doubt. Can He handle our sins, our doubts, our mistakes? Yes, if only we believe. With that faith, like the boy's father, we can receive new hope for any situation.

I'm so glad, Lord,
that You can handle all my sins and forgive them completely.
Thank You, Jesus, for the ever-new hope I have in You.

And they said, Go to, let us build us a city and a tower,
whose top may reach unto heaven;
and let us make us a name,
lest we be scattered abroad upon the face of the whole earth.

GENESIS 11:4

What are you building with your life—a reputation, an ability to help others, a name for faithfulness? Or are you building a career that will make your name?

The people of Babel were building their own name and future on their own terms. They wanted the world to know them, and for many centuries it did. But the Tower of Babel and the city were finally destroyed. Eventually the Persians conquered the Babylonians. The people who wanted to be engraved on others' memories became part of history.

Our careers easily become part of history, too. A few years from now, no matter how much we do for our companies, our only trophy may be, "Oh, do you remember so-and-so?" Like the Tower of Babel, we fall into the back of others' memories.

We can seek to become important to other people, or we can seek to be important to God. To do that, we build up His name, not our own; we try to build His kingdom instead of our own reputation. Which are you building today?

Lord, I want Your name to be greater than mine.
Help me build Your kingdom, not my own.

I want you to know how much I am struggling for you. . . .
My purpose is that they may be encouraged in heart.
COLOSSIANS 2:1–2 NIV

"Faithful Christians should never suffer." Has anyone ever said words like those to you? They imply that anyone who really knows Jesus has a smooth, flawless life. Any troubles that come are small and easily overcome.

Those who say such things have never looked at the life of Paul. Who could have been more faithful? Yet he suffered "on the job" from Christians who would not listen to his teachings, persecution from unbelievers, and the struggles that went with his constant travel as he preached the gospel to the world.

It happens on your job, too. You're working hard and expect that things should go smoothly, but an irritating problem remains. No matter what you do, it's still there. You feel like Paul, who was doing good and getting bad in return.

Look at the problem. See if you are causing it, and fix anything that's wrong. Pray about it. Do whatever God leads you to do. But don't assume that every struggle results from a spiritual flaw. Don't let how much you've suffered determine your success.

Today, does any Christian think Paul's a failure?

Lord, when I face struggles, I want to face them with You.
Don't let discouragement keep me from
bringing my troubles to You.

For I say, through the grace given unto me,
to every man that is among you,
not to think of himself more highly than he ought to think;
but to think soberly,
according as God hath dealt to every man the measure of faith.

ROMANS 12:3

You do a good job, and you're proud of your skills and your work. Maybe you've been complimented on your abilities. Great! But are you getting a swelled head about it?

Whether you're a big fish in a small pond or a small fish in a big pond, beware of letting praise or compliments make your head the size of a weather balloon. Remember, you'll never do everything perfectly. Also remind yourself that other people have skills and abilities that you lack, and having them as your partners in the workplace makes a company run smoothly. After all, you don't want to do every job in your place, do you?

Occasionally, we all are tempted to decide we're terrific. That's okay, as long as we keep our self-opinion in perspective. It's nice to feel good about ourselves sometimes, if we treat others respectfully and appreciate their abilities, too. So today compliment someone else on a job well done. After all, you aren't the only one who needs appreciation.

Lord, help me to see myself as You see me—
in a balanced way.

God, who gives life to the dead
and calls those things which do not exist as though they did.
ROMANS 4:17 NKJV

When you work, you use tools to create something. Without a computer, pens, pencils, or other equipment, you couldn't get very far on the job. From the beginning of time, people needed fire and clay to create pots, plows or sticks to turn up the earth, and sheep to use for clothes and food.

But God creates *ex nihilo*—"out of nothing." He didn't have to have something to create another thing. Out of nothing He made the earth and heavens. Rivers began to flow and stars to twinkle in a night sky, formed from the mind of God alone.

Humans can be incredibly creative, using artistic talent, a bent for words, or physical skills that allow them to make furniture, homes, and equipment. But none of us can create with just a thought. As you work today, give thanks to the One who gave you a computer and the other items you need. Appreciate all He has done for you, and be amazed at the incredible creativity of the Creator.

Thank You, Lord,
for creating me and giving me the abilities I need to work.
I praise You for Your wonderful imagination and love.

For I heard many mocking:
"Fear on every side!" "Report," they say, "and we will report it!"
All my acquaintances watched for my stumbling, saying,
"Perhaps he can be induced;
Then we will prevail against him,
and we will take our revenge on him."

JEREMIAH 20:10 NKJV

No matter what you do, there are times when you'll get someone's back up. Maybe it's a coworker who's jealous that you got your last raise when she got none. Or perhaps it's someone who had an idea that you critiqued in the line of work, and he'll never let you forget it.

Jeremiah knew what that was like. He'd been a good prophet, but what he did was not popular. He spoke out against "Pashhur the son of Immer, the priest who was also chief governor in the house of the LORD" (v. 1), and it got him into big trouble. Even his friends were against him. On the one hand, Jeremiah felt that compulsion from God to preach, but preaching had become dangerous.

Work isn't always a "safe place." We put ourselves on the line every day in many minor ways. But no matter who goes against us, like Jeremiah, we can trust in God as our protector. When we follow His will, even the most danger-ous place will be safe.

Thank You, Jesus, for protecting me on the job.
When I'm there, like Jeremiah, I want to be faithful.

"'Jonadab son of Recab ordered his sons
not to drink wine and this command has been kept.
To this day they do not drink wine,
because they obey their forefather's command.
But I have spoken to you again and again,
yet you have not obeyed me.'"

JEREMIAH 35:14 NIV

What does it take for a father to get his child's attention? Sometimes you may feel you need a brass band to get your child's ear. If so, you know just about how God felt when He inspired Jeremiah to tell this story of the obedient sons.

Jeremiah's brass band took the form of a story. He used this example to grab the attention of the people of Judah and point out to them how little they obeyed God. Unlike these boys who leaped to do their earthly father's command, Judah was not even lending an ear to the heavenly Father. They were off in their own world, doing their own things. Eventually, Jeremiah warned, their disobedience would bring God's wrath on them.

Sometimes it's easier to hear an earthly voice than that heavenly One that calls you to obedience to Him. Will it take a brass band—or an embarrassing story—to grab your attention? God's calling you to hear His voice today.

I want to obey You, Lord.
Let me listen to Your softest song to me,
not make You send a brass band to get my attention.

"Why do you call me, 'Lord, Lord,'
and do not do what I say?"

LUKE 6:46 NIV

Lots of people claim the name of Jesus, but how many call Him Lord and ignore Him? Don't be mistaken; Jesus knows the difference between the person who talks a good line and the one who really obeys.

God knows our thoughts before we say a word, so saying one thing and doing another is perfectly useless. We may hide our true intentions from a pastor, friend, or coworker, but not from God.

When He looks at your Sunday, does God immediately know it has nothing to do with Monday, Tuesday, and the rest of the week? Did the sermon that went in one ear on the Lord's Day go out the other as you started the workweek? Or are the same ideas and ideals that you talked about at church lived out in your other six days?

If you aren't living the same way each day, you're calling on Jesus' name, then ignoring Him with the rest of your life. The only one you're fooling is yourself, so open your mouth and say, "Lord, Lord," then do what He's already commanded.

Lord, I want to claim Your name in everything I do.
Help me to live each day for You.

My soul finds rest in God alone;
my salvation comes from him.
PSALM 62:1 NIV

Whom do you really trust? In this life perhaps you have some good friends and family members who are reliable. Maybe you have a few whom you'd prefer to trust carefully because of their past track records. People can have varying degrees of "trustability." But David tells us that God was the one he *really* trusted in—the one he could trust even with his soul.

Right now, you may trust that your sister will keep your secret, your friend will return the garden tools he borrowed, or that your parents will come through with the down payment on a new home. If none of them happened, it would only affect you for a short time. You'd manage something else or get over it. Yet David's trust is not for a few days, weeks, or months, but for eternity. He has hung his heart on the truth that God will save him, both in this world and the next.

Who are you trusting with your soul today? Some people wrongly trust in tarot readers, psychics, and others as they look to the future. Others assertively deny that there is any future after this life. But everyone is trusting in something. Many bank on sliding into an eternal nothingness, but even they trust that there is no eternity. Where are you looking for your eternity?

Lord, let me trust in You alone.

Now when a man works,
his wages are not credited to him as a gift, but as an obligation.
However, to the man who does not work
but trusts God who justifies the wicked,
his faith is credited as righteousness.

ROMANS 4:4–5 NIV

You probably don't work for free—you need money to live on, pay the rent with, and save for a rainy day. The Scriptures recognize that a valuable worker deserves fair recompense.

Though the Bible recognizes the need to earn a living, it also tells us God's kingdom isn't like that. We can't work our way into heaven, because we can't do anything to make ourselves right with God. The only one who can do that is God's perfect Son, Jesus. When we believe that He died in order to forgive our sins, we agree with God on the subject, and our eternal destination becomes heaven. God gives us that gift for doing nothing more than trusting in Him.

So today, instead of spending time catching up on office work, why not trust in God? Spend time in worship, not work; and instead of trying to enter heaven on your own credit, you'll arrive there safely on your trust in Jesus. It's the only way you *can* get in.

Thank You, Lord,
that I can only enter into heaven by trust in You.
I could work 24/7 and never build up
the righteousness You offer as a gift.

And Caleb stilled the people before Moses, and said,
Let us go up at once, and possess it;
for we are well able to overcome it.

NUMBERS 13:30

Caleb didn't go with the popular vote when asked about the people who inhabited the Promised Land. When most of the other spies who'd gone in to scope out Canaan said the people living there were too powerful to overcome, this faithful man resisted the idea. "We can win over these guys," Caleb said. But in the back of his mind was surely the idea that God had brought them this far, and He would never desert them. They could certainly conquer in His power. Hadn't He promised them this turf?

On the job, you may feel as discouraged as the worrying Israelites. The work looks so hard, and the obstacles seem large. When they appear that way, are you seeing with faithful eyes like Caleb's, which saw *everything* as being small compared to God? Probably not.

God has brought you this far, and He'll never let you down, any more than He would have let down Caleb and his people. But it's up to you to trust in Him. If you do, you can have all the success He has in store for you—spiritually and in the workplace.

Lord, I don't know if I can be as faithful as Caleb,
but my heart wants to.
Help me to trust You to overcome every obstacle.

But the men that went up with him [Caleb] said,
We be not able to go up against the people;
for they are stronger than we.
And they brought up an evil report of the land. . .
saying, The land, through which we have gone to search it,
is a land that eateth up the inhabitants thereof;
and all the people that we saw in it are men of a great stature.

NUMBERS 13:31–32

Have you ever gone to a meeting and later heard two people's response to what went on? Amazing how different their take on it was, right?

People can be in the same place, see the same things, and listen to the same words, and still not be able to agree on what was said. Maybe that's what happened here. Faithful Caleb and Joshua went up into Canaan and saw the lovely place God had promised to lead them to. The doubting spies saw only huge, dangerous people. The ten who brought back that bad report ignored the riches of the land and only saw the inhabitants. Fear overcame faith. So they reported out of their feelings, and God calls their report evil.

When you hear differing reports, remember that people bring their fear or faith into the workplace and see things in light of them. You can't change their reports, but you can decide which will influence yours—fear or faith.

Lord, help my report be a faithful one.

*And there we saw the giants, the sons of Anak,
which come of the giants:
and we were in our own sight as grasshoppers,
and so we were in their sight.*

NUMBERS 13:33

The ten fearful spies who joined Caleb on the trip into Canaan may have had what we'd call a poor self-image. Compared to the Canaanites, they seemed to be small potatoes—grasshoppers even! And they imagined that their enemies would see them as these irritating insects. When the Israelite spies described themselves that way, they were relying on their own power. And looking at it from that perspective, they were probably right. They didn't have the ability to overthrow people who had cities and villages in Canaan. The Canaanites were entrenched in the land, and moving them out was a big project.

Unlike Caleb and Joshua, these men didn't consider doing the job under God's power. They forgot who had led them there and what He'd promised them.

When you feel like a grasshopper compared to co-workers, huge projects, or anything else, are you looking at yourself through the right lens? Are you seeing your working life through God's eyes or your own?

*Lord, lead me in my working life.
I know You've brought me here for a reason,
and I want to fulfill Your will.*

[Joshua and Caleb] spake unto all the company of the children of
Israel, saying,
The land, which we passed through to search it,
is an exceeding good land. If the LORD delight in us,
then he will bring us into this land, and give it us;
a land which floweth with milk and honey.

NUMBERS 14:7–8

God had only good things in mind for the Israelites: Before them lay a good land, one that would sustain the people with rich crops. In His generosity, God planned to give them everything they needed and more.

But right on the border, most of the Israelites felt determined to go back to Egypt into certain slavery. Suddenly, an easy trip back to food and "peace" looked better than the battle to gain the land. Terror must have filled their souls once they heard the spies' majority report.

We've known fear in the face of good things, too. The company is going like gangbusters, but the new hire could compete with us—and maybe we'll lose out. We're up for a raise, but will the boss remember one mistake that marred our year's performance? Like Caleb and Joshua, we can trust in God. We know He delights in us and will bring us to just the right place in His will.

Now, *will* we really trust Him?

Lord, take fear away and help me trust You.

And the LORD said unto Moses,
How long will this people provoke me?
and how long will it be ere they believe me,
for all the signs which I have shewed among them?
I will smite them with the pestilence, and disinherit them,
and will make of thee a greater nation and mightier than they.

NUMBERS 14:11–12

Many people today think that God never gets angry—surely would never do anything like this. But it's foolish to expect to be able to use God as an emotional punching bag and get no response.

God had graced the Israelites with impressive miracles. He'd brought them across the Red Sea, led them through the wilderness, and now they perched on the edge of His Promised Land. But the unthankful people planned to turn around and head for Egyptian slavery again. No wonder God became angry and threatened to wipe out His nation. Humble Moses pled with God to give the Israelites another chance—and He did. But the rebels lost the opportunity to enter the Promised Land. He'd send their sons and daughters in, instead (v. 31).

God is no gentle pushover. Obey, and we are blessed; disobey, and He'll make us do laps in the desert. Before we turn down His grace, we need to ask ourselves if we want our own plot in the desert or a piece of our Lord's Promised Land.

I don't want to wander away from You, Lord.
Keep me in Your path each day.

I say unto you,
that likewise joy shall be in heaven over one sinner that repenteth,
more than over ninety and nine just persons,
which need no repentance.

LUKE 15:7

Has God ever thrown a party for you? Do you know how much doing that would thrill Him?

When a soul enters eternity by faith in Jesus, all heaven rejoices over that new member of God's kingdom. You might say God throws a party just for the new believer. All heaven celebrates for each person who comes to God through His Son. If you know Jesus, there was a day when God gave a celebration with your name on it. Invitations went out to all heaven, and everyone had a great time rejoicing in what God had done in your life. It was a great day!

If you've never had such a great day in your life, it can still happen. All you need to do is admit to God that you need to turn your life around. Tell Him you know you've sinned and need His forgiveness and that you're trusting in Jesus for that forgiveness.

Do I hear a party starting?

Lord, thank You that all heaven rejoices
at the salvation of one person.
Thank You that You were willing to let all heaven
celebrate because I came to faith in You.

And the multitude said,
This is Jesus the prophet of Nazareth of Galilee.
MATTHEW 21:11

With a joyous celebration, palm fronds waving, the people gathered in Jerusalem were happy to see Jesus. But what Jesus did they want to see? Not the one who was "very God of very God," as the creed says. Who would have seen Him as being more than a prophet? Not until after the Resurrection would even the twelve disciples know who He really was.

We have a wonderful advantage over the people of Jesus' day. We know He is God and have known that from the moment we believed in Him. There's no confusion in our hearts and minds.

Or is there? On this Palm Sunday, many who claim to bear the name of Christ want to join the celebration but aren't quite clear why they are celebrating. They want the good things Jesus brings: that whole, clean feeling of sins forgiven, the joy that floods the soul. But ask them to give up sin, and they may balk. Not live with a girlfriend? Be faithful to your spouse? Be honest with everyone?

This celebration is so much more joyous when your heart is really clean. Today, confess sin and clean the slate with God so you can see Him as king, not just a prophet. He yearns to be king of your heart today.

Lord, make my heart clean from sin.
I want to celebrate with You.

For the good that I would I do not:
but the evil which I would not, that I do.

ROMANS 7:19

You want to do a good job. You're committed to doing well and building a good career. But something just grabs ahold of you. You know it's wrong. God would never approve; still, you start heading in the wrong direction.

Though we know God and want to serve Him whole-heartedly, at times that old sin nature sticks its head up and seems to commandeer our lives. We struggle to resist, and sometimes we aren't fully successful. Occasionally, we don't even want to oppose sin. The apostle Paul knew what that was like. He knew full well what the right thing was, yet he balked at doing it. Something inside drew even this spiritual giant back to the wrong way.

None of us entirely escapes sin. As we grow in Jesus, temptations may lessen, but they'll always hang around at the fringes of our spirits. Every day we need to alertly guard against evil desires. When one tugs at our souls, we must rush to God and cling to Him for aid. No sin situation is hopeless: In Him, we *can* still do right.

Lord, I need Your help to stand firm.
In Your Spirit I can resist evil,
so fill me with Your strength today.

"If a righteous man turns from his righteousness and does evil,
he will die for it."
EZEKIEL 33:18 NIV

Righteousness isn't just a once-and-for-all thing. You can't accept Jesus, then simply ignore Him for the rest of your life. If you expect to do that and still want all the benefits of heaven, you're just kidding yourself.

Treating righteousness that way would be like going to a job interview, getting the job, and never showing up for work. Who among us would expect to receive a regular paycheck if we did that? What company would last a day allowing "employees" to take such advantage of it?

God doesn't allow people to take advantage of Him, either. Those who don't show up for His kingdom day by day don't get the reward of the ones who are there, working in His fields each and every day. The person who has no interest in God's kingdom doesn't receive heaven at all. The true believer who walks away from His commandments may receive heaven, but he'll pay a price for disobedience, even to the point of losing his earthly life.

You know what it means to show up at the job every day. Do the same for God. Show His love in action at work, home, or wherever you go.

Lord, not because I think I can earn heaven,
but because I love You,
I want to seek righteousness each day.
Help me start at this moment.

> *"And if I say to the wicked man,*
> *'You will surely die,' but he then turns away from*
> *his sin and does what is just and right—*
> *if he gives back what he took in pledge for a loan,*
> *returns what he has stolen,*
> *follows the decrees that give life, and does no evil,*
> *he will surely live; he will not die."*
>
> EZEKIEL 33:14–15 NIV

Have you ever made a mistake on the job? How did your boss treat it? Chances are that if you immediately took steps to clean up your act, you stayed with the company. You showed you cared, and your boss cut you some slack.

It's the same with God. He isn't a pushover who never punishes sin. But neither will He hold sin against someone who recognizes his wrongdoing and turns from it, faithfully trying to make right the wrong he's done and showing his change of heart by obeying God's commands. What point would there be in God's punishing a person who was no longer wicked? It would go against everything in His Word. When we do what He asks and follow His Law, God forgives. No matter how bad that wickedness was, it's gone forever.

God offers to clean each of our slates today. We only have to ask Him to use the eraser on our lives.

> *Forgive me, Lord, for my sins.*
> *I want to make them right,*
> *when possible, and follow Your decrees.*

> " 'Then they will know that I am the LORD,
> when I have made the land a desolate waste because of
> all the detestable things they have done.' "
> EZEKIEL 33:29 NIV

Sin creates desolate lives. We don't have to wait for God to take our country and denude it or give us terrible leadership. To find the damage sin does to our personal worlds doesn't require a microscope. Signs appear in a coworker's divorce or the career-minded selfishness of one person who ruins an efficient team. We know the desolation sin created in our lives when we failed to walk with God.

Though we might like to, we can't control the sin in other people's lives. No matter how much we encourage friends and family to make right choices, think of others, and turn to God, we cannot make them choose wisely. We can only bear the message, letting them know how sin destroys relationships and ruins happiness. We do that by sharing examples of how sin hurt our lives and showing blessings God's given as we've followed Him. Through our personal testimony and the way we live each day for God, we can fight back against the wasteland. Like Ezekiel, we may not always find our message welcome, but it's one that needs to be told with kindness, gentleness, and care.

*Lord, use my life to turn people away from sin
and toward life in You.*

"My people. . .listen to your words,
but they do not put them into practice.
With their mouths they express devotion,
but their hearts are greedy for unjust gain.
Indeed, to them you are nothing more than one who sings love songs
with a beautiful voice and plays an instrument well,
for they hear your words but do not put them into practice."
EZEKIEL 33:31–32 NIV

Are you a Christian who claims to love God but never acts on that concept? Then the Bible compares your faith to entertainment, not commitment.

People you work with can tell which you are. They can identify the "entertainment Christians," who are in it just for the fun, from the ones who really mean it. Maybe unbelievers don't give less serious Christians as much grief as the committed ones, but they know which ones mean what they say. And when they need to know about God, whom do you think they go to?

Are you listening to God's Word but not living by it? Then maybe, like the people in these verses, something other than God is first in your heart. You're listening to Him and treating Him as a singer with a lovely voice instead of the omnipotent Holy One who has words of life you can live by.

O omnipotent Holy One, I don't want to entertain
but show commitment. Help me live for You.

" 'The way of the Lord is not just.'
But it is their way that is not just."

EZEKIEL 33:17 NIV

"How could God ever forgive Robert?" Sally wanted to know. "He brought such sorrow to my sister Ellie while they were married, and it hasn't even stopped since they got the divorce. He's turned her children against her. Why, it isn't fair!"

Sometimes our aching hearts have a hard time understanding God. We wonder if He's really the just, righteous God He claims to be when He does not grind our axes but offers forgiveness to those who have done us wrong. We may want to accuse Him. But before we do, we need to look at our own motives.

When we feel that way, we aren't much different from our non-Christian neighbors and coworkers who hold an undying grudge against a family member. Maybe a disagreement occurred twenty years ago, but the hurt party still doesn't speak to the offender. Perhaps that grievance has spread to other family members.

We are not more just than God. Our ways are not the perfect ones. And we do not have the power to work things out in a new and more wonderful way. So before we point the finger, we should consider our own hurts and hates. Then we need to pray and wait on God, who can work wonders—even in places where injustice seems to reign.

Lord, help me see Your justice in the world.

When the morning was come,
all the chief priests and elders of the people
took counsel against Jesus to put him to death.
MATTHEW 27:1

If Jesus had "just happened" to die—if it had been an accidental thing—it would not be so shocking. But the thought that the important people of Jerusalem, the leaders and priests, plotted against Him makes us aware of the horror of this act. How could they, who supposedly experienced relationship with God, do such a thing?

It is horrible, but what's even more horrible is that the sins we've committed have brought Him to Good Friday. Jesus did not hang on the cross for only the wrongdoing of first-century Jews. He died for the sins of all humanity, down through the ages. Our names are on that long list of evildoers who caused His death.

Some of us may have "small" sins. We've never murdered. But we have cut people down with our tongues. A multitude of little things separate us from God. Sin really has no size.

But, gloriously, all our willful sin can be swept away in a moment of confession—the Resurrection declares that we have new life in Jesus, the author and finisher of our faith (Hebrews 12:2). Jesus died not to make us feel horror, but to give us new, fresh life. Rejoice in that life today!

Lord, I rejoice in Your freeing love.
Thank You for Your horrifying sacrifice that brought me life.

Yea, he loved the people;
all his saints are in thy hand:
and they sat down at thy feet;
every one shall receive of thy words.
DEUTERONOMY 33:3

Did you know that if you have faith in Jesus, God calls you a saint? No one has to find miracles you've done or show just how holy you are in order to receive that name. A biblical saint is a "holy one," someone called to show the difference God makes in human lives by being set apart for Him.

Some liturgical churches have named a select few saints, and many of them have exciting Christian testimonies to be shared with the world. The biblical saints, Peter, Paul, John, and so on, started the newborn church on its path. In the Middle Ages, St. Patrick and St. Columba helped spread the gospel to new lands. We can rightly admire their faith and work.

But let's not allow our less-exciting testimonies to make us feel so inferior that we never reach a hurting modern workplace, where those without hope surround us. The ancient truth bearers are not the only ones God wants to use. Are you showing the world His difference through your life?

Lord, I'm honored to be one of Your saints.
Let me bear Your light to those I work with today.

[Deborah] held court under the Palm of Deborah. . .
and the Israelites came to her to have their disputes decided.
JUDGES 4:5 NIV

What an unusual person Deborah was! Judges were usually men, yet she held this position of importance, deciding major issues for the people of Israel. In a time when most people thought of women as being fairly unimportant, she held a powerful position and seems to have been a good leader.

Like Deborah, we can find ourselves in unusual jobs. Perhaps you're the only person of your sex on your job. Maybe you are young, working with people greatly senior to you. Or perhaps you are the only person of your race on the job. Being the one who's different can be a challenge. Your position can be one to complain about or one to learn from. The Scriptures don't show Deborah whining or complaining. She took charge of the situation. She did her best for God, and an impressive best it was.

Whether you fit in completely or find yourself in a tough spot, you're there to serve God, not complain or quit easily. So make even your differences work for God, no matter what they are.

I may feel different, Lord, but You've given me this place.
Let me serve You by doing my best every day.

*"I will go with you.
But because of the way you are going about this,
the honor will not be yours,
for the Lord will hand Sisera over to a woman."*

JUDGES 4:9 NIV

God gave Barak a message through Deborah. He was to fight his enemy, Sisera, and God would give the Canaanite commander into Barak's hands. But nervous Barak wanted security—certainty that Deborah was right and God would do what she said. He'd only obey if she came with him. God granted Barak's desire, and Deborah went with him; but because the Israelite commander lacked trust, Deborah told him a woman would kill Sisera and get the credit for it.

In the workplace, we, too, sometimes want both the security and the glory when our company lands a big contract. We don't want to risk a lot on the sale, but we want the raise or bonus after the job comes through. Just like Barak, we can't have our cake and eat it, too.

We shouldn't take every risk that's out there—it would be foolish to do so. But when we have looked at every angle and the risk seems worth it, when we've prayed about our decision making and feel that doing this would please God, it's not time to hold back. Not to listen would be foolish.

*Lead me, Lord, when I face risks.
I need Your guidance every day.*

Ask the LORD for rain in the spring, and he will give it.
It is the LORD who makes storm clouds that drop showers of rain
so that every field becomes a lush pasture.
ZECHARIAH 10:1 NLT

By and large, we're no longer an agrarian culture, so the meaning of this passage loses something in the cultural translation. We cart in our vegetables from countries around the world, so if there's a drought nearby, we may pay more, but we don't fear for our lives.

The small farmer of the Old Testament period didn't have that option. No rain, no crops, no life. Asking God for rain was no unimportant matter. Yet the people of Judah had ignored God's ability to provide their need. Instead they turned to idols, expecting them to give an "easy out" without expecting the obedience Judah refused God.

We may not need rain except to water our lawns and shrubs, but we still need God's providence. He's the One who provides us with our jobs, our homes, and our daily food, even if we don't work in a field and harvest its fruits. So when we face problems on the job or need money to pay our bills, we can still turn to Him and ask for the rain of His wisdom. It provides for us as surely as the wet stuff from the clouds waters the fields.

Lord, I need Your help in so many ways.
Give me Your rain on every portion of my life.

And Jesus answered him, saying, It is written,
That man shall not live by bread alone,
but by every word of God.
LUKE 4:4

We don't live by bread alone. Dieticians tell us we need a
more varied diet than that, so we consume a diverse diet of
bread and meat and vegetables and fruit. But Jesus uses
bread to symbolize the edibles that sustain life. He compares our need to take in the cereal, milk, bread, ham and
cheese, and chicken with veggies to our desperate need for
God. Without food, our lives would end, but without God's
Word, our spirits also fast and die.

We often think we're depending on our bosses to provide for our needs. We ask for a raise or object to the one
we got because we feel we need more money to pay the
bills, raise our families, or put bread (and other things) on
the table. When our bosses fail us, we feel disappointed. Yet
if they deny us, God still will not—His Word promises His
care. As we obey His truths, He provides even for those
physical needs. Even when there's only a crust of bread in
the larder, we can always depend on Him.

Lord, thank You for caring for me
even when I'm not sure my boss does.
How glad I am that You're always there,
especially when bill-paying time rolls around.

Go ye therefore, and teach all nations,
baptizing them in the name of the Father,
and of the Son, and of the Holy Ghost.
MATTHEW 28:19

Just the other day, our doorbell rang. On the doorstep stood a couple of people who wanted to share their faith. So my husband spent a few minutes chatting with them. It didn't take long for him to figure out that orthodox Christianity was not what they cared to distribute with their literature. When the conversation turned to the Trinity, these men horrified my husband when they claimed it was not in the Bible, and they didn't believe in it.

Too bad these folks hadn't paid more attention to this verse, along with Galatians 4:6; 1 Peter 1:2; and John 15:26, all of which connect the three persons of the Godhead in an unmistakable way. The authority for spreading the gospel—the real gospel—comes from all three persons.

I doubt my husband's faithful witness changed these men's hearts, but perhaps God opened the door to His kingdom by just a crack. In time, we pray those faithful words bear fruit, based on the love of God the Father, the sacrifice of the Son, and the inspiration of the Spirit.

Lord, I cannot change another person's heart.
But let me always testify to Your truth.

"He is not here, but is risen!
Remember how He spoke to you when He was still in Galilee, saying,
'The Son of Man must be delivered into the hands of sinful men,
and be crucified, and the third day rise again.'"

LUKE 24:6–7 NKJV

Jesus had given His disciples a clear message of what would happen to Him, but in the fear, shock, and disbelief that surrounded the events of that terrible week, His words escaped them. So the angels remind the women at the tomb of Jesus' prophecy.

Sometimes we relate to the women's forgetfulness of the Lord's words. God gives us promises, but in the hustle and bustle of life, we lose track of them. He tells us all will work out to our good and His glory, but we don't always see it that way when we're in the midst of a frustrating situation.

Thank God that we need not rely on our own perceptions of our troubles. He has sent His Son, who provides us with new life and a new way of living that life. Our trust is in the risen Lord, not just a man slipped into an early grave. In our lives, too, He is risen indeed!

Lord, I praise You for the gift of Your Son
and the new life He offers.
As I trust in Him, I, too, rise to new life.

One who is slack in his work is brother to one who destroys.
PROVERBS 18:9 NIV

If you've slacked off at work, have you thought of yourself as being destructive? Probably not. But ask the person who had to take up that slack and had to rush through something else if it destroyed his opinion of you.

If you weren't up to speed because you just had a new baby and sleep had become foreign to you, perhaps your coworker didn't think that harshly of you. Eventually you got more shut-eye and improved. Perhaps you found some ways to make it up to your coworker.

But the person who habitually slacks off causes real problems in the office or factory. People resent someone who habitually won't pull her weight. For awhile she can get away with it, but eventually the boss begins to see the effects of that slackness, and she moves on, either fired or demoted into a job where she won't do much harm.

More than that, working hard isn't just something Mom and Dad told you to do so you could earn the big bucks. It's an attitude God designed you to have. So don't slack off—work to please the One who created you to honor Him, from nine to five or at any other hour.

Lord, I want to build up, not destroy.
Keep me working faithfully for You.

A fool's mouth is his undoing,
and his lips are a snare to his soul.
PROVERBS 18:7 NIV

"I should never have opened my mouth," Kate lamented. "It was a foolish thing to tell Sam about our boss's plans, even though they weren't confidential. If I'd known it'd backfire on me like this, I would never have said a word." Kate knew what she'd done was unwise; unfortunately, she hadn't realized that before she spoke.

Thinking before we speak is a wise workplace decision. We need to weigh the impact of our words, what response the person we're talking to may have, and other issues specific to our workplaces. We don't want to tell a confidence to the biggest gossip in the company, even if she is so nice. Nor do we want to hurt the feelings of someone who is particularly sensitive on a subject.

Unwise words may show we are not living in God's wisdom but our own sin; or even if we are not doing wrong, they can land us in impossible situations. Taking this practical advice from God's Word and thinking before we speak saves us a lot of trouble and heartache.

Lord, I want to speak wisely and keep my soul clean.
Keep me from doing wrong with my words.

The words of a gossip are like choice morsels;
they go down to a man's inmost parts.
PROVERBS 18:8 NIV

Let's face it—occasionally most of us like a good bit of gossip. We like to "hear the news" or "know what's going on." But what seems so tasty going down can give us an incredible case of indigestion.

Scripture says a lot about gossip—none of it good. God takes it seriously and never hands out exceptions for those things that we "just had to" pass on. Nor does He allow us to explain away our foolishness in bearing tales about other people, hurting their feelings, and ruining our own testimonies. So the next time someone offers you a "choice morsel" of gossip, let it end at you. Don't pass it on, talk about it to the person it concerned, or comment on it if someone else brings it up. Do all you can to defuse the situation by encouraging others to end it, too. Sometimes all it takes is one gently disapproving comment.

You'd appreciate it if others had a similar reaction when a story about you made the rounds. Let the meal end here, before it upsets more than one stomach.

Lord, give me strength to resist gossip in all its forms
and help me make it stop with me.

But we will give ourselves continually to prayer,
and to the ministry of the word.
ACTS 6:4

Many non-Christians don't think of prayer as "practical." They see it as some airy thing that "doesn't get the job done" and wonder why Christians even bother with it. These doubters haven't experienced prayer's power. But the apostles recognized prayer as an element critical to their work of spreading the gospel. Without God's guidance and blessing, the work could not be accomplished.

Though we may not preach to multitudes, prayer is important in our lives, too. With it we can do our jobs better and lift up coworkers who are under stress or have personal problems. We can even pray for the decisions our bosses have to make, so that they will make wise choices.

Sometimes, those who pooh-pooh prayer have a real crisis: They have an ill child, or their lives have been impacted by a family member's layoff. Then it's amazing how open they can be to the words "I will pray for you and your situation." So offer to lift those unbelievers up in prayer, both for their own salvation and the need at hand.

Remember, the work does not go on without prayer.

Today, Lord, I know some coworkers who need prayer.
Even if they do not want to know You,
I know You soften hearts.
Turn them to You through this situation.

MARCH 28

*If any man see his brother sin a sin which is not unto death,
he shall ask, and he shall give him life
for them that sin not unto death.*

1 JOHN 5:16

"I'm so disappointed in Joyce," Sarah admitted. "After all those years far from the Lord, she was walking with Him again, and now she's gone back to her old ways. I can't understand it."

Sarah thought she'd helped Joyce when her witness seemed to help return her coworker to God, and it was hard to accept that Joyce had slipped away from Him again. But suddenly Joyce didn't want to hear about God at all.

It's hard when a Christian seems to forget the joys of knowing God and returns to sin. But we don't need to write that person off. Instead, God calls us to pray. What may seem to us to be the end of the story may just be another turn in the plot. God may have more work to do—and this could signify a time of humbling that will eventually reap spiritual benefits.

Know someone on the job who's turned in the wrong direction? Even if she won't listen, you can still bend God's ear on the subject. When He acts, you may see some real changes in your coworker's life.

*Lord, work in the life of my coworker.
I want to see her living totally for You.*

Then the servant girl who kept the door said to Peter,
"You are not also one of this Man's disciples, are you?"
He said, "I am not."
JOHN 18:17 NKJV

For three years Peter publicly followed Jesus. The disciple stood near the Master during the miracles, the messages, and all the good times. Everyone could see him sticking by Jesus.

But when Jesus came before the high priest, His life in danger, Peter caved in to fear and denied his Lord to a simple servant girl. Why would he care what a slave thought? Perhaps he feared that word of his presence would get back to the ruling priests.

Like Peter, we've caved in because of what others we barely knew thought of us. Instead of obeying the Lord we've loved, we've sought approval of both people who barely matter and those who could have some earthly authority over us. In a split second, love for the all-powerful Lord hardly seemed to matter.

Instead of allowing fear to rule our lives, we need to steadfastly rest in Jesus' love. He who holds the entire world in His hands can direct our lives in the face of bad opinions from those who think ill of us. When we're faithful to Him, we hold firm to the One who really matters.

Lord, I want to hold on to You and please You only.
Give me strength to do what I cannot do under my own power.

So they rushed back to tell his eleven disciples—
and everyone else—what had happened. The women...
told the apostles what had happened,
but the story sounded like nonsense, so they didn't believe it.
LUKE 24:9–11 NLT

The most important message of history and its bearers couldn't even get anyone to believe them! How frustrated the women must have felt. They probably told the disciples, "If you don't believe us, check it out for yourselves!"

We know what it's like to bear an important message and receive unbelief for our troubles. We've risked such responses from our family, friends, and coworkers as we've told them of Jesus.

Just like the women, we can encourage others to check our message out for themselves. Jesus' empty tomb has never been credibly disproved. John and Luke reported that many saw Jesus after His Resurrection (John 20; Luke 24; Acts 1:3), a hard-to-deny multiple testimony. The labors of the first-century Pharisees and Sadducees could not prove their testimony wrong, and subsequent attempts at "debunking" these events are no more convincing.

We can have confidence in the Resurrection, more certainty than those who attack it. Let's share the good news and encourage people to check it out with biblically based sources that will show them that Jesus has conquered the grave.

I want to share Your truths with those
who have not understood them, Lord.
Give me the confidence I need.

Therefore, laying aside all malice, all deceit,
hypocrisy, envy, and all evil speaking.
1 PETER 2:1 NKJV

Certain attitudes, actions, and ways of thinking are not compatible with Christianity. The apostle Peter was absolutely clear on that subject. Though he spoke to the church, and this would be particularly true between fellow believers, it's also true that Christians on the job, at home, and anywhere else need to avoid these negatives that usually show up on their tongues.

As a Christian, don't speak one way at work and another way at church. To do so shows a lack of consistency of faith. It's as if you are saying that Jesus' truths are only sometimes valid—that they are true on Sunday but not for the rest of the week (except maybe Wednesday night).

You can't be malicious on Friday, then experience a personality change over the weekend. After all, part of the reason God has you on earth on all seven days of the week is to be a testimony—a good testimony—to Him. A malicious comment, a web of deceit, hypocritical or envious attitudes, or nasty words attract no one to Jesus. Instead, people will be more likely to conclude that you've been serving the evil one.

So not only in the church, but at work, home, and in the community, lay aside all these things. You'll be blessed without them.

Lord, keep my tongue clean and consistent
as a testimony for You.

But now they that are younger than I have me in derision,
whose fathers I would have disdained to have
set with the dogs of my flock.

JOB 30:1

In today's marketplace, experience often isn't much valued. Kate found out how true that was when she got laid off. Her manager's youthful boss felt anyone who'd been on a job for more than a few years was "dead wood." It didn't make any difference that knowing the clients' past history made selling to them a lot easier. For some time, she struggled with negative feelings about that boss. It hurt to know she'd been judged so unfairly.

Sometimes we don't work with insightful people. Young or old, they may not respect our work or our value to the company. Though they hold a high position, they do not value God's wisdom. These may not be the folks we'd prefer to have around us—or prefer to have leading our company. But they hold that position of authority.

No matter what kind of person you work for, that person alone is not in control of your future. Like Job, you depend on God, not the people around you. Also like Job, you may find that in the end, a forced change turns out better than you expected.

Lord, let me focus on the fact that You are ultimately
in control of any manager or boss who touches my career.

In the days when the judges ruled. . .
there was a famine in the land.
And a certain man of Bethlehem [Elimelech]. . .
went to dwell in the country of Moab,
he and his wife and his two sons.

RUTH 1:1 NKJV

We don't control what goes on in the world. So when things change in the marketplace or the economy takes a downturn, we may have to move to a new location. As we make the move, we leave part of ourselves in our old home.

Elimelech trudged all the way to Moab with his family to avoid a famine. They settled down, and his sons married women from that country. Life was probably pretty good. But Elimelech's household never forgot the place they came from; Bethlehem still looked best when trouble came. When Elimelech and his sons died, his wife and one daughter-in-law went back "home" to Bethlehem.

We, too, never forget the places we live. Each has a special memory. And often we can return for a visit, share our love for the people who remain there, and reminisce about the joys we shared. No matter where we go, if God is leading us, a special piece of our heart remains there. When God gives a place to us, it's forever in our hearts.

Lord, I only want to live in the places You have set for me.
Wherever I go, let it be "at home" in You.

I went out full, and the LORD hath brought me home again empty.
RUTH 1:21

Ramon started a new job, and everything looked so wonderful. The company's promises for promotion looked good, and he was heading in the career direction he'd always wanted to go. He couldn't wait to jump in to work.

It didn't take Ramon long to see that what he thought he was getting into and what he really had to deal with were two different things. It wasn't that the company had lied to him, but his new boss just didn't seem to realize exactly how things were in the marketplace. After only a few weeks on the job, Ramon could see he'd better start looking again.

Sometimes a new job doesn't work out. Much as job hunting may be tough, it may be best to leave that place and look for a new one or to look around while you hold on to that less-than-wonderful position.

When something like this happens, it's easy to ask, "Where was God in all this?" Don't assume God has abandoned you. He may be taking you on a longer path, but He hasn't forgotten your needs. In the end, empty or full, He'll bring you home.

Lord, when I wonder where You are,
remind me that You're right beside me.

" 'Should you then seek great things for yourself? Seek them not.
For I will bring disaster on all people, declares the LORD,
but wherever you go I will let you escape with your life.' "
JEREMIAH 45:5 NIV

All Judah groaned under the punishments for disobedience God had placed on that country. That situation had gotten to Baruch, Jeremiah's faithful scribe. He complained that he wanted some good things from God, not this feeling of being worn out by agony.

But God, who sees all people as equal, refused to reward Baruch's faithfulness to his master with good things while the rest of the nation suffered. What Judah endured, the prophet and his companion would experience, too, so no one could accuse God of favoritism. God promised only to spare the scribe's life.

When the company we work for suffers, we suffer. Anything else would be wrong. When corporate officers drain their company while the average worker's pension is destroyed, a scandal ensues. Everyone recognizes that it's wrong for one to benefit mightily while others lose their jobs, their futures, and their investments.

If your company is suffering, do what you can to help. Don't expect to escape just because you're a Christian or a good worker. God doesn't treat people preferentially like that.

Lord, it's hard to suffer,
but I don't want Your name to be disgraced.
So if I need to live through hard times, be close by my side.
With You I can go anywhere.

Children are a gift from the LORD;
they are a reward from him.
PSALM 127:3 NLT

If you have kids, remember this verse the next time they wake you up on a Saturday when you'd planned to sleep in. Hold off that irritation just a moment, and thank God for His blessing.

You aren't being punished with that joyful voice caroling you awake. (Perhaps it's better to be thankful that it wasn't screaming!) Instead remind yourself that children are children, and their enjoy-every-moment attitude can't take account of Mom or Dad's late Friday night at the office.

Remember, too, that not everyone is as blessed as you. Plenty of couples would love to have a child and can't. They make do by showering affection on nieces, nephews, and friends' children, but it just isn't the same. Sure, they may not get awakened at 6:00 A.M. or earlier by a child's voice— it may be the garbage truck or the dog scratching at the door. Isn't the blessing of an unexpected "I love you, Mommy" or "I missed you, Daddy" worth a little shut-eye?

Lord, thank You for my children.
When I'm not so sure they're a blessing,
remind me of this verse.

Then they said to her, "Woman, why are you weeping?"
She said to them, "Because they have taken away my Lord,
and I do not know where they have laid Him."

JOHN 20:13 NKJV

Faithful Mary Magdalene didn't quite understand. Still she looked for Jesus' body. To her, the Master's disappearance must have seemed one big hoax, perhaps the work of the religious leaders who wanted to get rid of Him any way they could.

The alternative did seem pretty preposterous. What man who died that kind of painful criminal's death came back to life? Crucifixion was a particularly nasty way to end your life, and for that reason, people who died that way were not considered blessed by God. Jesus seemed the last person who would receive life again.

Sometimes the people God saves seem to be in the same situation. The "nice" folks we'd love to see come to Him don't. But that one-time biker or gang member does. God doesn't deal in the probabilities that something will be true or false. He works in His own way. What seems impossible one day is a glorious fact the next.

That's the way it was when Jesus was raised from death into new life. We only follow in His footsteps.

Thank You, Lord,
for bringing one as impossible as I to new life.
I glory in Your work in my life.

And Joshua the son of Nun, and Caleb the son of Jephunneh,
which were of them that searched the land, rent their clothes.
NUMBERS 14:6

Have you ever felt like Joshua and Caleb? You did your best on the job and knew just what you were talking about when you gave your coworkers the information they needed to do the work. To you, it looked really good, but your bosses didn't believe you and shot the idea down. It's enough to make anyone tear their clothes in anguish!

Joshua and Caleb knew how it felt. The only faithful spies into the Promised Land, they could see the good God had planned for His people. But the doubt of the other ten spies ended their "project" in a few minutes flat. The people didn't believe the honest report of these two men but went with the bad report of the majority.

When you're not believed, you can be gracious about it. Give your bosses the benefit of the doubt; after all, unlike Joshua and Caleb, you do not have biblical testimony to your rightness on this subject. Accept it without bearing a grudge. That's the Christian response.

If it's still too much, you can tear your clothes—if you can afford a new wardrobe. But it won't change the outcome.

Lord, sometimes I get frustrated enough to tear my clothes, too.
Keep me well clothed in spirit and even tempered, too.

But my servant Caleb, because he had another spirit with him,
and hath followed me fully,
him will I bring into the land whereinto he went;
and his seed shall possess it.

NUMBERS 14:24

Imagine following God fully! What a testimony to any believer's life. Aware of our own sinfulness, we'd hardly claim to follow Him so well.

Caleb was not perfect, any more than we are, but his heart was committed to God. You can see that by the way he stood up for taking the Promised Land, and through the years, his heart for God never lessened. Yet this faithful man still spent forty years in the desert, companion to the faithless Israelites. All that time, his eyes must have focused on the promise God made here. He would eventually see the land God had promised him and his children.

Caleb's heroic qualities appear larger than life in part because of his faithful waiting. Despite his own correct choice, he did not get an immediate inheritance. Yet the Bible never says he whined, complained, or blamed anyone else. He displays impressive composure.

When we pay the price for a coworker's fault, are we like Caleb? Or do we whine, complain, and seek the closest pity party? Which would God describe as following Him fully?

Lord, help me follow You fully
with my heart and tongue.

Now therefore give me this mountain,
whereof the LORD spake in that day;
for thou heardest in that day how the Anakims were there,
and that the cities were great and fenced:
if so be the LORD will be with me,
then I shall be able to drive them out, as the LORD said.
And Joshua blessed him, and gave unto Caleb
the son of Jephunneh Hebron for an inheritance.

JOSHUA 14:12–13

Caleb was eighty-five years old when he requested this of Joshua. All those years he'd walked beside the faithless Israelites, and now he was coming into his own as one of only two Israelites who'd made it through all forty years of wandering. He and Joshua alone had come for a second time to the Promised Land.

How God blessed Caleb's steadfast faithfulness. When things were tough, Caleb believed. When they didn't go his way, he held on to God. Now the fruit of that faithfulness became reality, and Caleb received his inheritance. Though it was not an easy one, he was eager to continue in the Lord's service by conquering the land.

When we face challenges on the job, do we respond with Caleb's faith? Or do we let doubt overcome us if we don't see immediate results? However long we have to wait, God will not be faithless—we are the only ones who can be that.

Lord, keep me faithful to You,
no matter how long I have to wait.

So he said, "I have been very zealous for the LORD God of hosts;
for the children of Israel have forsaken Your covenant,
torn down Your altars, and killed Your prophets with the sword.
I alone am left; and they seek to take my life."
1 KINGS 19:10 NKJV

When he reported to God on the work he'd done, Elijah could say he'd done a good job. In fact, he'd done so well that he'd offended the queen, endangering his life.

At some point, we all have to give an accounting for our work, whether it's at raise time or a project evaluation. Having that responsibility may not seem welcome, but it's a good idea. Accountability keeps us from becoming too caught up in ourselves and reminds us we have a responsibility to our bosses and the company at large.

Sometimes our skillfulness may even get us in trouble, though we probably aren't in danger for our lives, as Elijah was. We may seem to threaten our manager if he thinks we want to take his job. Or we may get that raise someone else wanted. We still need to do our best, without slacking off. After all, like Elijah, we are still accountable to the One we really work for—God.

Lord, help me do my best for You.
Then I can trust that whatever happens to my career,
it will work to my benefit and Your glory.

*So the wall was finished on the twenty-fifth day
of the month Elul, in fifty-two days.
When all our enemies heard of it,
all the nations around us feared and fell far in their own esteem,
for they saw that this work was done by our God.*

NEHEMIAH 6:15–16 AMP

Under Nehemiah's leadership, the people of Judah had rebuilt Jerusalem's wall in fifty-two days. Facing opposition had only spurred them on. Though half the workers had to stand by fully armed to fend off attack, they'd accomplished their mission. In record time, the wall was standing.

The nations around Judah didn't like it one bit. But it wasn't because of something powerful about the people of Judah—no, they feared this nation because it was clear God had helped them.

Do you face an impossible task today? Perhaps you need to get some work done before the end of the day, and you don't see how you'll do it. Start by asking God's help, then work as hard as you can, giving your best to your boss. But when it's all done, don't expect that you have no more to do. Give God the praise in a tactful way. Perhaps you only need to say, "That was an answer to prayer," but somehow let the message that God was with you be known.

*Thank You, Lord, for helping me with impossible tasks.
To You, nothing is impossible.*

"Therefore, behold, I will allure her,
will bring her into the wilderness, and speak comfort to her."
HOSEA 2:14 NKJV

If you've been caught in sin, have you heard God's voice calling you back to Him? How sweet that voice sounded in the midst of the mess you'd made of life.

When we do sin, and we all do from time to time, God does not condemn us and leave us to our own way. Instead, as a lover, He calls to us. He draws us to Him with His love, reminds us of our past devotion. In response, we have a choice. Will we again turn away from the joys of knowing Him, or will we return to the One who loves us? Turning away leads to despair, while rejoining Christ brings great delight. "I will give her her vineyards from there, and the Valley of Achor as a door of hope," God promises. "She shall sing there, as in the days of her youth, as in the day when she came up from the land of Egypt" (v. 15).

How wonderful is the God who loves us so much, He keeps coming back to woo our love. May we never stray far from Him.

Lord, keep me close to Your side and woo me with Your love.
I am too prone to being drawn to this world.

Now when she had said this,
she turned around and saw Jesus standing there,
and did not know that it was Jesus.

JOHN 20:14 NKJV

Jesus' first appearance after the most amazing event in history, and Mary doesn't even recognize Him. Not yet does He appear in all His glory, so she mistakes Him for a gardener (v. 15). This seemingly simple, average man is not what He seems.

Sometimes our faith, too, seems ordinary. We don't feel as if we're anything spectacular. What tribes of native peoples have we reached? Hasn't God used others more than us? Perhaps that's true, but if we stand in the right place with God, He will use us. The resurrection life of Jesus shines through any believer truly willing to reflect His love.

Ordinary things are not always what they seem. After all, that ordinary-looking Jesus was the only man to rise from the dead and live in eternity. We can only follow in His footsteps.

Lord, I want to follow You and reflect the love
You gave me on that Resurrection Day.

I pray you, let us leave off this usury.
Restore. . .to them, even this day, their lands,
their vineyards, their oliveyards, and their houses,
also the hundredth part of the money, and of the corn,
the wine, and the oil, that ye exact of them.
NEHEMIAH 5:10–11

Can you imagine losing your farm and house to those you owe money—even selling yourself into slavery to pay your debts? That's what happened to Nehemiah's people. Hard times fell on Jerusalem, and wealthy Israelites were bringing poor ones down to slavery. The needy borrowed from the well-to-do and soon lost their lands and homes.

A "well, that's business" attitude when it comes to money is not God's approach. He never places cash, checks, or investments above people's lives. And He knows when a lender is charging too much—He calls it usury.

If you are involved in a money-related business, take Nehemiah's words to heart. Bring compassion to your work. When Nehemiah confronted the wealthy Israelites, they listened and answered, "We will restore them, and will require nothing of them; so will we do as thou sayest" (v. 12). Recognizing their wrongdoing, they willingly made it right.

But no matter what kind of job you do, there will be times for compassion. Don't stand on your rights, but do what *is* right. God will bless you greatly if you do.

Lord, help me be compassionate in my work.
Teach me to follow Your way.

> *And Jesus answering said unto them,*
> *Render to Caesar the things that are Caesar's,*
> *and to God the things that are God's.*
> *And they marvelled at him.*
> MARK 12:17

This ultimately practical statement hardly seems like the sort of thing people would marvel at. Yet when you read the entire story, it's amazing how perfectly Jesus answered His opposition.

The Pharisees were trying to trap Jesus into a statement that would get Him in trouble with Rome. They wanted Him to say they shouldn't pay the pagan Romans any taxes. But if He stood up for taxation, they felt He'd lose His popularity with the Jewish people. This sage response avoided both pitfalls perfectly.

Sometimes we'd like to make the Pharisees' distinction between our faith and the world. We'd like to have an excuse to ignore the practical things of life, like taxes, and claim that we are above them because we believe in God. Jesus doesn't leave us that out. We're part of that world, too.

So on tax day, don't go to your employer and try to talk him into not taking taxes out of your paycheck—it's a plan that won't work for either of you. Just be thankful that government works to your benefit, too, and help shoulder the burden.

> *Lord, I appreciate the benefits of good government.*
> *When our government doesn't do the right thing,*
> *help me to find the right way of redress.*

And the blood shall be to you for a token upon
the houses where ye are: and when I see the blood,
I will pass over you,
and the plague shall not be upon you to destroy you,
when I smite the land of Egypt.

EXODUS 12:13

On Passover, the Jews did as God commanded and painted the blood of a lamb on their doorposts and lintels. He had promised them that when the angel of death went through Egypt, killing the firstborn children and animals, any house having such a mark would be passed by.

Like those ancient Jews, we, too, have been passed over, though not through the blood of a sheep. The blood shed for us was much more precious—that of God's Son. Where the lamb's blood saved only one nation, Jesus' blood has touched people throughout the world, from every nation and tribe imaginable—including ours.

While we deserved death, God has passed by us because of His Son. Are we awed by that truth? Has it changed the way we live, work, and act? If not, have we asked ourselves, "Out of the whole world, why would God choose me?" If that does not humble us, do we know what Jesus' death means?

Lord, I'm amazed that You had such mercy on me.
Thank You for Your gift of life.

Though I speak with the tongues of men and of angels,
and have not charity,
I am become as sounding brass, or a tinkling cymbal.

1 CORINTHIANS 13:1

You may be the most talented person in your company at your job description, but if you aren't gracious, too, you may just seem like noise to the people around you. Who can stand someone who toots his own horn (or clangs her own cymbal) so much that others can't wait to get away from the sound?

Obnoxiousness isn't part of a Christian's job description. The hallmarks of faith are graciousness and love (or charity, as this version calls it). So when you do well in your work, thank God for the gifts He's given you that allow you to serve Him well. Be thankful that He's given folks who helped you learn your job and who continue to make your work possible. And appreciate the particular gifts of others who work with you.

No matter how gifted you are spiritually or skills-wise, no one appreciates someone who's so full of himself that there's no room for God or anyone else. So have some charity on your job, and you won't just be noise—you'll shed the light of Jesus' love.

Lord, thank You for the abilities that
allow me to do my job well.
I know they come from You, and I want to avoid pride.

*Shouldest not thou also have had compassion on thy fellowservant,
even as I had pity on thee?*
MATTHEW 18:33

If you've ever worked for a compassionate boss when your life was filled with stress, you recognize what a blessing this attribute is. If your boss gave you sympathy, support, and encouragement while you faced challenges at home or in the workplace, you've been blessed with a wonderful person to work for.

But compassion is not wimpiness. Supporting a person through a trial doesn't equate with a lack of accountability, as the man in this parable learned. He'd been in debt, and his master forgave what he owed. In turn, the greedy servant tried to extract every penny from other servants who owed him some cash. When his master found out about it, he was extremely angry that the servant had not passed on a similar mercy.

We need to have compassion and respect it when it's given to us. For a time, we receive an unusual grace, but we cannot take advantage. That would be like taking for granted the mercy God has given us in saving us—which is what this parable is about, after all. God gave us His grace, and we are simply to pass it on in all things.

*Lord, thank You for forgiving me.
Let me extend Your compassion to others
so they, too, can understand Your love.*

*You have been set free from sin
and have become slaves to righteousness.*

ROMANS 6:18 NIV

In today's republican ideas of freedom, this doesn't seem like a good idea, does it? Why would anyone want to be set free just to be made a slave again? It doesn't seem to make much sense.

Paul knew no one is perfectly free. Complete freedom to do anything we want soon turns into anarchy, as one person's rights confront and overrun another's. One person wants to use the freedom to do good, but his neighbor wants to use it for evil, and suddenly all society confronts the interconnectedness we all live in.

Non-Christians find it hard to understand that slavery to God means both freedom from sin and a new kind of joy. Many see Christianity as a dismal, painful thing and imagine serving Him means giving up too much. Some fear accepting Him because they'd have to give up the sins they delight in. They don't recognize that their godless "pleasures" are not freedom, but slavery to evil. Their need for temporary gratification has them in its grasp, and even if they wanted, they could never escape. What looks so promising today will bind them to an empty eternity.

Today, you can be trapped by sin or free to be righteous. Which kind of slave will you be?

*Lord, I want to live as Your slave, in Your freedom.
Part me from anything that would keep me from You.*

Jesus said to her, "Do not cling to Me,
for I have not yet ascended to My Father;
but go to My brethren and say to them,
'I am ascending to My Father and your Father,
and to My God and your God.'"
JOHN 20:17 NKJV

Not only does Mary feel the shock of seeing Jesus alive again, He gives her this amazing message concerning His future. If any average person said such a thing, we'd conclude he was crazy and lock him away for his own safety. But who could debate his words with Jesus? This man, once dead, stands alive before Mary.

People have tried to theorize away the crucifixion, explaining that Jesus was never truly dead, that the disciples revived Him, and so on. But examine the biblical text and the methods used by the Romans in crucifixion, and those theories fade into unreality. Expecting life in a man who had been cruelly beaten with a metal-tipped Roman whip, to the point where He was half dead even before the cross, strains credulity more than the Resurrection. A purely human Jesus who experienced that would have needed critical medical care, not a stroll around the countryside.

This amazing Jesus *is* alive again. He sits on God's right hand. Where else should a man who died and rose again be?

Lord Jesus, I praise You as the Holy One
who was raised from the dead to forgive my sins.
Bless You for giving me Your new life.

Let no man despise thy youth;
but be thou an example of the believers, in word,
in conversation, in charity, in spirit, in faith, in purity.
1 TIMOTHY 4:12

Timothy was young, but he had leadership credentials. He'd grown up with a Christian mother, and he had experienced God's forgiveness for many years. But while he tried to minister to the church in Ephesus, he ran into trouble. He felt funny giving advice to people who were so much older than he. So Paul encouraged the young pastor with these words.

If you are young, you can do a good job. You may not have experience, but you have a brain. You can learn what you need to know and address yourself seriously to the work at hand. By being responsible, asking questions, and showing up on time every day and working a full day, you can do the work. Attend to the things you need to do every day, and your skill will grow. Use the things you already know and keep on learning, and soon people will forget how young you are.

After all, you won't always be this young, so make the most of the days you now have, knowing that God doesn't despise youth.

Lord, no matter what my age,
I can always be a consistent worker for You.
Help me learn the things I need to do.

Jesus Christ is the same yesterday, today, and forever.
HEBREWS 13:8 NKJV

Change is constant in our world. We change jobs, homes, and churches. On our jobs, clients change, technology changes, our bosses change. Just as we learn one computer program, the corporation changes to another, and we have to learn that part of our jobs all over again. Sometimes we wonder when it will end and how we can keep up, over a whole career of revisions.

Some of us are "go with the flow" kinds who adjust easily to change; others like a lot of structure. But none of us can stay in the same place we are today. To do so would kill our careers, indeed, our whole lives.

As we seek to adjust to the world around us, it's nice to know that one thing *never* changes: Jesus. He does not give us one rule to live by today and eradicate it tomorrow. He never loves us one week and hates us the next. He says what He means and means what He says; all we have to do is read His Word to discover His truths.

So when work, home life, and everything else is up in the air, grab onto Jesus. He always has both feet on the ground. He's the unchanging Rock on which we can base our whole lives.

*Lord, I need to plant both feet on You when
the rest of my life is being rearranged
or when nothing seems to alter.
In either case, I'm glad You never change.*

Ask, and it shall be given you; seek, and ye shall find;
knock, and it shall be opened unto you:
For every one that asketh receiveth;
and he that seeketh findeth;
and to him that knocketh it shall be opened.

MATTHEW 7:7–8

Before you made the decision to look for a new job, you prayed about it. Certain this was what God wanted, you sent out your résumé, put out the word, and checked online to see what was available. If God is in this job hunt, how come you don't quickly have a new job? Did you misunderstand? Doesn't God want to give you good things?

God wants to give you the best. Just because He encourages you to do something doesn't mean it happens overnight. Sometimes it takes hard work to find a job; other times one just falls into your lap. The waiting may be part of what God is doing in your life, or the company you will work in may not be ready for you to start just now.

But whatever happens, God is in control and will give you only the best, if you're willing to trust Him. Maybe that best is spending more time with your kids and spouse while you search for work. But if you're doing your part, the job you finally land will be just the one He had in mind all along.

Lord, I want everything in my career to glorify You,
even a job search.

So when Samuel saw Saul, the Lord said to him,
"There he is, the man of whom I spoke to you.
This one shall reign over My people."
1 SAMUEL 9:17 NKJV

God chose Saul to rule His people. You'd think, with credentials like that, Saul would have to be a success. But though he started out well, Saul eventually became an example of what a king should *not* be.

Where did Saul go wrong? He became angry at the popular warrior, David, and at God. Saul constantly fueled his wrath and blamed God for his situation. Rather than asking God's prophet for advice, he turned to a medium. Soon the heavenly Father had no real place in Saul's life. He became a proud, angry man who wanted things his way. The promise he had when God chose Saul turned to failure.

Each of us has success before us at some point. We start the new job, and everything looks promising. But in order to fulfill that promise, we need to continually make wise choices. What seems like a small choice one day may become a major stumbling block in a career if that decision was badly made. Pile up a series of poor choices, and a career suffers.

Don't make Saul's choices and lose the promise of your future to a moment of emotion.

Lord, help me make a success for You.
Don't let poor choices kill my promising career.

"But now your kingdom will not endure;
the LORD has sought out a man after his own heart
and appointed him leader of his people,
because you have not kept the LORD's command."

1 SAMUEL 13:14 NIV

These words made Saul angry at God. Instead of waiting for the prophet, Saul had taken his place and offered a sacrifice. It was kind of like a low-level manager in your company speaking for the CEO without permission. Only no officer in your company speaks for God. Less-than-holy Saul had taken on a holy task. God was affronted that the proud king thought he could do this. So God decided He'd appoint a new leader who would love and respect Him.

Do we respect God in our work, or are we trying to do things our own way? If we have constant run-ins with authority, maybe we need to take a look at our attitudes. Have we gotten too much like Saul, who wanted it all his way? If Samuel didn't get to the right place on time, Saul thought that gave him the liberty to take the prophet's place.

Want your career to endure? Be, like David, a person after God's own heart. It's the only way to be a successful leader—or a successful follower, if it comes to that.

Lord, keep me from being proud.
Instead I want to respect You in all I do.

And so it was, at noon, that Elijah mocked them and said,
"Cry aloud, for he is a god; either he is meditating,
or he is busy, or he is on a journey,
or perhaps he is sleeping and must be awakened."
1 KINGS 18:27 NKJV

What a wonderful story this is about Elijah and the priests of Baal. When the two face off, we see an unusual side of this bold prophet, who does not hesitate to mock his enemies. What had Elijah to fear? He knew their god was only wood. It could not hurt him. For a time, nothing seemed to faze Elijah.

Mocking unbelievers isn't a standard witnessing technique, though. It's more likely to set up backs than win people to salvation. In the same way, a bold witness needs to be a careful witness. Occasionally God may lead us to shock unbelievers into thought, but more often, we speak gently and kindly, reflecting His love instead of His wrath.

Today, do you need to give a bold testimony or a gentle reminder that God is there and always cares? Whatever is necessary, His Spirit will guide you. Listen to His still, small voice (1 Kings 19:12). It will lead you where you need to go and give you the words to say.

Let me listen intently to Your voice, O Lord.
I need Your guidance today.

But he said to them,
"Do not be alarmed. You seek Jesus of Nazareth,
who was crucified. He is risen! He is not here.
See the place where they laid Him."

MARK 16:6 NKJV

One damp Easter morning I walked by a neighbor's house. Wet, bedraggled bunnies, Easter decorations, adorned their railings. Though they'd looked cute the day before, now they hung limply, waiting for the sun to dry them out.

For many people, bunnies and colored eggs are the only symbols of Easter. They do not recognize the power of the cross. As Christians, we understand these worldly symbols are also ways of describing the new life Jesus bought for us on the cross, but do we live in a way that shows that more complete understanding? So often we could be accused of filling our lives with "wet, bedraggled bunnies" instead of the power of the cross.

Jesus is not still in the tomb: The disciples knew that truth, and it impacted their lives as no wet rabbit or colored egg could. So at this Easter season, color some eggs and enjoy the bunnies, if you want; but even better, live in a way that shows the change Jesus brings by obeying Him every day of the year. You'll need more than a few rabbits and eggs to do that.

Lord, thank You for giving me new life in Your Son,
not just a rabbit or pretty egg.

If you suffer, it should not be as a murderer or thief
or any other kind of criminal, or even as a meddler.
1 PETER 4:15 NIV

Christians will suffer; the Bible makes no bones about that. But if a Christian's testimony is to be successful, he must suffer for doing the right thing, not because he has taken another's life. She must be accused wrongly, not because she has stolen. If that were not enough, Peter says a Christian should not even be rightly accused of meddling in another's business!

Can we be that pure on our own? It's not likely. Who among us has never felt like taking a coworker's life in our hands and "improving" on it. Even if we have not killed a coworker, who has not wanted to compel a coworker to wiser ways?

As a Christian, at times you may suffer because of your faith. But let it be because you took a right but unpopular stand, not because you failed to do your work, harmed the company's image with dishonesty, or did wrong to your coworker. Instead, let God's Spirit control your life so completely that all people see is Jesus. Then the persecution they give you will really be aimed at Him.

What better company could you be in?

Lord, when persecution comes, I want to face it with You.
Give me the strength of Your Spirit.

*"If a man delivers to his neighbor money or articles to keep,
and it is stolen out of the man's house,
if the thief is found, he shall pay double."*

EXODUS 22:7 NKJV

When Alissa reported the theft of company property, she was amazed at the response she got. The security department called it "unauthorized removal" and never looked too hard for the culprits. She was horrified at how lightly they took the loss of materials that had cost the company a pretty penny. On top of that, she had to reorder everything, since her department had planned to use the promotional materials to attract attention at a major convention. Not having them could have cost the company even more business.

We often don't take theft very seriously. We call it by other names to make it more appealing, and we excuse ourselves if we take home company property and never return it. But the Bible does not take stealing lightly. In the biblical era, when authorities caught a thief, he had to pay double for anything he had taken. Imagine paying twice the value for those pencils that ended up at home or the company T-shirt that wasn't given to you. It doesn't seem quite such a good deal now, does it?

*Lord, keep me honest at work and home.
I don't want to take anything that isn't mine.*

The wife of a man from the company of the prophets
cried out to Elisha,
"Your servant my husband is dead,
and you know that he revered the LORD.
But now his creditor is coming to take my two boys as his slaves."
2 KINGS 4:1 NIV

This woman was in a tight spot. Her husband died, and the man he owed money to planned to enslave her two sons. Without them, she'd have no financial support. So in desperation, she cried out to God's prophet Elisha.

God didn't tell the woman not to pay the debt. Her husband had gotten the money; it was only right that the creditor should be repaid. But He provided a way for her to pay. Elisha ordered the family to collect every pot they could from their neighbors. The woman poured oil in each, and the oil multiplied until it filled every vessel. Then the prophet told her to sell the oil and pay the debt.

When we don't live within our paychecks, we, too, can end up owing thousands. If we look for ways not to pay, God will not bless it. But He *will* help us pay if we ask Him—a second job or an affordable payment plan is a better solution than wrongdoing.

If you're in debt, trust God. He wants to provide for you, just as He did for that widow.

Lord, help me avoid debt and pay the ones I have.

The man of God sent word to the king of Israel:
"Beware of passing that place,
because the Arameans are going down there."
So the king of Israel checked on the place
indicated by the man of God.
Time and again Elisha warned the king,
so that he was on his guard in such places.
2 KINGS 6:9–10 NIV

Listening to God is of benefit, even if you are the person in charge. We learn this lesson in a king who heard God by listening to His prophet. During war with Aram, Elisha and King Joram worked as a team. Because God told the prophet of the enemy's plans, Israel constantly confounded the Arameans. It enraged the king of Aram so much that when he realized Israel's prophet caused the trouble, he tried to capture Elisha.

Are there battles you'd like to win on the job? Maybe you'd like to feel secure about a new plan you're devising. Or you'd like to know whom you can trust with some information. Ask God for wisdom, and He'll provide it.

To hear, you have to be close to God. Anyone who does not often pay attention to Him may expect a loud, booming reply. But God rarely communicates that way. Only those listening to Him day by day hear His still, small voice, speaking to their hearts. Are your ears completely open?

Lord, help me listen to You every moment
so I can benefit from Your wisdom.

We were under great pressure, far beyond our ability to endure. . . .
But this happened that we might not rely on ourselves but on God.
2 CORINTHIANS 1:8–9 NIV

Pressured days come to us all. Perhaps it's planned: a project you knew was coming but could not prepare for. Or maybe it's a sudden work overload, when a coworker lands in the hospital. You wish there were more hours in the day, that you had more energy to complete your tasks. Though you may make plenty of overtime money, you have no opportunity to spend it—you aren't even sure how you'll find time to do laundry, eat meals, and take care of the rest of your everyday chores.

When pressure comes, rely on coworkers; it's good to share the load as much as possible. But even they may not take on enough to give you a forty- (or even sixty-) hour workweek. Then become deeply aware of your need for God's help. Without Him, you have no chance at completing the work. But God smooths your path and helps you make the most of your time.

Paul, who faced deadly perils much worse than our own, knew relying on God was his only chance. If he could trust God under such circumstances, it's a cinch we can.

Lord, I don't face Paul's dangers, but just like him,
I can rely on You.
I need to trust that You will be with me in this.

*Finally, all of you, live in harmony with one another;
be sympathetic, love as brothers, be compassionate and humble.
Do not repay evil with evil or insult with insult, but with blessing,
because to this you were called so that you may inherit a blessing.*

1 PETER 3:8–9 NIV

Peter writes these words right after his exhortation to husbands and wives. While many people have had heated discussions over the earlier verses in this chapter and some might want to erase them from their Bibles, who among them would object to these words?

Maybe a lot of folks who debate 1 Peter 3:1–7 need to take a look at these verses, which are addressed to *all* Christians, even those married to each other. As a husband or wife, wouldn't you like to live in harmony with your spouse under these rules? The world around us might pooh-pooh a romantic love that also included them. Such relationships might not make good newspaper copy or sell a movie. But it's a lot easier to live and love with someone who's not hard to get along with, who understands your struggles and is willing to respond to evil with good.

So this weekend, treat your spouse this way—and your children, too, if you have any. It could make a world of difference in your home.

*Lord, help me treat all the people I love this way.
Let these truths also reach the world through me.*

"My words come from my upright heart;
my lips utter pure knowledge."
JOB 33:3 NKJV

Job was down and out, and all his three so-called friends, Eliphaz, Bildad, and Zophar, could do was sling mud at him. For hours they went on about Job's sinfulness and God's righteousness. It's amazing Job didn't toss them out, just to get peace. But godly Job took their criticism for a long time.

When a fourth man, Elihu, spoke the words in this verse, Job must have bitten his tongue. This young fellow obviously had a very high opinion of himself: Elihu called himself upright and wise. He didn't seem very humble! But was he right? Perhaps Job continued to listen because he didn't have all the answers, and there was something in what this young man said. Elihu certainly had a high view of God's holiness—and at the end of Job, God corrects the other three "friends," but not this young man.

Less-than-perfect Christians may criticize us, too. We're tempted to write off their critiques as jealousy or carping. But just in case there's a grain of truth there, we'd do better to consider their words. We, too, are less than perfect, and like Job, we don't want to miss something God wants to show us.

When I'm corrected, Lord,
help me be a gracious listener and then follow the truth.

For we are his workmanship,
created in Christ Jesus unto good works,
which God hath before ordained that we should walk in them.
EPHESIANS 2:10

When we create something, it feels good to know we've done a good job. As we put the final touches on a report, a letter, or whatever widgets we make on the job, gladness fills us, not just that we've finished the job, but that we've done it well.

God enjoys creating things, too—like people. Imagine how He felt when He finished creating you. Did He smile, knowing He'd finished a masterpiece? Could He trust that here was a person who would do good works for Him out of deep love?

We may make a widget and never see it again. It becomes part of a car, building, or computer. A report or letter gets filed away, and few see it after the fact. But that's not so with God; He sees us every day of our lives and watches us fondly as we do the good works He prepared for us to accomplish. When that work is finished, He calls us home because He made us and wants to share eternity with us.

Is the work you're doing today something that will make the Creator proud?

Lord, thank You for making me to do good things
that make You proud.
Help me do those things today.

But I discipline my body and bring it into subjection, lest,
when I have preached to others,
I myself should become disqualified.
1 CORINTHIANS 9:27 NKJV

Paul recognized that preaching the gospel meant more than telling people how to act. If he didn't live the words he preached, he would have no base to stand on. No one wants to listen to a hypocrite. After all, if the apostle couldn't make Christianity work in his life, how could anyone else do that? If the man who had seen Jesus on the road to Damascus couldn't follow Him, how could the people of Corinth?

Paul's spiritual truth also applies to the workplace. What a leader says has some impact, but what he does will influence his staff even more. Managers who expect their staff to come in at an early hour had better be there at the crack of dawn, too. A CEO who expects her employees to take a pay cut had better not rake in a huge bonus at the end of the year, or her words to the troops will mean nothing.

The consistency Paul describes does not come easily. Living with congruity takes discipline, and discipline often goes against the grain with us. But before we break our own rules, we must look at the results that will have. Is the risk of disqualification worth it?

Lord, I don't always like discipline,
but help me live consistently for You.

I thank my God upon every remembrance of you,
always in every prayer of mine for you all making request with joy.
PHILIPPIANS 1:3–4

Have you worked with some wonderful people? You spend so much time on the job, chances are that you've made some work friendships. Maybe you rarely see these folks outside of work, but they still hold a treasured place in your heart.

If a coworker moves on to a new job, relocates to another state, or retires, those fond memories remain with you. As you look back, you may feel thankful, as Paul did when he thought of the Philippian church. But do you also thank God and pray for that person?

As a caring Christian who believes God can work through prayer, even when people are far distant, why not lift a special workplace friend up to Him? Thank Him for that friendship. If you still keep in touch, pray specifically for that friend's joys and needs. Even if you don't see each other, always pray for his or her well-being.

You may not see your friend this side of heaven, but when you meet again in eternity, the blessings of those prayers will touch you both.

Lord, I lift up my friend to You.
Thank You for the love You caused to flow between us,
and bless my friend today.

Ye have sown much, and bring in little;
ye eat, but ye have not enough;
ye drink, but ye are not filled with drink;
ye clothe you, but there is none warm;
and he that earneth wages earneth wages
to put it into a bag with holes.

HAGGAI 1:6

Sometimes, no matter how hard we work or how large our paycheck is, our ends don't seem to meet. We think our budget is balanced, then the washing machine or water heater goes. No matter what we do, we have to pinch every penny.

Have we looked at our money issues as spiritual ones, or do we think money's too "practical" to relate to God? In this passage, God told the Jews their practical problems stemmed from a spiritual problem—they hadn't built His temple. They'd disobeyed Him and were paying a financial price.

Not every monetary problem stems from spiritual disobedience, but it's a good place to start. Take a spiritual inventory of your life. Did God warn you to control your spending, and you've kept on with it anyway? Or are you refusing to take part in the church's ministry? Ask yourself some deep questions and pray, being open to God's correction. Do what He directs you to do. Then live on whatever He provides, because when God provides, you'll make it through the end of every month.

Lord, show me anyplace I may not be in Your will.
Bring glory to Yourself even in my financial choices.

*Is the seed yet in the barn? yea, as yet the vine, and the fig tree,
and the pomegranate, and the olive tree, hath not brought forth:
from this day I will bless you.*

HAGGAI 2:19

God had not forgotten His covenant with His people, and
He wanted to bless them as they put their disobedience
behind them. Once the work on the temple started, the lack
of food that they'd suffered through ended.

When we face trials, they may feel endless. *Tomorrow
will be like today, and how will we get through this?* we ask ourselves. *No matter what we do, how can it change?* Like those
Jews, we're tempted to feel depressed over our situations.

But nothing that's not eternal lasts forever if we make a
good change. The famine ended, and so do our problems.
What seems forever isn't, because situations alter. The economy improves, management is revamped, or we discover a
new, better way to work. Solutions appear for most things.

Troubles don't last, but the blessings God gives do.
When the figs and pomegranates are gone, the care He
provided is still a warm memory that draws us ever close to
Him. He wants to bless us today with all kinds of good
things. All we need to do is obey.

*Lord, as I obey, I know You will bless me.
Yet the best blessing I will ever have is the joy of Your love.*

Some trust in chariots and some in horses,
but we trust in the name of the LORD our God.
PSALM 20:7 NIV

We say we trust God, but do we? Don't we have trouble not trusting in things? Don't we naturally look for physical proof of our faith?

No question about it, trusting God is challenging. After all, we don't see God, and we're used to having hands-on proof of things we trust in. Each month we get a statement from our banks so we know how much money we really have. When we go to draw out money, the teller gives it to us. We can "prove" what we have.

But the spiritual world doesn't offer proof beyond what is in the Bible and our hearts. We never get a spiritual statement, describing what God thinks of each of us personally. Trusting in God is a completely different matter from our financial concerns. Yet when we do throw our whole trust on God, as we face difficult situations and need His aid, we discover the proof only He can offer. Again and again, God shows us His steadfastness. It's the sweetest proof in this world or eternity.

Lord, keep me from trusting in things that don't last.
I want to rely on You first and foremost.

Do not despise your mother when she is old.
PROVERBS 23:22 NIV

When it comes to honoring Mom, some people have it easy. They got Betty Crocker moms who whipped up delicious meals and put them on the table to the tune of a family's happy voices. Others got the mom of Proverbs 31, with her thumb in a million pies but who always had time for her children. But what of the kids who never got that kind of care? What about the ones whose families led soap-opera lives, filled with discord and agony?

Did you notice that God did not tell you to honor Mom if she was worth honoring? He didn't tie the way you're to treat her to the kind of mothering she offered. That's because He expects us to honor the great moms and the not-so-great ones.

As you age, you may begin to understand Mom. Maybe she had a rough life and just passed that on to you. Perhaps she made bad choices that she couldn't change, no matter how much she tried. But no matter what her lifestyle, God chose your mom just for you. There are good things as well as bad ones that came from her.

Honoring Mom is honoring God. So on this Mother's Day, don't forget to let her know that you love her just for being her.

Lord, thanks for choosing a mom just for me.
Help me honor her today.

"The God of Israel said, the Rock of Israel spoke to me:
'He who rules over men must be just, ruling in the fear of God.'"
2 SAMUEL 23:3 NKJV

Do you manage many people or just one? Then keep in mind that you are not simply accountable to your staff for how you lead. God is also concerned that you lead well.

This verse's description of leadership was among David's last words, recorded by the prophet Samuel. The king wanted to tell his son, Solomon, the best way to rule. But his words apply not to kings alone. Anyone who has authority over others should keep them in mind.

Leaders who give God's opinion no credence easily get caught up in their own ideas and may become self-centered and opinionated. A leader who always has to be right, cannot forgive, or has a low level of morality spells trouble for a company. One who does not care for the people he has authority over has trouble keeping a staff.

Ruling in the fear of God means wielding authority as one who is accountable to Him. Those who follow His rules, rule well.

Lord, help me rule well.
I can only do that as I keep Your rules in mind.

"But the sons of rebellion shall all be as thorns thrust away,
because they cannot be taken with hands.
But the man who touches them must be armed
with iron and the shaft of a spear,
and they shall be utterly burned with fire in their place."

2 SAMUEL 23:6–7 NKJV

While those who obey God rule well, David warns Solomon that rebellious sons are like thorns that will be completely destroyed. You can't deal nicely with a thorn—you either strip it off the plant or get rid of the plant entirely. Leaving thorn bushes to grow creates a sticky situation.

Rebellious people in the work environment are something like those bushes. Their anger flares up and attacks others and may keep them from performing their jobs well. Soon others, stuck with those thorns of anger, become resentful, and bitterness can quickly fill an entire department. Before it goes further, a wise leader removes rebellion by handling it with strong measures.

Leaders may not like this kind of action. It's easier to go with the flow than take a firm stand; but for the good of the entire company, it's best to confront the problem. A quickly solved situation has no time to grow into a sticky thorn bush.

Lord, when I deal with others, am I rebellious?
Teach me how to deal with those
who have rebelled against You.

Pray without ceasing.
1 THESSALONIANS 5:17

How can I pray all the time? you may be wondering. *After all, I have to work, don't I? Isn't God being unreasonable here?* Clearly you can't pray twenty-four hours a day; you do need some sleep! But that doesn't mean you can't engage in regular prayer for your company, coworkers, and the other needs God brings to mind. Remember them in your quiet time. Then, while you're doing one of those dull, mindless chores every job has, lift up your company executives, your boss, and others. Ask God to lead them in the right direction for decision making or encourage them through trials.

The seventeenth-century monk Brother Lawrence called this attitude of prayer that follows you through the day practicing the presence of God. While he worked in the monastery kitchen, with this method he brought himself and others before God.

You may not have much time to pray, but God responds even to lightning-quick intercessions. As you're walking to a coworker's office, waiting for a meeting to start, or on hold on the phone, remember your coworkers in prayer. Soon you'll find that even when you aren't praying, the spirit of prayer sticks with you—twenty-four hours a day!

Lord, keep me in prayer as often as I can be.
And don't let me forget my quiet time with You.

Rejoice in the Lord alway: and again I say, Rejoice.
PHILIPPIANS 4:4

Have you ever thought about the fact that knowing God is just plain fun? After all, you can't rejoice in something that's painful, can you?

People who do not know Him often look upon God as being a big, mean judge, waiting to pounce down on them and cause them misery. They don't rejoice in God; in fact, they'd rather avoid Him because they know He has every right to judge them. It's not their idea of fun, and who could blame them?

One of the quiet testimonies you can offer to your coworkers is the joy you feel in God. You may not have to say a word, because they may not be able to miss your confidence in the face of trouble, the joy that bubbles up in you when you say His name, and the peace that covers you.

That doesn't mean you should never share your joy in words, as God leads you, but be aware that words alone are not enough to share God's love. Your spirit can shine even when words can't explain how you feel.

Lord, help my joy in You shine through.
Thank You that You use my life
even when I don't say a word.
But help me speak joyfully of You, too.

Wisdom, like an inheritance,
is a good thing and benefits those who see the sun.
Wisdom is a shelter as money is a shelter,
but the advantage of knowledge is this:
that wisdom preserves the life of its possessor.
ECCLESIASTES 7:11–12 NIV

Did you know that the money you make on the job is not what keeps you alive? Sure, it pays the bills. It makes life a lot easier. But if you had to choose between money and wisdom, wisdom is really the better choice.

Money comes and goes. And if you use your money wisely, it will shelter you from hunger and homelessness. But if you don't live wisely, you will end your life in misery. A lack of wisdom leads many folks to make choices that lead them to illness, extreme poverty, or emotional trauma. In some cases, it can even lead to death.

But God's wisdom provides true life and protection, whether you have plenty of cash or just a little. You might get some benefit from money, but you will always benefit from wisdom, as it impacts every portion of your life.

The only wisdom you need is what God has to offer. He'd love to share it with you today. Are you ready to accept it?

Lord, I need Your wisdom to make the most of my life.
Help me to walk in it today.

Woe to the rebellious children, saith the LORD,
that take counsel, but not of me;
and that cover with a covering, but not of my spirit,
that they may add sin to sin.

ISAIAH 30:1

Rebellious people look in all the wrong places for advice on sin. Often they look to each other. They don't want advice that will help them change their lives—at least not much. Instead, they want someone to give their sin a seal of approval so they no longer need feel guilty. They want to ignore sin, not root it out, and they may fear God because they fear He will make them address the things they fear.

But all of us fear removing sin from our lives. Change is painful, and we'd rather stay in our comfortable spots, even if they prick us in some ways. And if we had to make the changes all on our own, we'd be right to stay where we are. People trying to change themselves rarely get far. The habits we work on endlessly tend to come back, even after a season of change.

When we feel rebellious, the only cure is God. He gives us the counsel we need, the power we must have to change. Instead of adding sin to sin, His Spirit releases us from that need to sin.

Be free today in Jesus.

Lord, free me from resistant thoughts
and change my rebel heart.

*"My anger burns against your shepherds,
and I will punish these leaders."*
ZECHARIAH 10:3 NLT

Are you a church leader? Perhaps you teach a Sunday-school class or hold a church office. Did you know that God keeps track of the things you teach others, the way you lead, and how you fulfill your duties? Give the flock misinformation, lead badly, and you are not just accountable to the people you lead. God will have a say on the subject, too.

That doesn't mean you have to quake in your boots anytime you open your mouth. But be aware of the awesome responsibility God's placed in your hands. Treat it with respect, and check out the ideas you're passing on. Don't do a third-rate job on whatever you volunteer to do for the church, but treat it seriously. If you can't treat it seriously, give up your position to someone who will do it effectively.

After all, anything you do for your congregation, you do for God. So do it well, for His approval, not for the good opinion of others. His anger is to be feared more than any human's.

*Lord, I want to do everything I do as if it were for You.
I need Your strength to be faithful every week.*

God is just:
He will pay back trouble to those who trouble you.
2 THESSALONIANS 1:6 NIV

If you get the unfair part of a deal, if someone does you wrong, are you tempted to strike back? Does retribution look really good? It doesn't have to, you know. God keeps in mind everything that's unfair, and in His own time, He works them out equitably.

So if you worked hard and didn't get a raise, don't take it out on the company. If a coworker spread gossip about you, don't do the same to him. Just leave it to God, and in awhile, it will all make sense.

People who strike back at those who hurt them may seem to win in the short run, but eventually they, too, get a payback for their sin. So don't sin to get retribution; instead, rely on God, and if there is any retribution required, He will mete it out. Count on it; God's retribution will be perfect in a way yours never could be. When He hands out justice, it completely suits the situation, not too hard, not too soft. And the person who receives it gets the point of the lesson.

Lord, I don't want to strike back at those who do me wrong.
I know I can leave each situation in Your hands.

Now the Bereans were of more noble character
than the Thessalonians,
for they received the message with great eagerness and examined
the Scriptures every day to see if what Paul said was true.
ACTS 17:11 NIV

Derek had often heard Gil witness. The problem was that though Gil was so emphatic about his beliefs, Derek knew they were not quite scriptural. Sure, Gil quoted a lot from the Bible, but only from the verses that supported his views. He ignored anything that would prove him wrong. To listen to Gil, you'd think God didn't want too many people in heaven and made it incredibly hard to get in.

When you're sharing the good news with coworkers and friends, are you sharing the whole news? Or like Gil, do you settle on a few verses and ignore the rest of Scripture? People need to hear a balanced view of God that includes His justice and compassion. You can best share that if you have a clear, broad understanding of the Bible—one that comes from reading the whole book, Old and New Testament. Read and study both, then you can judge what you hear to see if it's right or wrong.

Whether someone preaches to you or just shares his beliefs, take it back to Scripture. Then you'll know who is on target and who's not.

Lord, help me constantly learn from Your Word
so I can pass on a clear, full message.

All scripture is given by inspiration of God,
and is profitable for doctrine, for reproof,
for correction, for instruction in righteousness.
2 TIMOTHY 3:16

Do you have a friend who does not quite understand an issue about God? Perhaps you'd like to help her clarify a few things. How can you do that?

Before you open your mouth, pray about the situation. Your friend may need to speak to her pastor or another believer, or you may be the perfect person to carry the message she needs to hear. You want your friend to understand, no matter who brings the message.

When you feel compelled to speak, pray first. Then make sure you know what Scripture says on this subject. Do a thorough search so you know as many sides of the issue as possible. If you know some truths, expand on those, using as many resources as you can. Your Bible, a concordance, and other texts will help you out. But your answer needs to come straight from Scripture, and you need as great an understanding as possible.

Pray again before you speak. Whether you are teaching her something new or showing her where she's been wrong, the Spirit needs to speak through you. That way, you know you'll be saying the right things—those things God wants your friend to hear.

When I speak about You, Lord,
may my words also be from You.
I know they will be when they are Your Word.

Be wise in the way you act toward outsiders;
make the most of every opportunity.
Let your conversation be always full of grace, seasoned with salt,
so that you may know how to answer everyone.
COLOSSIANS 4:5–6 NIV

Do you use salt in your conversation with non-Christians? That does not mean you should say anything improper, but that your words to nonbelievers should taste good to them. God wants people who can share His love in a way that appeals to those who don't know Him. How would they want to meet Him, otherwise?

What seasonings cover your words? Love, hope, compassion? Or do yours taste of judgment, bitterness, and divisiveness? God doesn't expect Christian speech to be dull and boring. He wants us to have some spice to our talk, but not the kind that burns and hurts others. Salt is a cleanser as well as a flavoring that makes the most of food. So a believer's words should both clean hurting hearts and bring out the best in them.

Speak wisely to those who share your working hours but not your faith. Let salt, not chili peppers, season your words as you share God's truth with love.

Lord, I want to speak with well-seasoned words
that draw all listeners to You.

Those things, which ye have both learned,
and received, and heard, and seen in me, do:
and the God of peace shall be with you.
PHILIPPIANS 4:9

Cheri knew what was right, but she wasn't doing it. The right thing just didn't seem as convenient as doing things her way. And she tried to tell herself that God would understand. After all, He couldn't expect her to give up the fast track to success, could He? That would mean He wanted her to fail. But as time went on and her doubts that this was okay increased, she felt more and more confused. What did God expect of her?

Obedience to God and His peace go hand in hand—you can't have one without the other. Paul told the Philippians that if they obeyed the truths God had shown them through the apostle, they would have peace because God would be with them.

Are you living in peace or worldly success that ignores the things you've learned about God? You can't have both. But you can live at peace with God and have a career that honors Him. God doesn't say you have to be a career failure, just that you need to do what He commands to build a faith-filled career. When you do that, no matter what job success you find, you'll be at peace.

Lord, I need to obey all I know of Your truth.
Keep me in Your way in every moment of my day.

Let everything that has breath praise the LORD.
PSALM 150:6 NKJV

Why is the Bible always telling us to praise God? Is He really stuck on Himself? Or does He need praise to feel good about Himself? Instead, why doesn't God tell us to praise one another—or even share some of our own wonderful qualities with others? Doesn't He like us very much?

The Lord isn't some almost-human being who needs to be propped up by another human. The above questions are actually pretty silly once you realize the kind God you're talking about. He does not desire praise because He's a weakling. Instead, He tells us to praise Him because by doing that our hearts recognize His infinite greatness and powerfulness. Only by praise can we recognize who He is and how small we are in comparison. Praise opens our eyes to God's true character. With it we can voice how much we appreciate the world He created for us, the love He freely gives, and the thousands of other graces He offers us.

As we comprehend God's greatness, we more completely appreciate His mercy and love in sending us Jesus. Through Jesus, the all-powerful One stepped into our world and became one of us, though He already owned the entire universe and didn't have to respond.

He only took that step so that He could also own our hearts.

I praise You, Lord God, from the bottom of my heart.

*"Are you not in error because
you do not know the Scriptures or the power of God?"*
MARK 12:24 NIV

The Pharisees made a career out of faith. They were proud to stand on street corners praying, just so everyone would know how "holy" they were. But all their human effort was not enough to earn their way into heaven.

They'd taken a wrong turn somewhere and missed out entirely on the message God had for them—and for all Jews. Instead of the truths of Scripture, they'd focused on their own ideas about how to relate to God. Their replacements were weak, ineffective measures, much less powerful than the truths God had for them.

How can we avoid the Pharisees' wrong turn? The answer is also in this verse. We must know the Scriptures. It's not enough to revere them or claim that we want to live by them. We must know them intimately. We can do that only by reading them often and deeply. Drinking deeply of their life-giving spring will bring God's power into our lives.

*Lord, it's humbling to think that
I've missed Your power because
I've failed to read Your Word.
Give me a hunger for the Scriptures
and the desire to search them daily.*

They were stoned;
they were sawed in two;
they were put to death by the sword.
HEBREWS 11:37 NIV

On Memorial Day we recall those who've given their lives for our physical freedom. Having people who are willing to commit their lives to their country is important. Without them, no country would exist for long.

But they are not the only ones who pay with their lives. The writer of Hebrews reminds us that without people who came before us, suffered for their faith, and even willingly died for it, we would not know about Jesus. As Christians, we can be thankful for the apostles, who suffered much to bring the faith to the world, and to Christians, from the first century to today, who have given their lifeblood because they would not forsake faith in Jesus.

Thankfully remember the fighting men who gave their lives for our country, but also remember the Christians who gave their lives for our faith. And commit your life to be a testimony to God, whether you give up your life as a martyr or simply allow it to be used by Jesus every day you live.

Then you'll have a memorial worth living for.

Lord, thank You for all those who've died
that I might enjoy freedom—physical and spiritual.
Pour out Your blessings on those who suffer this day
for their faith, and make me a faithful testimony, too.

*By faith Moses. . .chose to be mistreated along with the people of God
rather than to enjoy the pleasures of sin for a short time.
He regarded disgrace for the sake of Christ
as of greater value than the treasures of Egypt,
because he was looking ahead to his reward.*

HEBREWS 11:24–26 NIV

Today's reward—or tomorrow's? That's what Moses had to weigh when he gave up the palace in Egypt for mistreatment with his own people. He made a hard choice that seemed to spell disaster for his future.

We, too, have to make seemingly disastrous decisions sometimes: when we don't take the promotion we're offered because we know we won't like the job; when we encourage the company to make a choice that is right, even if it won't be as profitable as the wrong one; when we stand up for someone who's made a mistake.

We may lose earthly treasure to follow God: It can cost us promotion in our company or a transfer to a job we'd really enjoy. But like Moses, we still look forward to a reward: Some of us will find new jobs in even better companies; others will see no benefit this side of heaven. But all of us will be blessed, and the heavenly recompense will be better than any under the sun.

*Lord, I want to live like Moses
and choose Your will over anything else.
Give me the faith to always stand for You.*

But among you there must not be even a hint of sexual immorality,
or of any kind of impurity, or of greed,
because these are improper for God's holy people.
EPHESIANS 5:3 NIV

Though Sandra wasn't perfectly sure what her boss meant when he spoke those words, it sure sounded like an improper romantic suggestion to her. In only a moment, she'd gracefully but firmly refused. But the offense stuck with her. What had he been thinking? They worked for a family company, and anything like that could easily get him fired. Sandra decided to say no more about it for the moment, but it remained in the back of her mind. When her boss was fired some months later for other improprieties, she wasn't quite as shocked as her coworkers.

It's sad but true, some people will make such inappropriate comments in the workplace. When they open their mouths, it's time to speak up and to do so firmly. A Christian's only answer is no, because Paul makes it clear that such wrongdoing should not be connected to God's holy people. Those whom Jesus has bought with His blood cannot take such actions lightly.

So if someone on the job says something immoral, deal with it quickly but as gently as possible. But be clear that you are saying no. To say anything else would foul the name of Jesus.

Keep me pure for You, Lord. I want to be holy for You.

"But as for you, be strong and do not give up,
for your work will be rewarded."
When Asa heard these words and the prophecy of Azariah
son of Oded the prophet, he took courage.
He removed the detestable idols from
the whole land of Judah and Benjamin
and from the towns he had captured in the hills of Ephraim.
He repaired the altar of the LORD that was
in front of the portico of the LORD's temple.
2 CHRONICLES 15:7–8 NIV

If, like King Asa, you had a message directly from God's prophet that your work would be rewarded, would it make a difference? Would you work harder, change your plans, or keep on doing just what you've been doing all along?

Asa received this message and cleared his land of idols. It wasn't an easy job, since Judah had long been involved in idol worship. No doubt he ruffled a few feathers of people who were happy with their worship just the way it was. But he did it anyway.

If we are following God's ways, we don't really need a prophetic message. His Word has already pointed us down the path we must follow. When we walk in God's way, He promises to bless us (see Jeremiah 7:23). What could be better than to follow His path?

Lord, I want to follow Your path today,
doing all that You have already commanded.
Draw me closer to You.

Do not let your heart envy sinners,
but always be zealous for the fear of the LORD.
PROVERBS 23:17 NIV

Does your heart turn green with envy when a coworker or friend who doesn't know God buys a bigger house than yours or can afford to go to the best restaurant in town? It shouldn't, because your coworker or friend may be settling for the riches of this world while bypassing more valuable eternal rewards.

Anyone who owns a huge house but has an empty heart is not completely blessed. Having a small house and a lot of love can be better than the finest mansion. Visit a well-to-do person who lives without Jesus and whose family problems have emptied his home of love, and that becomes apparent. But even the non-Christian with a happy family life only settles for an enjoyable eighty or so years, with no promise of eternal blessings.

The Christian who takes accountability to God seriously may not receive the earthly benefits of a large home or other extras. It may mean chili instead of filet mignon for the faithful family. But giving to the church and Christian causes that made up that difference has been stored up in heaven for all eternity. In the end, that blessing lasts infinitely longer than any steak dinner.

Thank You, Lord,
for eternal blessings that last more than a lifetime.
When greed tempts me, remind me that I receive
forever rewards when I do as You command.

I will be glad and rejoice in You;
I will sing praise to Your name, O Most High.
PSALM 9:2 NKJV

Did you know that God doesn't care how good your singing voice is—He still loves to hear it lifted in praise? Whether you're another Luciano Pavarotti or can't carry a tune in a bucket, God rejoices in the praises of His people (1 Peter 2:9), and that includes you!

So don't worry how you sound when you lift up your voice at home or in the church. It doesn't matter if you can't read music or can sight-read perfectly. Don't waste time critiquing yourself or worrying what others think. Instead, rejoice with the psalmist at the wonder of God's love. Even if your neighbors or family doesn't appreciate your voice, you're really singing to an audience of one: God. And He appreciates every note that shows how much you love Him.

Lord, I praise You!
I'm so happy to be Your child,
loved by an omnipotent Father
who cares about the praises I have to offer.

"But he answered and said to his father,
'Look! For so many years I have been serving you
and I have never neglected a command of yours;
and yet you have never given me a young goat,
so that I might celebrate with my friends;
but when this son of yours came,
who has devoured your wealth with prostitutes,
you killed the fattened calf for him.'"

LUKE 15:29–30 NASB

Jealousy—we've all felt the burn of this sin. And our hearts may go out to the "good" brother of the prodigal son, who tried to do everything right and seemed to get nothing for it.

But the good brother missed the point. None of us is truly good, apart from God. Doing all the "right things" won't get us anywhere, if our relationship with the Father is all wrong. This son had served his father, but something in his motivation seemed less than perfect. Instead of rejoicing at the return of his brother, he became jealous. "Look at what you've given him, the bad boy!" he might as well have cried. "I deserve so much more."

We understand how he felt; we've felt that way. We see other, less well-grown Christians getting "goodies" we've missed out on and feel the sting of jealousy. Non-Christians make more money than we, and we wonder why God so blesses them.

Are our hearts on our love for God or our own greed?

Lord, keep my heart from greed.

You foolish Galatians! Who has bewitched you?
Before your very eyes Jesus Christ was clearly portrayed as crucified.
GALATIANS 3:1 NIV

Have you ever felt like calling someone who works for you a fool? Paul knew what that felt like—he became so irritated with the Galatians that he all but called them that. But tactfully he said that they must be bewitched, not their normal selves, to think that way. He gave them an out, an excuse for their actions.

Paul knew what it was like to speak out honestly and even offend people. He did it often enough in his ministry. So though he speaks strongly, he also provides a tactful, hypothetical "excuse" for the people who had missed the point of his ministry.

When you want to yell "fool" at someone, remember that after you say that, you'll still need to work with your staff member. It's probably better to hold your tongue on that name. Instead, explain clearly what the problem is, and solve the issue that causes the word to leap to your tongue. You'll be glad you spoke so wisely.

Lord, help me hold my tongue on harsh words
and instead solve the real problem when
a worker irritates me.

When the turn came for Esther. . .to go to the king,
she asked for nothing other than what Hegai,
the king's eunuch who was in charge of the harem, suggested.
And Esther won the favor of everyone who saw her.
ESTHER 2:15 NIV

Imagine a simple Jewish girl, a captive in Persia, being considered for the position of queen. Esther knew nothing of palace life in a strange land or how to please King Xerxes, who held her future in his hands. Humbly, she recognized her need to rely on others for wisdom. So Esther looked to the king's harem eunuch, Hegai, for advice. Hegai must have responded to Esther wisely because she not only received the favor of all who saw her, she won the heart of the king.

No matter what your age or position, at times you need advice. Like Esther, do you choose your counselors wisely? Then do you follow their good advice, or does pride get in the way?

Humility often requires courage. We assume people will think poorly of us if we admit we don't know all the facts or the best way to proceed. But often just the opposite is true. Humility has an appeal all its own. Remember, too, people may undervalue this gentle opinion-making quality, but God never will. Perhaps that's why He so often blesses the humble.

Humility doesn't come easily to me, Lord.
Help me turn aside from pride and be meek instead.

Then Queen Esther answered,
"If I have found favor with you, O king,
and if it pleases your majesty, grant me my life —
this is my petition.
And spare my people — this is my request."
ESTHER 7:3 NIV

Humble Queen Esther knew the value of tact when she approached her husband, King Xerxes. Though he seemed to approve of her, the queen understood she was asking about a serious matter, one that touched his favored counselor, Haman. So instead of barging into discussion of the issue, she invited both men to dine with her. (You might call this a business dinner.) Then instead of demanding her rights as queen, she tactfully petitioned the king.

Do you demand things from your boss as if he owed them to you, or do you treat him with more respect? Are your words tactful or irritating?

Like Esther, you'll quickly find that tact receives a better response. Your boss and other managers enjoy receiving respect as much as you do and are more likely to say yes to it than rude demands. So consider this lesson from Esther, and no matter what your corporate position, speak tactfully if you want to hear a yes. Remember, honey always draws people better than vinegar!

Lord, ensure my words are always tactful when I speak.
Give me gracious words whenever I open my mouth.

A good name is rather to be chosen than great riches,
and loving favour rather than silver and gold.

PROVERBS 22:1

God says that a good reputation is valuable—more important than money. Today, it would seem He's got the minority opinion. But since God's truth never changes, we know that even if the rest of the world doesn't mind ruining their reputations, we need to value ours.

Reputations can come and go. You may get one when you take an unpopular stand, do something wrong, or make a mistake. Whether you've done something good or something wrong, unless it's something huge, that reputation usually passes with time. Let people know that it was a mistake or a wrong choice, and they'll start to cut you some slack if they see you've taken responsibility and made changes. They will probably eventually forgive you for an unpopular stand, especially if you stand for something good.

But the reputation that does not stop is the one you build carefully—the one that shows what you wholeheartedly believe, the one you act out on. Do right consistently, worship God with your whole life by following His will, and you will get a reputation worth keeping. Even if others don't like you for it, it will be better than "great riches" because it will earn eternal rewards.

I want a reputation for loving and serving You, Lord.
Guide me in making that happen.

You are my portion, O LORD; I have promised to obey your words.
I have sought your face with all my heart;
be gracious to me according to your promise.

PSALM 119:57–58 NIV

Ever felt as if you or a coworker was harshly judged by God? Did you feel as if He did not care? No matter how you tried to improve things, life remained disjointed, unhappy.

For Christians who make God their "portion," the most important part of their lives, a call for help receives a response. It may not come today or tomorrow, and it may not come in the expected package, but that help *will* come.

How can you be sure? Because God keeps His Word, and He has said He will have mercy on those who fear Him (Luke 1:50). The psalmist reminds God that he has obeyed His laws and expects God's promise of salvation (v. 41) to be kept. God comes to the aid of any faithful believer who is in trouble. He's as close as a prayer away.

Don't trust the circumstances that envelop your life—they can and will change. Trust instead in the changeless Lord, who will have mercy on you.

Lord, I need Your mercy today.
Help me trust You to save me in this need, too.

"Run to and fro through the streets of Jerusalem;
see now and know;
and seek in her open places if you can find a man,
if there is anyone who executes judgment,
who seeks the truth, and I will pardon her.
Though they say, 'As the LORD lives,' surely they swear falsely."

JEREMIAH 5:1–2 NKJV

God couldn't find a truly just person in ancient Jerusalem, and He isn't having an easier time today. In this sin-sick world, people often say they believe in God, but you couldn't tell it by the way they live. How can you know if a coworker who says he knows Jesus really does?

None of us get to judge who goes to heaven. Some amazingly unpromising-looking folks may be destined to walk through heaven's gates. But the best gauge on this side of eternity is a person's actions. If he who claims to share faith with you shows no evidence of a changed existence, he may be missing the new life he claims. Otherwise, he may be ignoring Christ's claims on his life because he cannot give up a favorite sin.

Are you doubtful about another's faith? Share your own with him. If he truly knows God, you may uncover hidden needs you can help with. If he doesn't know the Savior, you may lead him to that knowledge. Just a gentle witness can lead a wavering soul into truth.

Lord, lead me not to judge,
but to bear Your witness everywhere I go.

O taste and see that the LORD is good:
blessed is the man that trusteth in him.

PSALM 34:8

A wonderful crusty loaf of bread tastes so good when you're hungry. Those "artisan loaves" of old-fashioned bread are my favorite. A breakfast piece of toast often fuels the start of my day.

Jesus called Himself "the bread of life" (John 6:35), and as I crunch into a favorite slice of bread, I can understand that He's talking on two levels. First, He provides the sustenance we all need. Without Him, we're spiritually empty. But I think today's verse on taste also applies to Jesus the bread of life. Not only does the bread of Jesus fuel the spiritual day, it tastes good. We're blessed when we trust Jesus, not only because He brings new life, but because He brings a delight to life that's missing from unbelievers' existence.

Living for Jesus isn't a matter of gritting your teeth and living in a cheerless way. Instead, faith in Him brings new joys into our lives—even better than the taste of a nice, crunchy loaf of bread.

Lord, I delight in living for You
because You bring much joy into my life.
Even on the tough days, I'm glad I'm living for You.

Dishonest scales are an abomination to the LORD,
but a just weight is His delight.
PROVERBS 11:1 NKJV

Did you know that when you weigh out a product properly and charge your client the right price, God is pleased? *Could such a small thing really get the attention of God?* you may wonder. *It doesn't seem like much—could it really be that important?*

Yes, because God approves of honesty in all things. Over and over, Scripture enjoins us to be honest people because living honestly reflects the kind of God we serve. Unlike some of the pagan gods, who were sometimes portrayed as sneaky, God does not play games with us. He tells us what He expects of us and stands by that expectation. As honest as He is with us, He expects us to be with other people.

God hates any kind of dishonesty, so whether you work weighing out a product or charge a customer for a service your company provides, remember to be thoroughly honest. It's what you expect of Him, isn't it? And you don't want your actions to be abominable to God, do you?

Lord, make me honest in all my ways.

A gracious woman retains honor, but ruthless men retain riches.
PROVERBS 11:16 NKJV

The business world often values ruthlessness. Some see it as the way to get ahead in business. But where do they get in the long run? Eventually their greed ruins their reputations; they destroy their own lives through their wrongdoing.

While the money is coming in, the ruthless think they've beaten the system. They've got it made, and no one can outdo them. But while they're selling their reputations cheap, the gracious woman, whom they have ignored or accused of naïveté, beats them on a front they've never even considered: the spiritual one.

Someday these ruthless men may find themselves envying the "naïve" woman. She wasn't "important," until they needed her good opinion with others, because those people have lost respect for them. But even more surely, there's a day when they will see her value, as, loaded with unforgiven sin, they face a holy God. Then they'll understand that they were the naïve ones—thinking their sins would never find them out.

Over and over in Scripture, God tells us sin will not escape Him (Exodus 32:33; Numbers 32:23; Psalm 69:5; Ezekiel 18:4). Do we really believe that? Or when we watch the less ones, do we envy them? In a little while, face-to-face with Jesus, that envy will mean nothing as we glory in the right.

Lord, make me gracious, not truthless.
I want to please You.

There is one who scatters, yet increases more;
And there is one who withholds more than is right,
but it leads to poverty.
PROVERBS 11:24 NKJV

"You have to give to get." Have you heard that worldly version of this verse? It probably didn't sit well with you when you first heard it; after all, it could be so easily overdone. Not being wise in "scattering" could get you in a lot of trouble. Without God's wisdom, we don't make wise giving choices.

But used biblically, giving's a good idea. Freely give encouragement and support to others, and when you need some, it's amazing what you'll receive back. Hold on to every good word, and you'll rarely receive encouragement. Or share the money you have (not your credit card overdraft), and God will bless you. Squeeze every penny, even when you have plenty, and soon you may find yourself with a financial lack.

One warning here, though. If you make this into a tit-for-tat affair and give only to get, it's unlikely to work. Giving needs to be done from a generous heart that's thankful for God's blessings. That's sharing the greatest blessing with the world, and God loves to see it.

Lord, give me a generous heart
that wants to share with others.

Like a gold ring in a pig's snout is a
beautiful woman who shows no discretion.
PROVERBS 11:22 NIV

In these few words we get a clear message. This verse is a poetic way of saying someone can have physical loveliness that makes the world envious, but if she opens her mouth and spreads abroad the confidences people offer her, no one will think her beautiful. They'll recognize her weakness, and that one fact may well overwhelm everything else about her.

From Proverbs' pithy description, we also can imagine our innate reaction to this indiscreet human. We flinch away from her as we would a pig's gold snout ring. Beauty contrasting with ugliness can't make the entire person beautiful.

At work, home, and church, people appreciate others who keep their private business private. Whether it's a business plan that isn't finished, information on a client, or a friend's personal life, when someone else would benefit by not having the word spread around, we need to keep the news private.

After all, we wouldn't want people to associate us with a pig, would we?

Keep my manners from being piggy, Lord,
by keeping me faithful to You.
Remind me that I have some things I'd like kept private, too.

He who seeks good finds good will,
but evil comes to him who searches for it.
PROVERBS 11:27 NIV

In the short run, people may hassle you about your faith; but over time, if you live a godly life, you'll experience the goodwill of others. The hassles you get by coworkers are probably more a testing of your faith to see what you really believe than permanent oppression.

When people know what you stand for and see the results of your faith, they begin to respect you. They learn that you're a person of your word—you do what you promise; they know you'll always be honest. Even if they don't share your faith, they'll accept your good character. The ones who earnestly doubted your faith may come not to doubt you.

No matter what evil your coworkers seek, make sure you look to the good, seek to do right, and continually obey God. The evil ones you work for will eventually find the wickedness they're looking for—but it won't be with you.

Lord, I want to only seek good by doing Your will,
even when evil surrounds me.
Turn my coworkers to good, too.
I want them to know Your love.

He who brings trouble on his family will inherit only wind,
and the fool will be servant to the wise.
PROVERBS 11:29 NIV

Do you have a troublesome family member? Perhaps it's a sibling who often fights with you over family matters or someone who lords it over you. Whatever your situation, no matter how many troubles you face, take heart. God has not deserted you.

Remember that in God's kingdom, things are not always as they seem. In this world, the person who seems unimportant today may be powerful tomorrow. The humble person on this earth may be great in heaven. Whatever the situation, be certain God will bring justice. In the end the troublemaker will have her just reward, and the fool will discover that he's not in a place of authority.

The change may be a long time in coming, but God will not forget. He does not change, and He is with you every day. Count on Him.

Lord, I pray for that troublesome person in my life.
Bring Your Spirit into this situation and help us find peace.
But most of all, I ask that this person will come
to strong faith in You and live by Your Word.

His name is the LORD. . . .
A father to the fatherless.
PSALM 68:4–5 NIV

Did you have a perfect father? No. No human is perfect at raising his children. Our fathers have done their best, trying to pass on their strengths and avoid passing on weaknesses to us, but even the best dads make mistakes because they're human. And fathers who don't care for us well can mar our lives for years.

If you had a wonderful dad, thank God. Dad's protected you from a lot of troubles. He's given you a clear idea of what God's like. But if you didn't get a father who'd get a Dad of the Year award or you don't even know your dad, don't feel discouraged. You still have a Father who cares deeply for you. He may not take you to ball games, show you how to drive, or teach you math, but He watches over you, wants to spend time with you, and makes certain you're safe. He helps you in ways an earthly father never could. God is the Father of all those who believe in Him.

God cares for all children, no matter how imperfect their dads have been. He knows that all children receive hurts from their earthly parents, and He wants to help. So share your hurts with your Father and feel His deep comfort. Open your life to Him and learn what a Father really is.

Thank You, Lord, for being my perfect Father.

Do not be rash with your mouth,
and let not your heart utter anything hastily before God.
For God is in heaven, and you on earth;
therefore let your words be few.
ECCLESIASTES 5:2 NKJV

This is good advice for Sunday morning worship time (see v. 1), but it's also a good principle to guide your working life. Another way to phrase this verse would be the commandment not to take the name of the Lord in vain (Exodus 20:7). Don't treat God as if He and His commands were unimportant.

For example, don't promise God—in the office or at church—that you'll take that hoped-for raise and put it toward His kingdom's work unless you plan to follow through with that whole amount. If you plan to do it, think it through ahead of time. Don't make rash promises to God, but do what you say you will.

Remembering who you are (a human) and who God is (the omnipotent One) and treating Him accordingly is a wise decision, no matter where you are or what you're doing. You're talking to God, so don't make promises you cannot keep.

How would you feel if He didn't keep His promises to you?

Lord, help me think through any promises I make
before I make them.
I want to keep them well.

Thy word is a lamp unto my feet,
and a light unto my path.
PSALM 119:105

I didn't know much about my neighbor's faith until I mentioned I was writing a devotional. We don't meet that often because our schedules don't mesh well. Though I'd liked her immediately when I first met her, we'd never talked of faith.

What a joy to hear, one day, that she keeps a Bible at work and dips into it two or three times a day. Hers can be a pressured job, and I was glad to know she had the best working team before her, beside her, and behind her: God the Father, God the Son, and God the Holy Spirit.

When you're having a tough workday, are you tapping into your best resource? Do you take a few minutes on break or at lunchtime to connect with your heavenly Father, the Son, and the Spirit? If so, you're part of the best working team available—nothing has to faze you.

Lord, help me tap into You throughout my busy day.
I need Your help through each day of the workweek.

But in a great house there are not only vessels of gold and silver,
but also of wood and clay,
some for honor and some for dishonor.
Therefore if anyone cleanses himself from the latter,
he will be a vessel for honor,
sanctified and useful for the Master,
prepared for every good work.
2 TIMOTHY 2:20–21 NKJV

Have you ever bought a tool for the kitchen or shop, brought it home with great expectation, and discovered it was utterly useless? You felt irked that you'd wasted your money, didn't you?

God also has tools—some valuable and others less so—us. Some, filled with faith, shine like gold or silver before the world. They receive places of honor because they are willing to be used by Him and cooperate with His purposes. But not all God's tools are such successes. Others want to know Him but not obey Him. They live with a foot in His kingdom and one in the world, obeying when it's convenient, ignoring God's commands when they please. These vessels, made of wood and clay, easily broken by difficult situations, are put to use on the least important purposes.

Do you want to be gold or silver or wood or clay? Don't settle for being an easily broken Christian. Turn to God for strength to do His will, and soon you'll shine like gold.

Lord, I want to shine for You.
Give me strength to obey Your will.

" 'Keep my decrees and laws,
for the man who obeys them will live by them.
I am the LORD.' "
LEVITICUS 18:5 NIV

Over and over, God tells us to obey His laws, but nowhere in Scripture does He promise obedience will be fun. Extremely beneficial, yes, but not fun.

If you've lived by God's laws for more than a day—maybe more than an hour—you've discovered this truth. Our old sin natures resist so much holiness. Also, Satan doesn't leave us alone when we're obedient. He loves to distract us, tempt us, and otherwise lead us into rebelliousness because he knows the dangers of obedient Christians. Those who pray regularly, act out the instructions in the Scriptures, and follow God's will threaten evil. Satan doesn't want that.

Though obedience is often less than fun, its benefits far outweigh every trouble. God blesses us for obedience, and when He gives, He does so generously. Scripture promises good harvests (or maybe a good career that will provide for you and your family) (Deuteronomy 11:13–14), blessings on following generations (Deuteronomy 12:28), and mercy (Deuteronomy 13:17–18) to obedient believers.

If obedience isn't fun today, look to tomorrow. Those blessings are enough to keep anyone obeying, even when it isn't all joy.

Lord, help me trust that You will bless me if I obey today,
and keep me faithful when obedience is hard.

"I know all the things you do,
and I have opened a door for you that no one can shut.
You have little strength,
yet you obeyed my word and did not deny me."
REVELATION 3:8 NLT

God can open those stuck doors in our lives if we seek to obey and not deny Him.

But that's hard work! you may admit. Yes, standing firm for Jesus *can* be difficult. But when it is, perhaps it's because *we've* shut some doors on *Him:* the doors in our hearts that hide dark, sinful spaces. Jesus will not respond to our sin by forcing our doors open or running for skeleton keys. If we shut Him out, He lets us. Yet we'll hear His sweet, gentle voice right through that door. No matter how we try to avoid it, His Spirit calls to our souls.

When, in our feeble strength, instead of trying to clean out sin ourselves, we offer Him the keys to the portals we can't even begin to budge, His Spirit opens our nasty closets, empties them, and fills them to overflowing with love, joy, and peace. Suddenly, new doors fling wide before us, doors of Christian service and freedom from sin.

No one can shut a door Jesus opens. So today, offer Him the keys to your life's closed doors. Then walk through the doors He'll open for you.

Lord, here are the keys to my heart. Open each door to You.

Pray at all times and on every occasion
in the power of the Holy Spirit.
Stay alert and be persistent in your prayers
for all Christians everywhere.
EPHESIANS 6:18 NLT

Paul isn't saying you can't or shouldn't pray for non-Christians, especially that they should come to know Jesus, but the Scriptures talk quite a bit about praying for believers. The apostle tells the Ephesians to pray persistently for Christians everywhere. That means the folks in the church, pastors, and even people they didn't know.

Are you praying for Christians everywhere? Does that include the suffering church—people around the world who are persecuted for their faith?

Going to church isn't just a matter of showing up on Sunday morning, it's about being part of a Christian community that cares for one another throughout the week. Believers need to develop alertness to the needs of other Christians anywhere. Hear of a need? Then bring it immediately to prayer, and if possible, add that person or need to your prayer list so you can remember it for longer than a day.

Also pray wherever you are—on the bus or in the car going to work, during lunch hour, over your meals, or while you're doing your least-favorite household chores. Any time is a good time to pray.

I want my prayers to be alert and persistent, Lord.
Every day, keep me faithful in remembering
other Christians before You.

For as in Adam all die, even so in Christ shall all be made alive.
1 CORINTHIANS 15:22

My church's buildings are surrounded on two sides by a graveyard. Among the headstones is one that shows a birth date of 1875 but no date of death. What happened to this mystery woman? Perhaps the family placed the headstone and never put the body there. Or maybe some stonemason failed to do his work. But life at that age is pretty unlikely—on this earth, that is.

However, I wouldn't be surprised to hear that this woman *was* still alive—in heaven. If faith in Christ was the deciding factor in her life, she isn't in the grave, but enjoying a reward that far surpasses this earth.

For Christians, death—at one hundred or during youth—is not the end of existence. It's a spiritual fact that Adam's sin and the death that accompanies it can't last. New life in Christ displaces death even in this life, as sin is put aside and the spiritual joys of heaven appear in believers' hearts.

I don't know about you, but at one hundred twenty-something, I'd rather be enjoying a heavenly reward, healed of illness, age, and sin. Because new life that only lasted on earth wouldn't be worth a single bit of eternity with Jesus.

Thank You, Lord, for new life in You.
I'm eager for eternity in Your presence.

The heavens tell of the glory of God.
The skies display his marvelous craftsmanship.
PSALM 19:1 NLT

Everything God creates tells how glorious He is—everything, even you. So even on your lower-than-a-snake's-navel days, you can have confidence that He can make your life show His glory.

But, you're thinking, *the heavens don't have mouths to open and say the wrong things. They don't sin. They have a lot of advantages over me.* True, they don't do those things, but they also can't change much. They don't show how God has worked in their lives, and they can't witness to a friend and see her accept Jesus. God made humans as special creations that surpass even the glory of the heavens.

So today, even if you're competing with that snake's navel, remember that God is working in your life. You're made to glorify Him. So speak that word of encouragement or testimony to a coworker. Help a friend in need. And glorify God in all your ways.

I want to glorify You throughout my life, Lord.
Help me do that today.

> *"There was a man who had two sons.*
> *He went to the first and said,*
> *'Son, go and work today in the vineyard.'*
> *'I will not,' he answered,*
> *but later he changed his mind and went."*
> MATTHEW 21:28–29 NIV

Two brothers, asked to go to the vineyard and work, gave their father different answers. The honest one refused, while his less-honest brother promised to go but didn't. Which brother describes the way you treat your heavenly Father? Do you tell Him what you know He wants to hear on Sunday but fail to live it out by Tuesday? Or are you honest with Him even in your rebellion?

Giving God an honest response, even when we feel rebellious, puts our real feelings on the table. God won't approve of our attitude, but when we tell Him the truth, He deals with it, as He obviously did with the honest son in this parable. He showed the boy his wrong attitude and worked to change his mind about going to the vineyard. God could open that honest, if rebellious, heart to the truth.

Feeling as if you don't want to do God's will today? Tell Him that. Ask Him to aid your rebellious heart and turn it in the right path. You'll be glad you told the truth when you unexpectedly find yourself going the right way.

Lord, my heart doesn't always want to turn in Your direction.
Cleanse me from sin and turn my heart toward You again.

The life appeared; we have seen it and testify to it,
and we proclaim to you the eternal life,
which was with the Father and has appeared to us.

1 JOHN 1:2 NIV

If you were a first-century reporter doing a piece on this man who claimed to be Messiah, whom would you believe—an eyewitness, like John, who followed Jesus for three years or someone who never even saw Him? If you had to report back to your editor, how would you feel about telling him you thought the woman who had never seen Jesus was right? Would you expect him to believe you?

Today, it's popular to doubt the biblical testimony. People living twenty centuries later like to doubt and criticize the Scriptures. They act as if they know the real truth these ignorant first-century folks missed. But who's missing the point? Is it the people who watched these hard-to-believe events or those who lived centuries after who can't know what really happened?

John gives a powerful testimony in his gospel and letters. He saw what happened, and he was no naïve follower who missed the point of Jesus' words and deeds. His complex writings prove his sharp intellect and deep understanding.

Do the doubters you witness to today offer any better proof than his?

Lord, when I face unbelievers,
help me share the apostles' eyewitness truth,
not the uncertainty of a contemporary doubter.

Man's anger does not bring about
the righteous life that God desires.
JAMES 1:20 NIV

Anger burns in you for the wrong done to a coworker. How do you handle your emotions? Do you immediately attack the wrongdoers in an attempt to correct the wrong, or do you hold off, waiting for your emotions to cool?

When emotions burn hot, it's easy to think we need to correct that wrong immediately. We're in the right, after all, and such evil should not be allowed to exist. But if we open our mouths too quickly, we risk doing a worse wrong or being discounted because we cannot control our emotions. The good we seek to do is tossed aside by our bosses because we could not control how we felt.

Bringing about a righteous result doesn't take anger, but it may require a cool head and prayer. Emotions tend to beget emotions, so when you strike in anger, another person is likely to respond the same way. Instead of righteous solutions, you end up trapped in a circle of emotional turmoil.

No matter how good your intentions, don't use anger to try to please God. He says it'll never happen.

Lord, help me control my anger
and seek Your solution instead.

We continually remember before our God and Father
your work produced by faith, your labor prompted by love,
and your endurance inspired by hope in our Lord Jesus Christ.
1 THESSALONIANS 1:3 NIV

Face it, the Christian life is no piece of cake. Even Paul tells the Thessalonians he remembers them for the energy they'd expended on work, labor, and endurance. Certainly Christianity in Thessalonica wasn't simple. The entire church faced persecution, just as Paul had when he first visited this bustling port.

Perhaps, like many prosperous cities of today, the inhabitants were comfortable with their own undemanding form of worship to deities that fed their "felt needs" of the "good life." Work, labor, and endurance did not appeal to them.

But this church's efforts paid off. Paul used them as a model for other congregations, to show how Christians should be, how they should respond in troubles (vv. 7–10). Even today, we know the Thessalonian church as one to be admired when it comes to standing firm in trials.

Are you working, laboring, and enduring, while it seems to get you nowhere? Don't give up. Keep on being a good testimony in your workplace, and you also may become an example for others. God may lift you up in the right time and use your example in a powerful way.

Lord, I want my effort to be of benefit to You.
Keep me faithful all the way.

*Finally, brothers, we instructed you how to live
in order to please God, as in fact you are living.
Now we ask you and urge you in the Lord Jesus
to do this more and more.*

1 THESSALONIANS 4:1 NIV

You feel you've done fairly well in your Christian walk. Not that it's been done under your power, but Jesus has led you, and you've tried to follow faithfully. There's no "big" sin in your life, though you'd hardly call yourself perfect. What do you do now?

"You're being faithful, don't stop," Paul tells the Thessalonians. The Christian walk doesn't last a few days or even a few years. It's a lifetime event. Every day of your life, keep on pleasing God, doing what He has commanded. Add year after year of obedience to the time you've already stood firm.

If you keep the need to please God ever before you, the Christian life will not become dull. Each day, as He opens new doors of service before you, you'll feel the joy that comes from obeying Christ. If things seem less than lively, look at your spiritual walk and ask, "Am I still pleasing Him?" Seek out the things you should be doing or should not be doing, and correct them. The joy should return to your walk.

Don't stop living for Jesus; just do it more, every day.

*Lord, I want to live only for You the rest of my life.
Help me do just that.*

"Therefore you also be ready,
for the Son of Man is coming at an hour you do not expect."
MATTHEW 24:44 NKJV

Look at it from the non-Christian point of view: We Christians say the person we love most in all time and eternity will return to us, bypassing death and the grave and coming again in glory. This person isn't a sweetheart, spouse, or much-loved parent. As much as we're devoted to the folks we share earth with, we claim they cannot give us hope because they cannot conquer death.

This hope in Jesus seems silly to the world. Though we've never met Him face-to-face, we believe He still lives. Our hearts belong entirely to this unseen One. Without viewing Him in the flesh, we believe He will return. How can anyone understand such attitudes unless they, too, have met the Savior?

We tell them that the One we trust in said He's coming again. Do we completely rely on that seemingly impossible fact? Do we know He could come at any hour, any day? And are we ready for Him to appear? If we're ready, we're living every day as if we could see His face for the first time. Is this the unexpected hour?

Lord, I want to see Your face and share the joy.
May my life be pleasing to You.

JUNE 30

A patient man has great understanding,
but a quick-tempered man displays folly.
PROVERBS 14:29 NIV

You're rushing to get through your day's work, and suddenly your computer program or some equipment goes kaput. *How will I ever get this done?* you ask yourself. In answer to that question, you have two choices: You can get upset, making solving the problem more difficult, or you can calm yourself, show patience, and think through a good solution.

Complaining to everyone around you may seem more fun than exhibiting patience, but unless you're explaining your problem to someone who can give you a solution, you're simply wasting time. Venting your anger in other ways isn't any better. You may feel relieved for a minute or so, but your problem waits back at your desk for you.

Patience and understanding work together to solve your problem. As you restrain your frustration, you can concentrate on understanding the problem and getting the help you need or deciding what's wrong so you can fix it.

Don't be a fool—let patience guide you instead.

Lord, help me keep my temper when frustration strikes.
Even then, I want to show faith.

He will cause deceit to prosper, and he will consider himself superior.
When they feel secure, he will destroy many
and take his stand against the Prince of princes.
Yet he will be destroyed, but not by human power.

DANIEL 8:25 NIV

The moral of this verse is that wicked power doesn't last. That was true in ancient Israel, and it's still true today.

Ancient Israel suffered under Antiochus IV, the Seleucid ruler described in this passage. He wanted to Hellenize the Jews and began offending God's people by putting an altar dedicated to the Greek god Zeus in their temple. Many Jews did not respond as he expected, and his rule caused the Maccabean revolt, in which Israel rebelled against Greek rule. Antiochus simply pressured the Jews more to make them comply, but it did not work.

Antiochus died a few years later, after Judas Maccabeus, leader of the revolt, had liberated Jerusalem. When Antiochus V, the next emperor, ended the persecution, all of Daniel's prophecy came true.

God won't let wicked people or governments last forever. It's as true today of corporate leaders as it was of ancient rulers. Those who do not follow moral practices are found out and eventually go under. So if your company is headed in a wrong direction and you want to keep your job, help set it on the right path.

I don't want wickedness to prosper, Lord,
so help me to stand for what's right.

*Daniel soon proved himself more capable than
all the other administrators and princes.
Because of his great ability,
the king made plans to place him over the entire empire.*

DANIEL 6:3 NLT

*A Christian can't really get ahead in this world. Things are
stacked against him because others don't like his faith.* Perhaps
you've thought this way when life didn't seem fair, but it
isn't true. Read the story of Daniel, and you'll learn of a
faithful man who rose to the highest levels of politics. Sure,
he had jealous enemies, and they made him suffer by turning the king against him; but they couldn't have the last
say—God did. For when faithful Daniel was thrown in the
den with hungry lions, God shut their mouths until Daniel
was removed. Then the men who'd stood against Daniel
were put in his place, along with their families, and the
lions destroyed them all (v. 24).

You probably don't need help with large felines, but
you may face opposition as fierce as lions. Everyone, even
those who don't share your faith, has people who disagree
with them. What they don't all have is God's support. So
rely on Him when you face the lions, and He will bring you
out alive—even if no one ever agrees with you.

*Lord, protect me from the "lions" I face each day.
I only want to do Your will.*

But this is not to be so with you; on the contrary,
let him who is the greatest among you become like the youngest,
and him who is the chief and leader like one who serves.
LUKE 22:26 AMP

Most people like to lord it over people in their power. They often think of them as being "below" them. But Jesus made it perfectly clear to those who would lead the fledgling church that this was not the way they were to deal with others. The name of Christian leaders is not "boss," but "servant." Those who want to be greatest must put others ahead of themselves.

If you've worked for people with this philosophy, you've probably been a happy employee. Having someone who makes your job easier by providing you with all the tools, information, and encouragement to do your job well is a wonderful thing. Count your blessings if you work for such a person.

If you don't work for such a person, make certain you become the first example of servant leadership in your place. The same idea that worked in the church will work in the "real world," too.

Lord, help me to serve those I work with and work for.
I want to be Your kind of leader.

So God created man in his own image,
in the image of God created he him;
male and female created he them.

GENESIS 1:27

"We hold these truths to be self-evident that all men are created equal," wrote Thomas Jefferson in the Declaration of Independence. Try to write those words in a government document today, and you'd probably take some flak; but Jefferson had no problem in his day because even those, like himself, who were not committed Christians accepted certain facts about God. Though Jefferson himself did not believe in all the Scripture, he surely accepted creation as fact.

What wise men accepted several hundred years ago is now doubted by so many. But that has not changed the truth. You *are* created in God's image. Whether you are male or female, He values you deeply. And from Him you have the promise of a potential that goes far beyond your own meager skills and abilities.

Don't let those who doubt discourage you from believing what many of our founding fathers accepted without question. God did make you. You are valuable to Him and "endowed with inalienable rights." Better than the "life, liberty, and the pursuit of happiness" Jefferson propounded, He offers you life eternal with Him.

Thank You for creating me, Lord.
Because you made me unique,
I can trust that I have a special place in this world.

*And do not forget to do good and to share with others,
for with such sacrifices God is pleased.*

HEBREWS 13:16 NIV

All the sacrifices the ancient Jews made to God had one point: to show them how sinful people are and how much they need to give their hearts to God. Some first-century Jews got the message loud and clear, and others missed it entirely.

Today we don't slaughter animals in an attempt to appease God for our sins. God clearly put that in the past when Jesus died for all our sins. Because God doesn't expect such sacrifices, we don't make them. But that doesn't mean we need not give God anything. The sacrifices we offer today are the things God wanted in the first place: our hearts and lives.

We show those sacrifices not only in our attitudes and thoughts, but through actions that show others God loves them. When a neighbor is short on cash, we may help her buy food for her family. When the church takes up a collection for a need here or halfway across the planet, we give as generously as we can, according to God's leading.

When we do that, God is pleased.

*Lord, I want to please You.
Please take control of my heart and life.*

Can the fig tree, my brethren, bear olive berries?
either a vine, figs?
so can no fountain both yield salt water and fresh.
JAMES 3:12

When you're on the job, do you allow yourself to become involved in practices that displease God and expect to please God on Wednesday night, Saturday church clean-up day, and Sunday worship? If so, you probably feel frustrated with your Christian walk. You may even be tempted to say that Christianity "doesn't work."

There's a reason why that kind of "faith" doesn't work. God says that if you're a fig tree, you bear figs, not olives. You can't have it both ways. Either you're going to do good to honor Him or you'll do the acts of wickedness that show where your true allegiance is. You can't do some of both and be a true Christian testimony.

Christians, James says here, have to be consistent. They'll either be sweet, potable water or salt water that kills all growth. They can't run sweet and salty at the same time.

If you're trying to do some of both, is it time to find a new job—or even a new line of work—where you don't have to compromise your Christian faith? Or is it time to simply begin living the way you know you should?

Lord, I don't want to try to be two things at once.
Help me live for You at work, home, and church.

And the soldiers likewise demanded of him, saying,
And what shall we do?
And he said unto them, Do violence to no man,
neither accuse any falsely;
and be content with your wages.

LUKE 3:14

Kind of odd, isn't it, that soldiers would come to a holy man for work advice? You wouldn't think John the Baptist would have much to say to them. But these men recognized that they could not compartmentalize their lives. There was not one set of rules for work and another for their religious lives.

Most of us are not soldiers, but this advice not to take advantage of others, to be honest, and to live within our wages, not looking for dishonest gain to pad our incomes, still works for us. Whether we have a great deal of authority or just a little, through John, Jesus tells us we should treat others gently, treating others as we would want them to treat us. Intimidation tactics and false accusations are not for children of God.

Need more work guidance? Today, have you asked God, "What should I do?" Then have you listened to and obeyed His answer?

Show me what I should do today, O God,
and help me obey Your commands.

I am the vine, ye are the branches:
He that abideth in me, and I in him,
the same bringeth forth much fruit:
for without me ye can do nothing.

JOHN 15:5

Are you "connected"? You may have a cell phone, beeper, computer, and a thousand other gadgets, but that doesn't mean you have the right connection.

Jesus talked about having the one everyone needs: a connection with God. When we're tapped into God the way a branch taps into a vine, we've got an attachment that does more for us than any phone, beeper, or computer.

Can you use your cell phone from anywhere in the world? Probably not. Some places it just can't receive transmissions. But you can always reach God in prayer—more than that, you'll get an answer, not an answering machine. You don't have to wait for a call back, either. And unlike a beeper user, God won't forget to pick up the message.

Computers are wonderful machines, but not as wonderful as God. From them you can get a lot of information, and with them you can bring forth a lot of work, but they will not give you all truth. They can help you do a lot, but you'd never say you can do nothing without them.

Connect with Jesus today, and you'll surpass all technology has to offer.

Lord, I need to stay connected to You every moment.
Keep me attached to You as a branch is to a vine.

"Do not be afraid of those who kill the body but cannot kill the soul.
Rather, be afraid of the One who
can destroy both soul and body in hell."
MATTHEW 10:28 NIV

Your boss tells you to lie. You know it's wrong, and you feel uncomfortable doing so. So instead of following his directive, you tell the truth. But now you fear for your job. Will he fire you for disobedience? He'd have every right to.

At this point, you have a choice. You can obey your boss, who can control your working life but not your eternal destiny or the rewards that go with it, or you can obey God. It's a tough choice if you have a family to feed, but it may not be as impossible as you think. Because when God calls you to obey Him, He also provides for you. That provision may be a new job, even if it follows a time of unemployment. Or the situation may come to a head, and your boss may change his mind or be reprimanded by someone higher up.

But whatever the choice you need to make, you can be sure you've made the right one if you follow Jesus. He holds eternity, not just your nine-to-five life, in His hands.

When I'm challenged to tell the truth, Lord,
keep me faithful to You.
I trust You with my whole life.

*I consider everything a loss compared to the
surpassing greatness of knowing Christ Jesus my Lord,
for whose sake I have lost all things.
I consider them rubbish, that I may gain Christ and be found in him,
not having a righteousness of my own that comes from the law,
but that which is through faith in Christ—
the righteousness that comes from God and is by faith.*

PHILIPPIANS 3:8–9 NIV

Suppose you had to give up something in life—what would it be? Would it be a job you've outgrown, a home that's bursting at the seams, or something else that doesn't seem quite suited to you now?

Paul wasn't giving up anything old, worn, or too small. He wasn't trying to get rid of something that didn't work for him. He had lost his reputation, his position in the Jewish religious community, and probably a hundred other things that had felt comfortable. In exchange, he'd gotten a ministry where people often gave him grief, that had hard traveling conditions, and with opposition from many. You'd hardly think the exchange fair, would you?

But one thing made up for every trouble and problem —Jesus. All the religious rules and regulations Paul had lost were garbage by comparison. The apostle treasured the Savior's righteousness, given to him at his conversion, and his relationship with the Son. Paul didn't mind giving up man-made laws for this faith. Have you done that, too?

Lord, nothing's better than You in my life.

Not that I have already obtained all this,
or have already been made perfect,
but I press on to take hold of that
for which Christ Jesus took hold of me.
PHILIPPIANS 3:12 NIV

Some days it's tough to press on. Work isn't exciting. Life is hard or dull. We wonder why we do what we do and where it will lead us. If the weather's beautiful or we have something better to do at home, we may wonder what we're doing in the office or at the factory.

Why don't we just skip out? Maybe it's because even when we'd like to be sunning ourselves or working on a project at home, we have a commitment that won't let us escape from doing the right thing. Like Paul, we aren't perfect, but we're on the path to holiness, and that includes doing right by our employers.

Holiness isn't an overnight thing—Paul didn't find it so, and neither do we. It comes to us in bits and pieces as we follow Jesus, and He increasingly takes hold of our lives. The more we seek to please Him, the more our lives slowly transform. We haven't obtained it all, but it's increasingly coming into our lives as we do the things God commands and seek to be more like Him.

Jesus has grabbed ahold of you. Are you grabbing ahold of Him, too?

Lord, I'm holding on tight.
I need to be more and more like You—perfect.

Now the LORD God had formed out of the ground
all the beasts of the field and all the birds of the air.
He brought them to the man to see what he would name them;
and whatever the man called each living creature,
that was its name.

GENESIS 2:19 NIV

Do you have a pet God gave you? Then you're like Adam, whom God gave authority over the animals.

Our pets have often seemed to come directly from God. Our cat was a neighborhood stray that my dad found dining on leftover chicken bones the raccoons had dropped in the driveway. This starving, ill animal would not have lasted without swift medical help. And one of our dogs inexplicably moved from family to family 'til he found the right place—our house. The rescue worker we got him from told us that sometimes God just meant an animal to be with certain people. I'm sure she's right.

We're not the only ones who have been "given" a pet by God. He cares for each member of His creation, and many people have amazing stories about how they connected with their animals.

So whether you have a number of pets or don't like animals at all, remember, they're still God's creation. Treat them with respect and love.

Lord, thank You for all Your wonderful creations—
including the animals.
I want to treat them as You would.

And it will be said in that day:
"Behold, this is our God;
we have waited for Him, and He will save us.
This is the LORD; we have waited for Him;
we will be glad and rejoice in His salvation."

ISAIAH 25:9 NKJV

How often do we think how wonderful it would be for the Lord to come? With expectant anticipation, we imagine how that day will be, but our minds can barely comprehend it. Beyond that, we can hardly imagine what spending eternity with Him will be.

One day all our hoping and waiting will be over. We'll see Jesus face-to-face and know Him fully. And according to Isaiah, we will not be disappointed. All that time will seem as nothing compared to eternity with Him. We won't feel shortchanged or wronged but filled with gladness. The trials of the past will be over and hardly thought of.

So today, if waiting seems too hard, keep your eyes on that day when you will see Him face-to-face. Stay faithful, in expectation of that day when you will have waited long enough.

Then it will be enough to have been saved by Jesus.

Keep me faithful to You, Lord,
when the waiting seems so long.
My eyes need to focus on that day when
I will be completely saved from this world.

"Make yourself an ark of gopherwood;
make rooms in the ark,
and cover it inside and outside with pitch."

GENESIS 6:14 NKJV

Being saved in the ark was no cakewalk. Before it could happen, Noah had a lot of work to do. First he and his family had to make a ship, though they didn't even know what water was. Their land didn't run to watercraft because no one needed them.

God gave him directions on how to make a large but basic vessel. We're not talking the *QE II,* just a few basic amenities, like rooms and pitch to keep it watertight. But before they could enjoy these basics, Noah had to cut wood, shape it, and fix it together, all in the right way. Then he had to build rooms—some for the animals, others for his family. The worst was yet to come. Stinky, hot pitch had to be placed all over the ship to keep out the rain God promised to send.

What would we think if God asked us to take on such a task? Would it be too much trouble? Too dirty a job? God is looking for people like Noah, who won't complain but will take on messy jobs without complaint. Whether it's at work or in the church, He wants people who will be faithful to Him, no matter what He asks.

What is He asking of you today?

Make me willing, Lord, to do whatever You ask.

But with thee will I establish my covenant;
and thou shalt come into the ark, thou,
and thy sons, and thy wife, and thy sons' wives with thee.
GENESIS 6:18

God promised Noah that He would save not only him, because the man obeyed. This generous Lord also saved Noah's entire family, including the in-laws.

What was it like for the other members of the family to see the waters cover the entire earth and know that because Noah had been faithful, they were reaping an undeserved benefit? For the forty days and nights of rain and the days when the rain subsided slowly into the ground and seas, could those people have done enough to help their husband, father, and father-in-law? Every time he needed a hand with the lions or zebras, someone was probably ready to assist. How else could these undeserving people show how much they appreciated him?

Noah's story is a picture of salvation. None of us deserved to be saved. None of us could earn it, but all of us can be thankful that God chose to save us. To show that, we can work on our jobs, at home, and in the faith community to share that love. Whatever we do, like Noah's family, we want to show appreciation.

Lord, thank You for saving me.
Let every act I do show forth my love.

*"You are to bring into the ark two of all living creatures,
male and female, to keep them alive with you."*

GENESIS 6:19 NIV

If you've ever owned an animal, you know it can be a lot of work. Imagine having seven of every kind God had declared clean and two of the unclean to look after. First Noah had to get them all into the ark, then he had to feed, clean, and otherwise care for them until the water went down.

By the time Noah had all the animals in the ark, he was probably realizing what a huge job God had given him. But God had also given him a lot of trust. Without his care, some kinds of animals would no longer exist—he could have wiped out a species by simple carelessness.

When your job seems overwhelming, do you appreciate the trust that's placed in you? Whether you hold people's lives in your hands or do a more mundane job, your work is important to someone. How you carry it out is at least important to your boss—and God, who may not care if you flip burgers or do brain surgery, but who wants you to do your work to the best of your ability.

Appreciate the trust that goes with your job, whatever level you're on, and do your work to God's glory as well as for a paycheck.

*Let me work to Your glory,
not just for my own needs, Lord.*

And they that went in, went in male and female of all flesh,
as God had commanded him:
and the LORD shut him in.

GENESIS 7:16

As the door closed on Noah, his family, and the animals, doubts must have filled the humans' minds. Soon they'd be floating on the water, the only living creatures above the waves. Before them lay a lot of unknowns, and only one thing they knew for sure: God had saved them. He had a plan in this, but they hardly knew what to make of it.

Work must have filled their days, leaving little time to ponder the situation; but as they cleaned out stalls, fed recalcitrant beasts, and protected them from one another, the questions must have flitted through their heads. What would their new world be like? Where would they end up? How would they live?

We, too, face unknowns. How will the new job work out? Will we like the people? What will our boss ask us to do today, next week, next year? Will we get the new account? We can tie ourselves up with "what ifs" and doubts or accept that God is guiding us in this, too, and get on with the work.

Whether we're Noah or a twenty-first-century Christian, we can trust that God has saved us for a reason and live that out day by day.

Even when I don't know what's going on, Lord,
I trust in You.

*"Go out of the ark, you and your wife,
and your sons and your sons' wives with you."*
GENESIS 8:16 NKJV

Hearing these words must have ranked as one of the most wonderful moments in Noah's life. A praise party probably followed Noah's announcement that it was time to leave behind their cruise ship and step again on dry land.

The first thing Noah did, once they and the animals had left the ark, was to build an altar and worship God. How many levels of appreciation he must have felt: first, for the safety of him, his family, and the animals; then gratitude that they could finally leave what by then must have been a very smelly, noisy place. How Noah and family must have looked forward to their new life.

When we come to a happy turning point in our lives, do we rush to thank God? Or do we assume that our own abilities have brought us this far and take the credit for ourselves? We've never stepped foot on an ark, but He's surely cared for us, too.

*Thank You, Lord,
for every time you've saved me and kept me from harm.
I praise You for being the compassionate One
who guides my life each day.*

The LORD said to Samuel,
"How long will you mourn for Saul,
since I have rejected him as king over Israel?
Fill your horn with oil and be on your way;
I am sending you to Jesse of Bethlehem.
I have chosen one of his sons to be king."

1 SAMUEL 16:1 NIV

Whether at work or home, change often comes hard. Even if our lives aren't picture perfect, we resist any alteration to them, as Samuel resisted the fact that God had rejected the promising Saul as king. Samuel couldn't see God's plan, as he mourned for the ruler Saul could have become. Had Saul followed God faithfully, the prophet could imagine the blessings that would have followed. Perhaps he wanted to try one more time to change the king's mind and heart. So sadness for Saul echoed in his heart.

While the prophet mourned, God pointed the way to the new king, David. One king's disobedience had not changed God's plan or Israel's bright future. A man after God's heart (1 Samuel 13:14) would rule the land.

Are you mourning over something God has asked you to leave behind—a failed relationship, a financial loss, or a work-related change? Trust in God that what He asks you to leave He will replace with something infinitely better. Never fret about exchanging a Saul for a David.

Lord, it's hard to leave the familiar behind.
Give me trust in You that overcomes that pain.

Who among you is wise and understanding?
Let him show by his good behavior his deeds
in the gentleness of wisdom.
JAMES 3:13 NASB

Few of us want others to think we're dull witted or foolish. We'd rather have them believe we have smarts or wisdom, even if we don't expect anyone to compare us to Einstein. Too often, however, in our efforts to have others in the church admire us, we show off our intellectual abilities, using the world's measures of smarts. We like to prove our Bible knowledge or publicly show our ability to counsel someone properly. It seems better when everyone can appreciate our God-given spiritual gifts.

God says we don't really show wisdom or understanding that way. The kingdom method requires selfless good behavior and gentleness, not a show-off's attitude. Instead of appearing good to others at a new Christian's expense, we'll help that new believer gain a love of Scripture by helping her memorize it more easily. We'll counsel others not for our glory, but God's; it won't matter if no one but God knows how it happened.

Today, instead of making yourself look like a smart, well-grown Christian, be one. In love, offer to gently share the wisdom God's given you. Then you *will* be wise and understanding.

Lord, You have the wisdom I need to share.
Let me never forget where it comes from
or how to help others with it.

So Joseph naturally became quite a favorite with him.
Potiphar soon put Joseph in charge of his entire household
and entrusted him with all his business dealings.

GENESIS 39:4 NLT

Thrown into a pit by his brothers, sold into slavery to Ishmaelite traders—a state of affairs that barely saved him from death at his siblings' hands—Joseph had some tough breaks. When he reached Egypt and was sold to one of Pharaoh's officers, things looked pretty bleak for the young Hebrew.

But Joseph didn't spend a lot of time whining and complaining. He didn't go on strike because he had become a slave but deserved better. Instead, he drew close to God, and God blessed him (v. 2). His work went amazingly well, to the point where Potiphar noticed. The more God blessed the slave, the more authority he received in Potiphar's household, until Joseph was running everything.

If you face difficulties at work, do you complain or despair? Or do you draw close to God and do your best? The first responses won't get you far, but the second could benefit both you and your workplace. Be a Joseph on your job.

Lord, when I face work challenges and doubts, help me,
like Joseph, to remain faithful to You.

"No one here has more authority than I do!
He has held back nothing from me except you,
because you are his wife.
How could I ever do such a wicked thing?
It would be a great sin against God."

GENESIS 39:9 NLT

Tempted by Potiphar's wife, Joseph cried a firm "No!" Then he explained why in these heartfelt words. His master had placed great trust in him, and Joseph appreciated that. He would not betray him in such a way. Even more important, Joseph would never betray God. His Lord clearly defined right and wrong, and Joseph understood this was wrong. He resisted repeatedly (v. 10), until his master's wife lied about him, and her lie landed Joseph in prison.

Taking God's side in the office may not be popular. Sometimes it gets faithful believers in more trouble than if they'd just gone along with the flow. But in the end, like Joseph, they end up blessed for their fidelity.

So when anyone tempts you to fudge on the paperwork, approve of some seemingly small wrongdoing, or wink at a misdeed, beware! It would be a sin against your Lord, and one that may someday come back to bite you. Remember instead the trust your company and God place in you, and do the right thing.

Lord, no matter what the temptation,
help me remain faithful to Your truths.

The keeper of the prison did not look into
anything that was under Joseph's authority,
because the Lord was with him;
and whatever he did, the Lord made it prosper.

GENESIS 39:23 NKJV

No matter where Joseph went, whatever he did prospered. Even when tossed in prison, he ended up running the place. You couldn't call this young son of Jacob a slacker. But how did he do it?

Doubtless Joseph was an intelligent young man and a hard worker, but that alone cannot account for his ability to make the most of any situation. We, too, have some smarts and work hard, yet we don't necessarily end up running our companies.

Joseph's difference lay in his complete devotion to God. Instead of bemoaning his awful lot in life, Joseph called on God for help, did what he was given to do, and did it exceptionally well. Facing desperate situations, he had thrown himself totally on his Lord, not his own mental abilities or skills. By doing that, he received God's blessings on all he did.

Today, learn from Joseph. Place all you have and are in God's hands, to use as He will. Even if you never run your company, your blessings will surprise you.

Gracious Lord, I give You all I am and do.
Take control of my working life, my home life,
and every moment of my day.
May everything I do glorify You alone.

"It is beyond my power to do this," Joseph replied.
"But God will tell you what it means and will set you at ease."
GENESIS 41:16 NLT

Pulled from prison, hastily washed and dressed in court clothing, and brought before the pharaoh, Joseph must have felt stunned by the changes in his life. He had an opportunity to influence Egypt's ruler, who held the slave's life in his hands.

The last thing that might have seemed appropriate was to witness to this pagan king, who probably knew almost nothing about the Hebrew God. Yet Joseph didn't mince words with him, nor did he try to appropriate some of God's wisdom as his own. Courageously the Hebrew slave gave God the credit for his ability to help Pharaoh.

That doesn't mean we need to bring God into every work conversation. If we work for bosses who don't believe, we don't irritate them by bringing up Jesus every time. But there will be moments of need when they are open, as Pharaoh was, and we feel God's tug at our hearts to offer the truth we have to share. Then we can be certain we're speaking in turn and give a brief but honest message.

Lord, give me Your wisdom on
when to speak and what to say.
Let me consistently be a faithful witness to You.

*He was thirty years old when he entered the service of Pharaoh,
the king of Egypt.
And when Joseph left Pharaoh's presence,
he made a tour of inspection throughout the land.*
GENESIS 41:46 NLT

Before this, you probably won't have guessed that Joseph was on the fast track of success. Abused by his brothers, sold into slavery, lied about by a temptress, sent to jail. None of these sound like the path to becoming second in command of a nation. Yet each step led Joseph closer to greatness.

Our career paths may seem as checkered as Joseph's. We're out of work for awhile and end up landing a less-than-perfect job. We stay in the "wrong" job too long and fear it won't look good on a résumé. We don't have a perfect education for the job we'd like and can't afford to go back to school.

But somehow, even those weaknesses in our job histories can become strengths. Perhaps the job we thought would be ideal wouldn't work out for us, but another that we're perfectly trained for by our job history will be just what we need.

We are never entirely in control of our careers, any more than Joseph was, but God rules over everything. His plans will come to fruition in the end, if we follow His paths.

*Lord, I have little control over my career.
Take it in Your hands and use it for Your purposes.*

JULY 26

> *"I—yes, I alone—am the one who blots out your sins*
> *for my own sake and will never think of them again."*
> ISAIAH 43:25 NLT

Our awe-inspiring God demands perfection, and we so rarely give Him anything barely resembling it. When we look at our own imperfection, it's easy to become discouraged. Can we ever hit the mark?

When we feel that way, we're much like a child who has disappointed Father. We respond with fear, doubt, or even resentment because we've made a mistake or intentionally disobeyed.

Before negative emotion gains ground in our lives, we must realize that God never loves us because we act perfectly any more than we want to give our children that kind of conditional love. God blots out sin not because of our character, but because of His. He wants to love us so badly that even sending Jesus to die for us was not too great a price.

Discouraged by your own sinfulness? Don't give up—give it to God. He'll forgive your past wrongs and forget them all as He gives you strength for new life in Him.

> *Forgive me, Lord, the wrongs I've done*
> *and the attitudes that do not glorify You.*
> *Change my heart and soul and make me whole in You.*

Thou shalt have no other gods before me.
EXODUS 20:3

Some years ago, the lighthearted "Love Song for Number Two" hit the Christian recording charts. The gist of the song was that the writer loved her husband second best—after God. No, she didn't say her husband was second rate, just that God should take first place in both their lives.

If you're new to marriage or Christianity, that may seem confusing. How can your mate come second to God? Doesn't He approve of marriage? Of course He does, but a marriage that puts a spouse before God is backward; it's made the mate into an idol, and God does not tolerate anyone taking His place.

Amazingly, when God becomes part of a marriage in which both partners completely commit to Him, their relationship to each other improves immeasurably. Problems are often solved more easily as the Spirit works in their hearts. As they draw closer to God, they become more intimate with each other, too.

So don't turn your mate into an idol, but treasure your beloved as the gift God has given you. A godly marriage is a great blessing.

Lord, I don't want my marriage to
interfere with my love for You,
but I desire a great relationship with my spouse.
Help us cultivate that in You.

How beautiful you are, my darling!
Oh, how beautiful! Your eyes are doves.
SONG OF SONGS 1:15 NIV

Married? When you leave for work in the morning, do you grab a quick cup of coffee but ignore your spouse? Or can you take a few seconds to let your beloved know he or she is more important than work? A quick kiss, followed by an "I'll miss you!" could be just the encouragement your husband or wife needs—especially if your husband is unemployed or your wife will be spending the day at home, caring for the kids or working a home business.

God approves of marital love. After all, He created it! When two people enjoy each other within the bonds of marriage, they strengthen their relationship with each other and possibly even with God. Together, spouses draw closer to Him when they put Him first and each other next in their lives.

So today, before you step out the door, do you delight in your spouse? Or does that quick cup of Joe get in the way?

Lord, thank You for my spouse,
who brings such wonder into my life.
You've given me many gifts,
but my beloved is one of the best.

How fair is thy love, my sister, my spouse!
how much better is thy love than wine!
and the smell of thine ointments than all spices!
SONG OF SOLOMON 4:10

As you come home from work, do you long to reconnect with your spouse? Whether you're on to a meeting, helping get the kids ready for bed, or kicking off your shoes and spending downtime together, is it obvious you delight in being with your beloved? Can you share at least a few moments together to kindle the fire of your romance?

God designed marital romance to intoxicate in a purely beneficial way. As the king described it, love is better than wine. This powerful emotion draws two people into a commitment that overcomes many trials and brings spiritual and emotional growth to both, if they're committed to Him.

Don't allow the world to push out that time of reconnection with the one you love most of all people on earth. Protect the love that fills your senses and heart.

Lord, each night I need to reconnect with my beloved.
Keep me from being caught in distractions that
keep me from my spouse's love.

The king's heart is in the hand of the Lord,
like the rivers of water;
He turns it wherever He wishes.

PROVERBS 21:1 NKJV

Do you worry about decisions your boss, the government, or industry giants make that influence your working life? Occasionally, concern for changes you can't impact may even keep you awake at night.

Take comfort, then, in this verse. No matter what powerful person makes choices that influence your life and work, no decision, even from the rankest unbeliever, is beyond God's planning and mercy. Though you may disagree with the choices of the powerful or consider their judgments unwise, though their decisions may have made your life more difficult, nothing surprises God or disturbs His plan for your life. The all-powerful One really has all authority, ultimately even over those who do not believe in Him.

So if you wake up at night and start to worry, don't get caught up in a spiral of emotional defeat. Instead, pray for those corporate executives, government decision makers, and captains of industry. God may work through your prayers to turn their hearts and minds, like a river, to a better resolution.

I put my life in Your hands, omnipotent One,
and ask that You give wisdom to the
decision makers in my company and industry.
I ask that You might guide their way today.

*Like a city whose walls are broken down is
a man who lacks self-control.*
PROVERBS 25:28 NIV

Today, self-control isn't a popular concept. Our society tends to assume we must wear our emotions on our sleeves in order to be healthy. But that's not the advice the Bible offers. Often it counsels that we hold on to our thoughts and emotions, perhaps until we've had time to process them, pray about them, and make a wise decision.

God isn't saying we shouldn't express our thoughts and emotions, but that we need to do so wisely. If we quickly go on the attack, praise something to the hilt that tomorrow we'll wish we'd thought twice about, or hurry to make a decision, we may find ourselves without defenses. Like an unwalled city, any opponent can walk all over us when we've rushed off in another direction.

Self-control doesn't come swiftly or easily to most of us. It may take a few harsh lessons to teach us to value this quality; but when we recognize the need for it and seek it through God, we'll discover one of His great blessings.

*Though it doesn't much appeal to me, Lord,
I know I need to control my thoughts, emotions, and deeds.
Help me to put them all under Your control.*

The integrity of the upright will guide them,
but the perversity of the unfaithful will destroy them.
PROVERBS 11:3 NKJV

Years ago, after an accident, my dad needed some work done on his house. Unasked, a contractor offered to take it on; then, as if he were doing my dad a favor, he promised he'd tell the insurance company the job cost more than it actually did so my dad could pocket the difference. Dad, being a man of integrity, didn't even consider the offer.

You have to wonder what that contractor was thinking. After all, if he was so quick to extort money from the insurance company, why would my dad trust him? Why would anyone want to hire someone he knew was dishonest?

I suspect that contractor wasn't very busy because his reputation went before him and put folks off. But worse than that, his spirit was obviously so deeply mired in dishonesty that he couldn't see why he didn't get jobs or conceive of the benefits integrity would bring.

Your boss may never thank you for your integrity, and a client may not mention that it's one of the things she likes best about you, but it's still the oil that greases the wheels of your career. Don't let your career grind to a halt because of any dishonest act.

Integrity isn't very exciting, Lord,
but I know it needs to be part of my life.
Give me the ability to always be consistent for You.

"Your love for one another will prove to the world
that you are my disciples."
JOHN 13:35 NLT

Can people tell you're a Christian? If so, how do they know?
Is it because you always carry a Bible or collar people on the
street to tell them they're sinners? Carrying a Bible and
witnessing to your faith may be parts of your Christian testimony, but if it ends there, you're missing the crucial ingre-
dient Jesus mentioned in this verse—love.

Jesus didn't command His disciples to carry Bibles or
attempt to make wrongdoers feel guilty, but He did tell
them to love one another. Why? Because love has an attrac-
tiveness that reaches out to others as it shows what's truly
in our hearts. Few people can resist real, honest love.

People may not know much about your faith because
you do all the "right" Christian things like going to church,
giving to good causes, or carrying your Bible; but the love
you have for others will spill out on the world and convince
it that your faith is real. It will give you opportunities to
really share your faith—in a way that reaches the heart.

Lord, I want people to see Your love through
my love for other Christians—
and even people of no faith.

Then Jesus said,
"You would have no power at all over me unless
it were given to you from above."
JOHN 19:11 TLB

Was Jesus' crucifixion a great, cosmic mistake? For a short time, was God out of control of the world? Or was He being mean to His own Son?

Non-Christians may attempt to portray God in such ways. They see God as being powerless or cruel; but neither is true, as this verse shows. God the Father was in control even when the world did its worst to His Son. But God had a larger goal in mind—bringing about mankind's salvation through this horrible situation that showed how vile human hearts really are.

From this we know that in a seemingly out-of-control world, we can trust God makes no errors. If He was not powerless on the dark day of the crucifixion, He's not powerless in our lives, either. No matter what troubles or doubts we face, He's still in control. We only need to trust in Him.

Lord, help me see Your power in the blackest moments.
I know I can trust in You completely,
but sometimes my heart needs to feel
what my head understands.

*Now to him who is able to do immeasurably more than all we ask
or imagine, according to his power that is at work within us,
to him be glory in the church and in Christ Jesus
throughout all generations, for ever and ever! Amen.*
EPHESIANS 3:20–21 NIV

Have you ever had God answer a prayer you hadn't even gotten around to praying yet? Maybe your mind was on that problem at work or a coworker's troubles. You mulled it over, but somehow it never made it to your prayers, perhaps because the world got in the way. By the time you got to formal prayer, it'd slipped off into mental oblivion.

Then you went to the office one morning and learned that God had been at work all along and solved the problem you'd shelved. The situation came to a beautiful conclusion, without your having prayed at all. How awful you felt that you'd never even brought it before the Savior!

None of us should ignore prayer, and it's a good idea to keep a prayer list handy; but even when we fail, God doesn't. We may ponder something without prayer, yet in His grace He answers even that unspoken need. He did immeasurably more than we thought to ask for. How much He deserves our praise!

*I praise You, Lord,
for doing more than I'd even think of asking for.
I give You all the glory.*

Thus saith the LORD, Let not the wise man glory in his wisdom,
neither let the mighty man glory in his might,
let not the rich man glory in his riches:
But let him that glorieth glory in this,
that he understandeth and knoweth me,
that I am the LORD which exercise lovingkindness,
judgment, and righteousness, in the earth:
for in these things I delight, saith the LORD.
JEREMIAH 9:23–24

This world has many wise, mighty, and rich people. Though we might not like that, speaking in purely human terms, it's true. Such folks wield plenty of authority, whether or not they're Christians, and can do much good or ill for the world.

But God warns us not to focus on their wisdom, might, or riches. Though they may seem important when we need to know where the economy will go next, who should become president, or where to get cash for a good cause, even the most powerful people can only change a small portion of the world. They can't bring loving-kindness, fair judgment, and righteousness to every corner of it—some don't even have these in their own lives.

Each of us, even those who don't have much worldly wisdom, power, or wealth, can glory in something bigger than the brains, strength, or money that seems to rule this world. Our real glory is the One who's really in charge: our Lord God.

Remind me each day of who's really in charge—
You, Lord God.

Don't worry about anything; instead, pray about everything.
Tell God what you need, and thank him for all he has done.
PHILIPPIANS 4:6 NLT

Are you tuned into WWJD? You are if, every day, you ask, "What would Jesus do?" If you're tuned in to God, the first thing you'll do in any worrisome situation is lift it up to Him.

Worry, and where will it get you? Maybe you'll add a few wrinkles to your face or some extra acid to your stomach, but you surely won't find a solution. You're more likely to end up thinking in circles, feeling more defeated by the moment.

Prayer draws you closer to a solution. You may not have all the answers when you start; you may not even have them when you've ended your prayer; but eventually, God clears the path and shows you the way.

So instead of tuning in to a rock, classical, or even a Christian station when you rise in the morning, begin your day with God. You can catch up on the latest tunes, news, and worldwide church reports later. Right now it's time to tune into WWJD for the inspirational report.

Lord, I always need to tune in to Your will,
no matter what else I hear today.
Let me get Your message loud and clear.

Let your conversation be without covetousness;
and be content with such things as ye have: for he hath said,
I will never leave thee, nor forsake thee.

HEBREWS 13:5

Who among us would not be glad to receive some more money? We can always find a "good" use for it, whether it's fixing up the house or going on vacation. Or maybe we'd prefer to give the kids some advantages our salaries won't afford. What's wrong with that?

The problem isn't in the money; it's in the attitude people have about it. Some folks can live contentedly on what they make, though they'd never turn down a raise or windfall. Others are like the overweight person who doesn't eat to live but lives to eat. The person with a money problem has made money the focus of life and will no longer be content with "enough." "More, more, more" is the cry of the covetous. Make more, and still it's not enough.

Instead of loving money, the Christian appropriately loves the One who provides it. Money may come and go, but Jesus doesn't. When the checking account is empty, He never is. When the assets are frozen, He's still offering a warm heart. So don't love money, but the One who really controls it. His name isn't your bank president's or Uncle Sam, it's Jesus.

Lord, I know You really provide all I have.
Thanks for what You've given me.

I press toward the mark for the prize of
the high calling of God in Christ Jesus.
PHILIPPIANS 3:14

Though you may never list them on a piece of paper, you have career goals. You may want to stay in your field for the rest of your career and rise up the ladder in your company. Or, dissatisfied with your work, you may be looking for a new calling.

Whatever your goal, you probably aren't aiming to do the worst job you can or ignore everything your boss tells you to do. These are good ways to get fired, quickly. No sensible person considers them a reasonable goal.

But while you focus on your career goal, do you miss out on an even better goal that will end in more than a good 401(K) plan or a good-bye gift that sits on your mantel? Are you keeping your eye on service to God?

You can and should serve God on the job. But are you also giving Him the rest of your day? God provides you with spiritual gifts He does not intend to be left on a shelf, stuck behind a dusty Bible. That would be like ignoring your boss from nine to five. Instead, your use of your "spare time" should earn a prize with God.

Are you pressing on to God's high calling or being a spiritual couch potato?

Keep my eye on the goal of serving You with my whole day,
Lord. I want to honor You.

But these speak evil of whatever they do not know;
and whatever they know naturally, like brute beasts,
in these things they corrupt themselves.
JUDE 10 NKJV

When you speak of your faith, do you know what you're talking about? Plenty of leaders out there teach some fairly crazy things and call them Christianity but, like the heretics of the first century, have missed some of the main points of the faith. What something is called is not as important as what it is—and a faith that does not teach what the apostles said can be called many things but not Christianity.

Jude figured out that the teachers he mentions in this verse were not talking about the Jesus he knew. In verse 16 he comments that they're following their own evil desires, not the biblical faith. These men probably taught forgiven Christians that it was okay to sin because of God's forgiveness. They handed out a sort of license to do as you please once you asked Jesus into your life.

Some teachers today will say similar things, but their "eat, drink, and be merry" philosophy is not what Jesus or the apostles taught. So don't settle for a feel-good faith that disobeys God. Instead, cling fast to Jesus' love, forgiveness, and commands. Then you'll know what you're talking about and share a *real* faith.

Let me rightly share who You are, Lord,
and what You command.
I don't want to corrupt myself.

*When you sin against your brothers in this way
and wound their weak conscience,
you sin against Christ.*
1 CORINTHIANS 8:12 NIV

The young Christians of Corinth were probably a power-packed bunch when it came to witnessing. They keenly felt their past sins and appreciated the forgiveness they'd found in Christ. But they were also still so close to their unforgiven days that they did all they could to avoid every temptation. So they insisted that no faithful Christian should eat meat offered to the idols they'd recently worshiped. It obviously created quite a furor in the congregation, since Paul had to address the subject.

Paul explained some of this to the Corinthians who'd known Jesus longer and asked them to treat the new Christians gently by not condemning something they meant for good, even if it was inconvenient. He asked them not to harm a brother by pushing him to do something his conscience said was wrong. To do so was to also hurt Christ.

Real Christians can differ on many minor issues of doctrine or practice. Those small things can become like sand in the wheels of faith, disrupting the church on many levels. Or they can become opportunities to show the love we share. Which will they be for you today?

*Lord, help me treat others with
tender consciences gently and in love.
I don't want to sin against You.*

*Servants, be obedient to them that are
your masters according to the flesh,
with fear and trembling, in singleness of your heart,
as unto Christ.*

EPHESIANS 6:5

Obeying your boss can appear to be a pleasure or curse, depending on what kind of boss you have. When you feel part of a team and know that your obedience will benefit your entire company, it's easy to obey. If your boss is good at his or her job and offers excellent leadership, you want to do the right thing.

But what about the days when you wonder if obeying will be a good thing? Do you hold your peace and obey blindly, or do you open your mouth and perhaps put your foot in it?

The best place to start is by lifting your situation up to God. Don't begin a prayer marathon, but briefly ask for guidance. If you can wait a bit, it might be best to hold off an hour or two, because sometimes such problems solve themselves. Then if you can, chat with your boss about your doubts.

But ultimately, God holds you responsible for obedience. So if your boss holds firm, lift a quick prayer up for this circumstance, and as long as what you're doing doesn't go against God's Word, follow your boss's direction. During your daily quiet time, lift it up again. And trust that God is in control of everything—even your boss's choices.

Lord, help me obey—but not blindly.

For verily I say unto you,
Till heaven and earth pass,
one jot or one tittle shall in no wise pass from the law;
till all be fulfilled.

MATTHEW 5:18

Have you ever worked for someone who insisted you follow every company rule—even if that rule made no sense and slowed down productiveness? Made you crazy, didn't it?

The Pharisees were something like that—they could identify every single Old Testament rule (and more that weren't there) and demand that people follow each. In the process of seeking to know God on their own terms, they lost out on the real meaning of His forgiveness.

When Jesus came along, He made the Pharisees nuts. Here He claimed to be God, yet He didn't know how to keep score "properly." The legalism that meant so much to the Pharisees was foreign to His nature. When Jesus said He fulfilled the Law, the Pharisees must have been livid.

Rules are needed in any workplace. They're guidelines that keep everyone working together. But just as the Old Testament Law was designed to show God's holiness and love, not create a "who can top this?" game, rules aren't meant to be the be-all and end-all of work.

Follow the rules, but don't make a god of them. God isn't just a rule maker. He's using His Law to show you how much He cares.

Today, Lord, show me how to use rules wisely.

Exhort bondservants to be obedient to their own masters,
to be well pleasing in all things, not answering back.
TITUS 2:9 NKJV

You know what it's like. While you're trying so hard to say the right things, awful words trip off your tongue. It's so strange, you feel like turning around and asking, "Where did that come from?" You'd had thoughts on the subject but never intended to share them publicly. Now here your doubts are, out there for your boss and everyone else to see.

Eventually the things on our hearts and minds come out somehow. The ideas, hurts, and fears that bubble below our conscious level churn up unexpectedly, perhaps at the most troublesome moments. It can be embarrassing when they show up in our speech.

Avoid such incidents by clearing each problem up while it's small. Deal with minor concerns, and they'll never become major. Instead of waiting for bitterness or anger to trip off your tongue, confront your boss before final decisions are made, when you can have input and changes can be made. Dealing with large issues while the concerns are still small may keep you from making a huge mistake that will affect your career. Better than that, you'll be pleasing God, too!

Lord, keep my tongue in check
and let every word I speak please You.

Likewise the tongue is a small part of the body,
but it makes great boasts.
Consider what a great forest is set on fire
by a small spark.
JAMES 3:5 NIV

Damaging a promising career may not take much. Open your mouth and publicly complain about your boss, pass on some gossip, or give a client misinformation, and you can find yourself looking for a new job. That's why James warned his fellow Christians about the tongue and its dangers.

Do you think and immediately speak? Then wisdom escaped you. God's Word never says, "To think is to speak," but gives many warnings about our words and the way they impact others and our faith.

A thoughtful Christian checks on her thoughts before she opens her mouth. Will saying this harm someone? Will it wrongly portray a person's motives? Is it simply not true? Is it simply wishful thinking? If any of those questions can be answered yes, it's time to close her lips. No matter how much she desires to speak out, she'll hold her tongue.

So instead of speaking out boldly, check your thoughts at the door of your lips. If what you have to say is something God would call good, open up and speak.

Lord, help me check my words before my lips open.
I don't want to hurt anyone with my speech.

For it is God's will that by doing good
you should silence the ignorant talk of foolish men.
1 PETER 2:15 NIV

Hold your tongue, speak wisely, and you'll still have a few people who don't return the favor. Once in awhile, you'll hear that someone has slandered you, doubted you, or misunderstood your reasoning. In an instant, you may want to respond in kind.

Whether the issue is your faith and your ability to share it or your work performance, take a deep breath, bite your tongue, and deal with the problem peaceably. Do all you can not to fire up the situation with harsh words or deeds. Instead, return kindness for evil and faith for doubt. Do the best you can in the situation.

By answering responsibly or even by ignoring a small, meaningless wrong, you'll gain the respect of your bosses and coworkers. Eventually, the talkers will fall silent because they recognized their misdeeds or got nowhere with them. The wrong will turn to right as your good deeds silence the foolish ones.

No matter whether it's world politics or your reputation, good always becomes evident, and evil is undone. Just be patient and prayerful, and you'll see it in your own life.

Lord, I want to see Your good triumph in every situation.
Help me be part of it by holding my tongue when I need to.

she did not consider her future.
LAMENTATIONS 1:9 NIV

Long-term sin has no future. No one engages in it after carefully considering the benefits and brightness of its results. Satan knows that and suits his tactics to the weakness in his plan by keeping people ignorant of the direction sin carries them in. Unable to see the ending of their bad choices, humans only view their wrongs as ways to dull the pain in their lives.

Sin's results appear clearly to its practitioners only after they've been caught in its net. By then, it's hard to escape from, and many never do make the break. But Satan's future is not God's future. God has plans for a good, prosperous future for those who love Him (Jeremiah 29:11). Holiness, not wrongdoing, is the result of His plan.

Do you have a friend or family member who's caught in sin? Perhaps that individual had a powerful impact on your life, one you can't escape, hard as you try. You cannot change that person's life or make his future better. But you can take his life as a warning and head in another direction. Run into the arms of God, not to alcohol, drugs, or other wrongdoing. In Him you'll find a blessed future.

When sin pulls at me, Lord,
remind me of my future with You.
Turn me from evil and into Your arms.

Then he said to me,
"Write: 'Blessed are those who are called to
the marriage supper of the Lamb!' "
And he said to me, "These are the true sayings of God."

REVELATION 19:9 NKJV

"Where two or more are gathered together, there shall be food" was a popular saying at a church I attended. It seemed that no matter what the get-together, we were breaking bread (or doughnuts or cake or even a roll with sausage and peppers) together. Most churches aren't much different when it comes to eating. It's a favorite Christian pastime.

Sharing food and drink seems to aid fellowship. Put a piece of cake in one hand and a cup of coffee in the other, and you reach right into a newcomer's heart. Chat over a muffin and tea, and an old friendship is revived. Get to know a longtime church member you've seen often and rarely talked to over a luncheon meeting.

So it's not surprising that our heavenly reward will have a church supper at its start. As we feast on the joys of knowing Jesus, the Bread of Life, it's only proper we should gather as one huge fellowship.

Then, with bread in hand, we will *really* praise Him properly.

Thank You, Lord Jesus, for the joys of fellowship,
both here and in our heavenly home.

And David enquired of God, saying,
Shall I go up against the Philistines?
and wilt thou deliver them into mine hand?
And the Lord said unto him, Go up;
for I will deliver them into thine hand.

1 CHRONICLES 14:10

While David fought and fled from King Saul, he learned a good lesson: Everyone has to choose which battles to fight and which to avoid. The anointed but not crowned king also knew where to go for the wisdom to make such decisions: God alone was his advisor when the Philistines were seeking to do battle.

We may not fight against warriors armed with swords and shields, but we also need to choose our battles. On the job, we face issues that are not important enough to be fought and others that will become a losing battle. Fighting over a vacation day that you and a coworker both want to take has no long-term value and is usually better not done. Trying to replace the boss's son on a job will be a battle you can't win.

As we face battles large and small, we, too, need to look to David's source for guidance. Instead of relying on our own wits and wisdom, as we turn to God, we can know where our efforts will be most effective. When God sends us on a mission and we follow His direction, our battles will be won.

Lord, help me choose which battles to engage in
and which to avoid.

*Then the local residents tried to discourage and frighten
the people of Judah to keep them from their work.*
EZRA 4:4 NLT

Though Cyrus, king of Persia, declared the Jews should
rebuild their temple, the neighboring peoples didn't like it.
First they tried to horn in on the work; and when the Jews
refused, they tried to stop it with a campaign of fear and
discouragement. They even hired counselors to advise the
king against the project.

Then the opposition also wrote Cyrus's heir, King
Xerxes, pretending to have his best interests at heart and
warning him against the rebuilding of Jerusalem. Should
the Jews have given up then? No, because a few verses later,
they're also writing King Artaxerxes. Despite their repeated
efforts, the opposition had little success. In the end, the
temple was rebuilt, just as God wanted it to be.

No matter who you are or what you do, at times people will threaten or discourage you. When they seem to
have more power than you, their efforts can seem daunting.
Should I go on? you ask yourself.

What was true for the Jews is also true for you. You
may not triumph over every bit of opposition, but follow
Him, and God will keep you building. Finally, your work
will be a temple that brings glory to Him.

Lord, keep me building to Your glory every day.

"For I know the plans I have for you," declares the LORD,
"plans to prosper you and not to harm you,
plans to give you hope and a future."
JEREMIAH 29:11 NIV

How secure would you be if you knew your life had a plan
no one could thwart? Would you step forward with confidence and hope? Would it mean the difference between
mediocrity and the best in your life?

God has just such a well-planned future for the believer
who trusts in Him. He pointed out His plan for the nation
of Judah, when it was completely disobedient to Him. The
people were not going in the right direction, and God had
so much more for them, if they would give up their wicked
ways and walk into the blessings He had in mind for them.

Sin never offers the benefits of God's plan. At best it
offers quick thrills, followed by long-standing regrets. Its
eternal plan is miserable: an eternity separated from God,
filled with suffering. Compare that to the blessings of a life
on this earth that serves God and an eternity of joy in His
presence.

Don't settle for Satan's second-best plan. God has a
plan for you!

Lord, I want to follow Your plans, not my own,
so I can build a blessed life in You.

And now, dear brothers and sisters,
we give you this command with the authority of our Lord Jesus Christ:
Stay away from any Christian who lives in idleness
and doesn't follow the tradition of hard work we gave you.

2 THESSALONIANS 3:6 NLT

Is there such a thing as a good Christian lazybones? Not according to Paul. He made it perfectly clear that he didn't appreciate some Christians sitting around and awaiting the second coming in frivolous living, sticking their noses in other people's business and expecting others to support them (vv. 11–12).

It's one thing to be temporarily unemployed and another not to work and to expect never to work. Not using your hands in a worthwhile fashion does not make you a better person. Paul says just the opposite when he tells Christians not to become friendly with those who have this attitude.

God anoints hard work done for Him. Think of the blessed people of the Old and New Testaments. Can you think of one that did not work? Noah kept a whole zoo for months and months; Deborah judged her people; David ruled a nation; Paul and the other apostles spread the gospel to much of the known world. No one sat on his or her hands, waiting for whatever God planned.

Putting our lives in God's hands doesn't mean we do nothing. Instead we do all He puts in our hands.

Lord, give me something to do for You today.

All who hear of your destruction will clap their hands for joy.
Where can anyone be found who has not
suffered from your cruelty?
NAHUM 3:19 NLT

Fear filled the hearts of the people of Judah as Assyria seemed poised to attack. This nation of fierce warriors had already conquered Judah's northern neighbor, Israel. That's when the prophet Nahum (whose name means *comfort*) spoke to God's people of the conquerors' eventual destruction. The pain the Assyrians inflicted in the prophet's time would not last more than about fifty years.

If you're faced with a cruel attack, God comforts you, too, with the knowledge that it won't last. Wicked people are not eternal, though we may feel they are. At some point, they bring on their own destruction, and that's when the rejoicing starts. Then the good and innocent happily declare God's proven protection and love.

Those who obey God suffer trials and troubles. Their houses may be smaller than a wicked coworker's. But they don't die empty, meaningless deaths because no one could love their ways. Unlike Assyria, no one claps joyfully at their demise.

Lord, I need Your comfort in trials.
Help me stand firm and respond to cruelty with Your good.

I say unto you, If ye have faith as a grain of mustard seed,
ye shall say unto this mountain,
Remove hence to yonder place;
and it shall remove;
and nothing shall be impossible unto you.

MATTHEW 17:20

A little faith goes a long way, according to Jesus. You don't need buckets of it to do amazing things. But we often feel that the more the better, and we seek to "get more faith." It doesn't take long for us to discover our own failure; for the harder we try, the worse things seem to get. We can't conjure up faith on our own. No matter how hard we try to achieve it, we're doomed to failure.

Unable to force our own faith to grow, where do we go? Should we sit and wait, doing nothing until it just happens? That's hardly biblical. God tells us to exercise our faith in many ways.

Though the apostles' faith might have seemed microscopic, God could grow it to a mustard-seed size that spread the gospel to the world. No matter how small our own is, He's willing to do the same for us, if only we trust in Him.

Lord, only in You can my faith grow.
Give me all I need to glorify You.

I have no greater joy than to hear
that my children walk in truth.
3 JOHN 4

Families can be curious things. They can be a great support in times of trouble or so irritating that you wish you could trade them in for a new model. But whatever kind of family you've been blessed with, no matter what its trials or joys, you've got an even larger and perhaps happier one. That's your Father's family, founded on the work of His Son, Jesus, on the cross.

But the family doesn't end there. God's children pass on the message, and when others accept it, the sons and daughters get that family feeling toward the new believers. John described those who'd received the gospel through His ministry as His children.

If you've been instrumental in someone coming to Christ or growing in Him, you can feel a proprietary interest in them. You want to see her put aside the sins that have entangled her for so long and see her increase in faith. When your "spiritual children" glorify God, it makes you happy.

Then you're feeling the emotions John described in this verse—and you know you've begun to experience the joys of heaven on earth.

Thank You, Lord, for Your extended family.
I pray for each life I've influenced,
that it would grow in faith today.

*For he who is called in the Lord while a slave
is the Lord's freedman.
Likewise he who is called while free is Christ's slave.*
1 CORINTHIANS 7:22 NKJV

If you had a job similar to yours (but redefined to fit first-century work) in the Roman Empire, it's not unlikely that you would have been a slave. Slaves held down many jobs, including the ones we'd consider professional. Scribes, farm workers, and teachers could all be slaves. Though slavery wasn't as common in Paul's homeland, the Corinthians would have had a sharp mental image of what he was talking about.

Paul told them that no matter whether they were slaves or free, they'd had to serve someone. Before they'd known Jesus, they served Satan, who controlled them no less than a wicked master who forced them to do his will. Now, though they served a kinder master in Jesus, they were just as obligated as they'd been before.

Today, we may punch information into computers, guide a train into a station, or fly above the earth on our jobs, but we're still obligated to obey someone. Are you obeying Jesus or only calling Him Lord and giving your life to the evil one?

*Lord, I want to be Your slave, no one else's.
Help me serve You on the job and in the rest of my world.*

Watch therefore:
for ye know not what hour your Lord doth come.
MATTHEW 24:42

You may not even know what time you'll get to work, if you run into frequent traffic jams. You leave early and do your best to get to the office on time, but if a truck's overturned along your route or an accident is blocking the way, you'll get there when you get there. As you drive on, you hope your boss will understand, especially when you get into the office on time tomorrow.

People are marvelous beings, made by God to do amazing things. We've developed complex computers, medical solutions for numerous diseases, and thousands of other things. But for all our gifts and graces, we still don't know everything—and this side of heaven, we never will.

If we can't be sure when we'll get to work, how could we possibly have an inkling of when Jesus will return? He told us none but the Father will know (Matthew 24:36), yet many people continue guessing or developing elaborate methods for figuring it out. These disobedient ones have missed the point—God expects them to live every day as if He could appear. Always ready, faithful believers put their trust in Him that what day will not matter if they've been following Him consistently.

The day doesn't matter, but our faith does. Are you ready now?

Lord, each day I want my service to be worthy of You.

Six days shalt thou labour, and do all thy work.
Exodus 20:9

Those "down" times of slow work, when you have little or nothing to do, prove why busyness, as irritating as it can be, is not the worst state of affairs to be in.

What do you do during your downtimes? Clear out unnecessary E-mails? Catch up on filing? Do all the boring chores you've put off for awhile? Remember, your company pays you—even when business is slow. So as long as you have something to do, keep working. Be as faithful as possible in putting in your required hours.

When you completely run out of anything to do, can you help another department that's bogged down? If your offer is turned down, do something quiet so you don't disturb those who *are* working.

Remember, God has only given you so many days to work; and while you're working, He expects you to do your best. How else could you effectively honor Him?

Lord, I'm glad I only have to
work on my job five days, not six.
I need that extra day to do my own chores.
But don't let me take advantage of
what should be my boss's claim on my time.

The same came therefore to Philip,
which was of Bethsaida of Galilee,
and desired him, saying,
Sir, we would see Jesus.

JOHN 12:21

Greeks came to Philip, asking to see Jesus. Perhaps they had questions they wanted answered or wanted to see if He really could be what He claimed to be. Was this the Son of God?

Was there a time when you wondered about Jesus? How were your questions answered? You couldn't go meet Him like those Greeks. You probably came to a saving knowledge of Jesus because you met people who reflected His love. Perhaps they had a quality missing from many folks, or they offered solutions no one else seemed to have.

Today you may meet someone who would see Jesus. He doesn't know all the answers, though he'd never admit it. He's caught in a terrible romantic relationship and can see no way to escape. You don't have all the answers, either, but you know where to go for them. All you need to do is point the way to Jesus. They'll see Him in your love.

Lord, may others see You in me as I go about my life today.
Let me clearly show Your love.

And when Peter came up to Jerusalem,
those of the circumcision contended with him, saying,
"You went in to uncircumcised men and ate with them!"

ACTS 11:2 NKJV

No sooner did Peter get back from a business trip than his fellow apostles were complaining about the job he'd done. To a Jew, eating with pagans was wrong, and they couldn't imagine why Peter had done this. What was he thinking? But instead of tactfully asking that, they jumped down his throat.

Doubtless the apostles weren't trying to mount a major offensive against their brother, but they felt concerned for the state of the church. Was Peter going to set a bad precedent here? What could come of it? So they overreacted a bit.

You may know what it's like to be on the receiving end of similar criticism. It's a human failing to attack first and ask questions later. When it happens, do you follow Peter's example in the next verses and explain what you were thinking? Do you publicly ignore the talebearers who told your management what you did and speak graciously to everyone involved? Do you deal privately with anyone who did wrong? By reacting this way and not in anger, the apostle turned the situation around and gained the agreement he was seeking. A soft answer is the best answer when attacks come your way.

Lord, help me speak softly but clearly when I'm attacked.

"Do not my words do good to him whose ways are upright?"
MICAH 2:7 NIV

When sin enters our lives, we often stop reading Scripture. We may excuse ourselves by saying we aren't getting anything out of it, but often the real reason we don't want to read is that we're afraid we will get something out of it—a truth we'd rather avoid, a change we need to make in our lives.

God never promised His words would not cause us pain. Giving up sin can be painful when it's entrenched in our lives. But He does promise that those who live upright lives will find His words good.

The words that are good for us may taste like nasty medicine, but we wouldn't decide not to take a medication that would save our lives just because we didn't like the momentary flavor on the tongue. In the same way, avoiding the Word because it may hurt for a short time means we'll also avoid its eternal benefits.

Take a short-term pain that can help you become upright. Live in His Word for the rest of your life, and you'll avoid a lot of pain.

Lord, I want to be upright.
Help me to consistently stay in Your Word.

Jesus saith unto him,
I am the way, the truth, and the life:
no man cometh unto the Father, but by me.

JOHN 14:6

How could Jesus have said it any more clearly? He is the way, the only way, to God. But according to one recent poll, 77 percent of those who call themselves Christians believe that Christianity is not the *only* right way. Have they read this verse? Do they really believe it?

Many poll respondents felt Christianity was true for them, but not a universal truth. That's like saying, "Hey, it works for me, but if it doesn't work for you, that's okay, too." The problem is Jesus didn't say that; He didn't say it because it wasn't what He meant. If He'd meant it to be that way, He'd never have opposed the temple leaders of His day. That means He probably wouldn't have died. And if He hadn't died, sin would not be forgiven.

Hard as you try, if you look honestly at Scripture, you can't have a live-and-let-live attitude about whether or not people know Jesus. That's like saying you don't care if they spend eternity in hell. Because "No man—or woman," says Jesus, "comes to the Father, except by Me." Not one, not your brother, your best friend, or someone across the world whom you've never met.

Show them the way—the only way.

Lord, help me see You as the only way—
and share You with others.

Then man goes out to his work,
to his labor until evening.
PSALM 104:23 NIV

We put a lot of effort into our jobs, whether we work in a fast-food chain or an emergency room. And we have those jobs because someone needs what we do. We serve a purpose as we serve other people. Without our work, our country could not continue. Even if we don't get a lot of credit through the year, we are important to our bosses, our customers, and our world.

We may enjoy serving others and like to go to work each morning. But no matter how we feel about working, we all appreciate a day off, one that's designed to say to each of us, "Job well done!" Everyone should get some appreciation and praise at least one day a year.

So this year, as you celebrate Labor Day, even if your boss hasn't told you or your company hasn't said it, accept the compliment. You are important, and you do a worthwhile job. Well done!

Lord, thank You for this job You gave me.
I want to do well in it,
and I appreciate the praise.

*Whoever pursues godliness and unfailing love
will find life, godliness, and honor.*
PROVERBS 21:21 NLT

Managers spend a lot of time trying to find ways to motivate their staff to do better work. Some feel they have to force employees to "toe the line." They institute plenty of rules and regulations to keep people working hard. The problem is, this method often backfires, creating a negative working environment.

God is *the* expert at motivating people. He sets the agenda, then offers generous rewards. His plan is evident in this verse. "Follow My way, and I will bless you with life, righteousness, and honor," He says.

Notice the large size of the benefits. God doesn't offer a one-time reward, a pat on the head, or a big promise that's never fulfilled. Those who follow Him earn lifetime blessings that affect them forever. He also doesn't give people things they don't want or need—another vacation day when they'd prefer the cash or cash when they'd rather take a vacation. The benefit is uniquely suited to the need.

If you're a manager trying to motivate your staff, consider what they really want or need. You may not be able to fulfill every wish, but chances are there is something they'd like, whether it's a more positive work environment or financial compensation.

*Lord, thank You for giving me the best motivation.
Whether I'm working with staff or encouraging another worker,
help me give just what's needed.*

He said to them, "Listen to this dream I had:
We were binding sheaves of grain out in the field when
suddenly my sheaf rose and stood upright,
while your sheaves gathered around mine and bowed down to it."
GENESIS 37:6–7 NIV

Seventeen-year-old Joseph had an amazing dream he couldn't wait to share with his brothers—he was going to be great! When this young man told his siblings what he'd dreamed, he got a great shock. His brothers didn't like the idea that they would serve him.

Like Joseph, we as Christians believe the best about others, but we can sometimes be a little naïve. Yet work has a way of making us realists. It wakes us up to the way other people think and feel and makes us consider others. We learn to take account of coworkers' strengths and weaknesses, as well as our own.

Becoming realistic in the work world is fine, as long as we don't become cynics. Joseph could easily have become one when his dream led his brothers to sell him into slavery. He worked many difficult years before that dream came true and he all but ruled Egypt. Though he lost his naïveté, Joseph remained faithful to the God who gave him the dream. Realism aplenty Joseph developed, but never a hard heart.

Can we say the same of ourselves?

Lord, make me a realist, not a cynic.
I want my heart to be all Yours.

Tell the righteous it will be well with them,
for they will enjoy the fruit of their deeds.
ISAIAH 3:10 NIV

One of our basset hounds expects to constantly get paid for his good deeds. Whoever owned him originally must have trained him to come indoors by giving him a treat. Now every time he goes in, he wants something. To keep him healthy, I only give him a small treat each time.

God has promised to give us good things if we obey Him. But are we like my dog and expect immediate repayment for every good deed? Do we expect a raise every year, even when the company is not doing well? Do we want frequent promotions, even if the new jobs would not be suited to us? Do we irritate God with our constant demands?

God may not repay our good deeds today or even tomorrow. We may not get the treat we expect now. But we can always trust God to give us the fruit of our deeds—the thing that is healthy and good for us. It may not come this week, this month, or even this year, but it will come eventually.

So if you haven't gotten the fruit yet, don't despair. It may just not be ripe yet.

Lord, I know You give me only good things,
even if I have to wait for them.
Help me be patient and expect only the best from You.

As a prisoner for the Lord, then,
I urge you to live a life worthy of the calling you have received.
EPHESIANS 4:1 NIV

No matter how difficult living for their faith was, the Ephesians had it better than Paul, who sat in a Roman jail. They could move about freely and worship together, even if they feared suffering for their faith. Yet the apostle had urged them to courageously live out the message he passed on to them during the three years he ministered in Ephesus.

Paul pointed out that this was not the time to live for themselves alone, give up what he had taught them, and fall into selfishness. Even as a prisoner, Paul lived for God, preaching to all who came near and writing letters to the churches he'd founded—and without those letters, we'd be missing a large part of the New Testament. Wherever Paul was, he served his Master.

Today, you are not in prison. Though you may face trials, you are free to live for Jesus. What are you doing with your ability to move through the world? Do you use this time to share your faith with others, whether it's helping another Christian or speaking to someone who has never heard of God's love?

If you don't live out your faith, you're more a prisoner to fear than Paul ever was in his Roman cell.

Lord, I don't want to be fear's prisoner.
Help me live actively for You.

But the fruit of the Spirit is
love, joy, peace, patience, kindness, goodness,
faithfulness, gentleness and self-control.
Against such things there is no law.
GALATIANS 5:22–23 NIV

When someone dies and the family or friends go through their household goods, there are some things worth keeping and others that are not. Good things get sold off or given to loved ones. The others go in the trash.

Spiritually, some things also deserve to be kept, while others need to get tossed. Paul makes it easy on us by outlining the keepers—spiritual fruit that shows our faith. From them we can identify the things we need to toss from our lives: hate, grief, fighting, impatience, harshness, wickedness, unbelief, disobedience to God, and so on.

If we keep and toss the right things, when our days on earth are done and people go through their memories, they won't find a lot of junk they need to forget. Instead the memories will be sweet and our testimony to God's grace will be effective. Who would make a law against that?

Lord, make the fruit of the Spirit effective in my life.
I want to get rid of anything that
will not bring glory to You.

Now I urge you,
brethren, note those who cause divisions and offenses,
contrary to the doctrine which you learned, and avoid them.
ROMANS 16:17 NKJV

"Keep an open mind" is the philosophy of many in our culture. They pride themselves on accepting many different ideas at the same time—though they probably aren't particularly fond of Christianity. Much as they'd tell you they're open to anything, they really aren't.

An open-minded philosophy isn't Paul's, and he didn't mind admitting it. Paul didn't tell the Roman Christians to listen to every doctrine and choose among the most appealing ones. He knew that would spell disaster for the church as division increased. Instead, he told the Romans to keep away from people who taught anything that contradicted his teachings.

Paul wasn't just trying to keep others off his turf. He sought to create single-minded Christians who followed the gospel. God had entrusted him with His message, and the apostle didn't want it confused by sweet but unbiblical concepts that had nothing to do with Jesus. Paul knew there was a single truth for all people, and he wanted his people to learn that, not waste their time in empty philosophies.

So don't listen to every doctrine out there without sifting each to see how it agrees with Scripture. And when you find the unbiblical ones, don't walk away—run.

Lord, help me discern which teachings
are of You and which are not.
I want to listen only to Your Word.

"Let more work be laid on the men,
that they may labor in it,
and let them not regard false words."
EXODUS 5:9 NKJV

This was Pharaoh's method of keeping his Hebrew slaves out of trouble: pour so much work on them that they'd be exhausted and unable to listen to Moses. Though it may have controlled his slaves for a short time, the ruler could almost have counted on rebellion breaking through. It was as if he'd put a lid on an over-full, boiling pot but not taken the fire from under it.

Quelling trouble or solving problems with oppression doesn't work for long because it doesn't bring about change. Emotions rise as people feel they've been wronged, and the situation escalates. It was true for Pharaoh, and it's true for leaders today. Putting a lid on the problem never solves it.

The Hebrews didn't revolt, as many might have. God's solution to a problem is never rebellion. But Pharaoh didn't keep his slaves.

Have a work-related problem you want to end? Don't use Pharaoh as your management expert and put a lid on it. Solve the underlying problem instead.

Lord, help me find a solution for my problem,
instead of trying to control others.

I say then: Walk in the Spirit,
and you shall not fulfill the lust of the flesh.
GALATIANS 5:16 NKJV

"I just can't do this on my own. It's overwhelming!" Have you ever thought or spoken those words on the job? If so, you were crying out for help. Maybe you were asking your boss for assistance from another staff member because you recognized your need for help.

Work isn't the only place we face an overwhelming need for help. Sometimes we require it in our spiritual lives, too. We've tried to be good and do the right thing. We want to serve Jesus alone, but temptation keeps getting in our way. We can't get the best of it, though we pray, study Scripture, fellowship with other believers, and ask their advice. Nothing seems to work.

Overcoming sin isn't our job. If it were, it would be a hopeless one. It's the Spirit who works on sin in our lives. Where all our efforts fail, His gentle touch works a miracle of grace.

As we throw ourselves on God's mercy, admitting our own need and helplessness, the Spirit can enter our spirits and work that grace. When we completely offer up our sin-battered lives to Him, He changes them entirely. Suddenly we're walking in the Spirit, away from that lust that once held us in its grasp.

Lord, I need help! Only You can free me from this sin.
Take my life now.

For the flesh lusts against the Spirit,
and the Spirit against the flesh;
and these are contrary to one another,
so that you do not do the things that you wish.

GALATIANS 5:17 NKJV

When sin has us in its grasp, it's impossible to let go. Just as the charge of direct-current electricity will not allow the muscles to relax but keeps the hands holding tight to its deadly charge, sin cannot be escaped by the sinner.

How, then, can anyone escape such a deadly spiritual situation? A cry of "help!" to God is our only answer. We know we're doing wrong and don't desire to stop. So we start with a prayer asking Him to change our hearts. It may seem like a small, useless, or even hypocritical prayer, but God's powerful response may surprise us.

The next time temptation comes, we find ourselves able to say a tiny no to it. It's not us but His Spirit that gives us this power. We hardly know where it came from, but relief floods our souls—until the next temptation comes. Again we turn to God; again His Spirit sets us free.

Over and over, we cry for help, and God's Spirit increasingly frees us from sin. As we repeatedly stand in Christ's freedom, temptation lessens; and when it reappears, we know how to resist.

Jesus diverted that electrical charge.

Lord, turn my heart from sin.
I need to say no to it.

O LORD, I have so many enemies;
so many are against me....
But you, O LORD, are a shield around me,
my glory, and the one who lifts my head high.
PSALM 3:1, 3 NLT

On September 11, 2001, the destruction of the World Trade Center and part of the Pentagon rocked America. As the towers fell and a chunk of the Pentagon was destroyed, so was the security of a nation.

On that day, many people had an inkling that they trusted in the wrong things. Compared to these tragedies, the small irritants of life seemed so tiny. Feeling violated, many began to ask how they could trust again. Broken trust is so hard to repair.

For a time, many turned to God—at least, they gave lip service to Him. But as a revival, the spiritual situation fell flat. Nothing big really came of it. No great spate of conversions took place. Again, people began to trust in those wrong things—or new things that were equally powerless to save them.

Real salvation doesn't last for a few days or weeks or until we feel better about our situation. The glory doesn't depart but stays a lifetime and the following eternity. Trusting in anything more short-term is trusting in the wrong thing.

Lord, I need to trust in You, not smaller things.
Turn my heart to You alone today.

"Moreover, because I have set my affection on the house of my God,
I have given to the house of my God,
over and above all that I have prepared for the holy house,
my own special treasure of gold and silver."

1 CHRONICLES 29:3 NKJV

King David knew how to motivate people. Instead of telling them they had to give to the temple-building project, he set an example. He gave an especially generous gift to start the work, and Israel's leaders followed suit (vv. 6–9). The temple was well on its way to being built.

At work, you probably don't have to give a fortune to inspire people, but what you do can be worth thousands of dollars. If you expect others to be considerate of the staff, be that way yourself. If you want people to turn work in on time, do the best to get yours done in a timely fashion.

Asking people to do anything you won't do is an exercise in futility. People see right through that kind of attitude. You might get cooperation for a short while, but it won't last when they see how little the principle means to you.

So take David as your example and set the pace. No one will go ahead of you.

Lord, I don't want to ask others to do one thing
and do another myself.
Keep my mind and actions consistent.

So teach us to number our days,
that we may apply our hearts unto wisdom.
PSALM 90:12

Numbering your days is fine, but do you often feel as if you have to number your hours? There's so much to get done in a weekend. Household chores, time with the kids, a sports event, whether it's a Little League game or a major-league contest. Life tends to get crammed full. Every moment has something going on.

Maybe numbering our hours isn't such a bad idea. After all, hours make up the days, and God only gives us so many days to our lives. We need to consider the fact that we'll only spend so many of them on earth. So each hour should count for something.

That doesn't mean we should never rest. Everyone needs downtime. But it needs to be productive downtime that recharges our batteries, not simply another event to add to our to-do list.

Perhaps that means we put off the major-league event and go to the backyard instead to throw a ball with our kids, or maybe it means taking a nap so we recharge our batteries. But whatever we do this weekend, may every hour be of benefit to someone else or ourselves. It's only wise to plan what we do.

Lord, I want to use my time on earth wisely.
Show me every hour just what to do.

I do wish, brother,
that I may have some benefit from you in the Lord;
refresh my heart in Christ.

PHILEMON 20 NIV

A powerful preacher and writer, a most faithful Christian, Paul would hardly be expected to need to be refreshed by a much more ordinary Christian. After all, wasn't he the spiritual giant? What could Philemon do to refresh the great apostle?

No matter how great the preacher or teacher, each one needs encouragement. Earlier in the book, Paul says Philemon "refreshed the hearts of the saints." Obviously, this was a man of real faith who knew how to love and encourage others. Perhaps Paul had already experienced this after a long day's preaching or travel; Philemon had met a need in the apostle, and he appreciated it.

Do you know someone who needs to be refreshed today? Perhaps your pastor, spouse, or a friend could use encouragement, prayer, or a sign of love. The Lord's Day is an appropriate time to remember that person. Wouldn't you love a time of refreshment, too?

Lord, help me refresh another's faith today.
I know I will benefit as much as
he or she will from this time.

"No one knows about that day or hour,
not even the angels in heaven, nor the Son, but only the Father.
As it was in the days of Noah,
so it will be at the coming of the Son of Man."

MATTHEW 24:36–37 NIV

Jesus made it very clear: No one knows when the second coming will be. Just as Noah's friends and neighbors had no clue when destruction would come, today's nonbelievers have no idea when their destruction will be. And Christians don't, either.

That doesn't keep some people from trying to guess when it will happen. All kinds of tricks and imaginations have been used to set a date for the return of the Lord; but over the centuries, if history has taught us anything, it's the truth of these words Jesus spoke to His disciples.

We feel uncomfortable thinking that Jesus might not let us in on some things. But He told the disciples even He did not have the time line. God the Father alone knew the whole plan and did not intend to tell His children.

Some things are just a matter of faith and trust. God wanted us to trust Him on this large issue, and none of our imaginations or nagging will make Him tell. One day He will let us in on the secret, when Jesus appears before us.

What a day that will be!

Lord, I look forward to Your return.
Keep me faithful till then.

"Where is the promise of His coming?
For since the fathers fell asleep,
all things continue as they were from the beginning of creation."
2 PETER 3:4 NKJV

"Things will always be the same. Nothing changes." One way or another you've heard people say or live out those words. They expect life to continue in the same, perhaps dull, path. Work was here yesterday, it's here today, why won't it be here tomorrow? Like the first-century doubters who spoke this verse, they voice similar objections about Jesus' return.

With two thousand years having passed since the Lord left the earth, it's not hard to imagine that some would doubt that Jesus would come back to earth. Then, too, the Book of Revelation describes His return in words that seem to the unbeliever more like science fiction than reality.

But the years are not what really make the difference. These doubts reflect more than logical questions. People prefer to live as if Jesus will never hold them to account for their actions, so they follow the natural path of denial.

Jesus is slow in coming, not because He's forgotten, but because God has another plan. There are more people to be saved, and at the right time, He will come. Then doubters will see the truth of the promise. How sad that it will be too late for them to change their eternal destiny.

Lord, I know You keep Your promises.
Help me wait patiently and faithfully.

This is the day which the LORD hath made;
we will rejoice and be glad in it.
PSALM 118:24

Having a bad day? This morning you woke up tired and grumpy, and things haven't gone right from that moment. You took the dog out and he wouldn't come back in, so you spent a lot of time coaxing him in the house. Either you didn't have time for breakfast, or it burned. Traffic on the way to work was horrific. Now you've opened up your computer, and it's giving you one of those messages that you can't interpret but you know means you can't do your work until you find out what's wrong.

We all have days that go awry, ones where we'd like to be able to go back to bed, pull the covers over our heads, and sleep away twenty-four hours. If only we didn't have to work on them!

It's hard to recognize on tough days that this, too, is a day God made and one He made, at least in part, to benefit us. But unless the day is already gone, it's not beyond repair. Turn around your less-than-impressive days by giving them back to God. He knows what you're going through and wants to help, but He won't barge in. Ask Him to take over those awful twenty-four hours, and you will be able to rejoice in them.

Lord, take this day and make of it what You will.

His ways are always prosperous. . . .
He says to himself, "Nothing will shake me;
I'll always be happy and never have trouble."
PSALM 10:5–6 NIV

Did you know that most people think a 20 percent raise is all it would take to make them happier? Just that much money and they could be really at peace, cover all their bills, and maybe even give a little more.

But if you've been working for a number of years, you should know the falseness of that idea. You've received 20 percent more money, and it hasn't solved all your financial problems. It hasn't been a quick solution to every trial.

The prosperous fellow described in these verses is evil; he thinks God has forgotten people (v. 11). So he places his trust in his house and lands, his bank account, and the other things he owns. He treats others wickedly (vv. 8–10). When he thinks worldly goods have made him happy, he's deluding himself. He makes more and more, owns more and more, yet never finds peace.

If you get a raise, rejoice. Be glad God has provided, but don't trust in the things He's given instead of the One who's given it. You don't want to be like the prosperous evil fellow the psalmist called on God to correct.

Lord, I want to trust in You, not money or things.
Keep me faithful always.

*And when she hath found it,
she calleth her friends and her neighbours together, saying,
Rejoice with me;
for I have found the piece which I had lost.*

LUKE 15:9

If you've lost an important piece of paperwork, then found it in an odd place, you know the joy this woman felt. While you rushed around looking for it (or made someone else rush around to find it), tension mounted. But when you found it, your whole body relaxed. Joy flooded your emotions, and life could go on again normally.

Just like your paperwork or the coin the woman in the story found, you are important to your heavenly Father. While you're lost spiritually, He feels concern. He seeks you out to bring you home to heaven. When you turn to Him and enter His kingdom, He sets His angels to rejoicing. The tension concerning your salvation is finished, and your forever home is chosen.

We understand the importance of paperwork that's key to a project or a coin that provides for earthly needs. But do we comprehend the importance of a soul to Jesus? It's so easy to assume the lost person will never accept the Lord and bypass him. The search for that soul seems harder than finding a lost coin or paper.

But what fun to rejoice when that person is saved!

*Lord, I'd rather rejoice.
Help my testimony lead others to You.*

> *"For three transgressions of Edom, and for four,*
> *I will not turn away its punishment,*
> *because he pursued his brother with the sword, and cast off all pity;*
> *his anger tore perpetually, and he kept his wrath forever."*
>
> AMOS 1:11 NKJV

Anger can be a good thing when we use it to show us where we have a problem. If we feel angry at a brother and go to him, addressing and solving the issue, we've used it well. As a marker for things we need to deal with, anger is good.

But when we let it fester and grow, it's a bad thing. Anger that's held causes sin.

God planned to punish Edom, the nation descended from Esau, because they had been constantly hostile to Israel. Instead of attempting to solve the problems between them, Edom had pitilessly fought Israel, with no desire to end the battles.

Do you have a sibling with whom you are angry? Try to settle the issue. If it's a long-standing problem, it may take time. But begin by inviting God into the relationship through prayer. That way, even if you never see eye to eye, you won't have to pursue each other with hatred. That wrath that seems to last forever may be ended today.

> *Lord, help me use anger in a healthy way.*
> *I don't want to be angry forever.*

"Ho! Everyone who thirsts, come to the waters;
and you who have no money, come, buy and eat.
Yes, come, buy wine and milk without money and without price."
ISAIAH 55:1 NKJV

Have you wandered away from God? Perhaps following Him just seemed too hard. The goodies of the world seemed more attractive. You didn't completely forget God; maybe you even think warmly of the times you spent together. Or maybe you spend some time together, but it just doesn't seem the same as when you first knew Him.

Those are all signs you're feeling thirsty. Life without God is dry, empty, and sometimes seems so worthless. By giving you a desire to taste of His spring, your Father's reminding you just how wonderful your fellowship was; no earthly rewards can take its place.

As the thirsty ones come to drink, they not only receive water. The gift of God's mercy provides them with extravagant blessings, symbolized by wine and milk. You can't pay for such blessings—God doesn't need your money. But He does want your love; that's why He went seeking after you.

If you're feeling thirsty, come to the water and drink deeply. Your Father holds the cup in His hand.

Lord, I want You to have my whole heart.
I give it to You now.

*"Go to the great city of Nineveh and preach against it,
because its wickedness has come up before me."*

JONAH 1:2 NIV

God gave Jonah a mission: Go to Nineveh to preach. He
didn't ask Jonah if he felt like preaching or if he wanted to
visit Nineveh. After all, wasn't God in charge? Didn't He
get to make the decisions? Just as you don't often question
your boss, it wasn't part of the prophet's job description to
second-guess God.

Though Jonah didn't like the job, he couldn't quit.
How could he just stop being a prophet? God might still
tell him things he didn't want to hear. After all, God was
the One who called Jonah to his job.

Has God given you a message to bear that you'd rather
leave behind? Has He told you to start a Bible study, mow
the church lawn, or share your faith with a neighbor? You
may not head for Tarshish, like Jonah, but you can still run
away. There are a thousand ways to avoid doing what God
commands.

But running away wasn't the end of Jonah's story, and it
won't be the end of yours, either. Because God doesn't give up
on His children even when they disobey for a season.

*Lord, help me not to run away from You
even when I don't like the task You've set before me.*

"Pick me up and throw me into the sea," he replied,
"and it will become calm.
I know that it is my fault that this great storm has come upon you."
JONAH 1:12 NIV

Jonah knew he'd made a mistake before he even hit land.
Out in the middle of the sea, while he was traveling to
Tarshish, a storm hit. When the other passengers on the
ship cast lots and discovered he was the cause of their trouble,
the prophet immediately admitted to it. Jonah was big-
hearted enough to be willing to have them toss him into the
sea just to save the vessel.

When we make mistakes, are we quickly willing to do
whatever it takes to make them right? Jonah might not
have wanted to go to Nineveh, but neither did he want his
disobedience to cost the lives of his fellow travelers. He
took responsibility for the wrong and found a way to fix it,
even at the cost of his own life.

Everyone makes mistakes on the job, but not many are
brave enough to admit them. That doesn't mean the boss
can't figure it out, just that it takes a little more time or
effort. Admit to your mistakes, and maybe, like Jonah,
you'll find that your coworkers aren't in a rush to slip you
over the side.

Lord, help me be humble enough to admit my mistakes.

*"Those who cling to worthless idols
forfeit the grace that could be theirs."*
JONAH 2:8 NIV

By taking part in pagan worship, the Ninevites forfeited God's grace, but Jonah was no more deserving of grace as he ran from God. Though he'd never bowed down before an idol, he'd set up his own will against the Almighty's. Stuck in the belly of a fish, the prophet recognized his wrongdoing and called out to the God he'd deserted.

Idols constantly compete with God for our attention. When we land ourselves in a fish's belly, we don't often start out consciously wanting to disobey God, but we want to do things an easier way. Though we may not realize it as we start toward our idol, we settle for what Dietrich Bonhoeffer called "cheap grace." We look to get only the best at no cost to ourselves.

There's a saying that goes, "If it seems too good to be true, it probably is"—the unspoken ending being "too good to be true." That truth applies in many ways to spiritual things. The promise of an easier religion probably isn't Christianity—and in the end, what claims to be easier than Christianity will turn out to be very hard.

After all his running, it would have been simpler for Jonah to just go to Nineveh in the first place and see how God would work things out. Disobedience made him go far and get nothing, just as it can do to us.

Lord, help me cling to You, not idols.

And the LORD commanded the fish,
and it vomited Jonah onto dry land.
JONAH 2:10 NIV

Jonah asked God for forgiveness, and he didn't have to wait long for a response. *Sluuurp!* He was spewed out on dry land. You have to wonder where God dropped him off, but it couldn't have been far from some travel method that went to Nineveh, because the next thing we know, the prophet headed toward the city he'd turned his back on.

Sometimes, like Jonah, when we ask God's forgiveness, it's amazing how quickly He sets us on the right path again. It's as if He is waiting by our side for that change of heart. Quickly we find the job that had been eluding us for so long—one where we can really obey Him. Or that family situation that's beleaguered us for so long is swiftly solved. God can act right away when it serves His purposes.

But even if God doesn't work a quick change, we know He's faithful. Just as He came to Jonah's aid, He comes to ours. Whether it's fast or slow, because we know He never gives up on us or wants the worst for us, we can trust we'll reach dry land.

That fishy destination might even be closer to our Nineveh than we expected.

Lord, I know Your forgiveness is there for the asking.
Help me to quickly call out to You.

He prayed to the LORD,
"O LORD, is this not what I said when I was still at home?
That is why I was so quick to flee to Tarshish.
I knew that you are a gracious and compassionate God,
slow to anger and abounding in love,
a God who relents from sending calamity."

JONAH 4:2 NIV

This is a great Scripture verse. We finally find out the truth: Jonah didn't want to go to Nineveh because he feared God's compassion. The people of Nineveh were Israel's enemies, and the prophet didn't want them to be saved. Imagine spending eternity with your greatest foes!

God did save the Ninevites through Jonah's preaching. It made the prophet so angry, he asked God to let him die (v. 3). How could he live through such a situation? How could God do such a thing?

Though the prophet had obeyed God, his heart still hadn't been in it. Perhaps he hoped God would change compassion into destruction at the last minute. Maybe He'd do what Jonah wanted after all. But the merciful God he served poured out mercy on even these wicked ones.

How often do we, like Jonah, seek destruction when God wants to send compassion? Are we tuned in to His will or seeking our own agenda? Could God wonder if saving us from the belly of the fish is worth it after all?

Lord, Your compassion is infinitely greater than mine.
Let me learn to be more like You.

And because of his words many more became believers.
JOHN 4:41 NIV

Often we like to think we can witness to people only with our lives. If we live honestly, faithfully, and so on, they'll get the point. But is that really true?

If anyone could have gotten the gospel message across with His life, it was Jesus. After all, He lived perfectly. Yet nowhere in Scripture do we hear that He relied just on His life to get the point across. And if you think about it, if He'd done that, we wouldn't know many things about God that we learn in His words. Jesus was constantly speaking, telling people about the Father and what it took to please Him.

That's not to say we need to become Jesus' chatterboxes. We don't have to bring Jesus up at the drop of a hat, annoy all our friends and fellow workers with the good news, and alienate our families with our witness. Jesus didn't do that, and neither must we. But there will be times when we'll just know God wants us to share our faith, times when we can help a person with a choice or hurt.

Words alone are not enough, but a witness without words leaves out something important, too.

Lord, show me when to speak for You
so that many can become believers.

Jesus said to her,
"Go, call your husband, and come here."
JOHN 4:16 NKJV

Jesus spoke to the Samaritan woman about faith in God, but He didn't stop there. He also listened to her concerns, answered some of her questions, and eventually got to the root of her problem. Her questions about God might have been real, but they weren't prompted by a deep faith. She was a seeker who had heard about Him but had never connected to Him.

Surely, just as Jesus knew the woman was not married when He asked her this question, He knew the state of her soul. He could have jumped right in and told her all the ways in which her life was wrong. But He didn't. Concern for her and her spiritual state led Him to approach her gently. Only after they'd spoken awhile and she felt some confidence in Him did He bring up the touchy topic.

Do we take Jesus as our example when we share our faith? Or do we jump right in, criticizing others? If we do, it's not surprising they don't listen. No one wants a critic when he needs a helping hand. No one responds to condemnation when she's looking for life solutions.

Do we listen when we witness and respond to the internal needs of others? If so, we're following in the steps of Jesus.

Lord, help me listen and speak to others
when I share my faith.

Woe to the city of oppressors [Jerusalem], rebellious and defiled!
She obeys no one, she accepts no correction.
She does not trust in the LORD,
she does not draw near to her God.
ZEPHANIAH 3:1–2 NIV

Do you obey anyone, or are you a free spirit who resents correction and wants to do things your own way? In America, where independence rules, we can become too independent, too caught up in our own ways and inconsiderate of others.

That kind of attitude creates a difficult worker. When an employee expects the boss to explain every decision, resents being told how to do things, or tries to change every way of doing them, the workplace becomes a stressed place. Not that workers should never question the boss or try to find a better way to work, but they also need to comply with the leaders' plans.

God connects a rebellious attitude that refuses obedience with a lack of trust in Him. When we believe He is at work in our jobs, we can trust that even the bad decisions can be retooled to improve the workplace, that even if it isn't done our way, it can be done well.

Don't follow Jerusalem's example. Instead accept your boss's correction and that of God. Show obedience instead of rebellion.

Lord, I want to obey You on the job.
Help me be graciously obedient.

Then Jesus said to those Jews who believed Him,
"If you abide in My word, you are My disciples indeed.
And you shall know the truth, and the truth shall make you free."
JOHN 8:31–32 NKJV

With these words, Jesus turns all our popular notions of freedom upside down. No longer is freedom the ability to do what you want; it's the ability to do what God wants. Instead of falling into sin's traps, Jesus' followers are made free of them when they do as He commands.

This freedom isn't just a matter of intellectual or spiritual knowledge. Even memorizing the entire Bible couldn't make anyone perfectly free. We could hold God's truths in our heads and hearts and still never really understand them. The only way to know God's truths fully is to live them out—to abide in them. Then experience brings their reality into our lives in a new way.

Living daily in the truth and experiencing the ups and downs that come with it shows us ever more truth, and that kind of truth increasingly frees us from sin and this world.

Are you living in freedom today?

Lord, show me Your truth today.
I want to follow You.

*"Do not remember the former things, nor consider the things of old.
Behold, I will do a new thing, now it shall spring forth;
shall you not know it?
I will even make a road in the wilderness and rivers in the desert.*
ISAIAH 43:18–19 NKJV

"If such-and-such hadn't happened to me, I could have had
a *real* career," a friend lamented. Through others' wrong
choices, her life had been harmed. Now, years later, she
mourned the past she never had.

All of us could have done better. Sin—ours or others'—
has marred our lives and made us less than we could be.
Even those who have not had extraordinary circumstances
affect them could have been better and done more. But
none of us are all that we could be on this earth. None of us
fully find God's potential in our lives.

But that doesn't mean God is finished with us. What's
left of our careers can be impressive if we give Him control.
And perhaps the shoulda, woulda, coulda plans we think up
wouldn't have been as wonderful as we'd like to imagine.

Most of all, even though we have missed the mark, our
lives are still in God's hands. Perhaps He's building a road
we'd never have imagined, and we just aren't able to see it. In
the end, we may have accomplished more than we expected.

*Lord, take my whole life,
even the mistakes I've made,
and let them bring glory to You.*

"Even from eternity I am He,
and there is none who can deliver out of My hand;
I act and who can reverse it?"

ISAIAH 43:13 NASB

Who's in charge here? you may wonder when life gets crazy. When terrors strike our world or the workplace seems confused, life appears to be out of control.

Maybe the government isn't acting logically. Perhaps your company has made some poor choices. You may be heading in the wrong direction in your personal life. But none of it is so crazy or so disorganized that God is unaware of it and can't deliver it. Nor has God forgotten you, your coworkers, or family. He's in control when life is normal or not so normal.

Others may declare that God made the world, then forgot it. Or they may say there is no God or that He can't or won't do a thing to help you. You know better. Just as the Israelites who worshiped idols had lost out on God's power, your coworkers or friends who don't know Him can't appreciate what He's really like. They don't appreciate His ability to save both your soul and life situations.

When God has you in His hand, He's in control of your life, no matter what happens to the rest of the world.

Thank You, Lord, for being in control of my life.

Moses my servant is dead; now therefore arise,
go over this Jordan, thou,
and all this people, unto the land which I do give to them,
even to the children of Israel.

JOSHUA 1:2

No sooner had Joshua received the position of Israel's leadership than God set him a large task. The inexperienced leader was to take the people into the Promised Land. Surely he remembered the problems Moses had when he was last in this place: reports of a large, fierce people who would be hard to overcome. No one could have blamed Joshua for feeling a little nervous.

But Joshua was not going in alone. Not only did he have the hordes of people who made up the Hebrews, God promised to give them the land (v. 6). He would be with them as they walked into this new land. And what God promised, He did. The new land did not come without a battle; but in short order, Israel owned the new turf.

Are you facing something new? Does fear enter your heart at what you're taking on? It's not surprising. We all have fears at starting a new job, getting a promotion, or making a change in our personal lives. But if it's something God has brought into our lives, we can count on Him to see us through. Like Joshua, we can count on Him to bring us into the blessings of our new land, as long as we obey His will.

Thank You, Lord, for this new blessing.
I trust You to help me use it wisely.

They have not known nor understood:
for he hath shut their eyes, that they cannot see;
and their hearts, that they cannot understand.
ISAIAH 44:18

What an accurate description of those who do not know God. You may try to tell them about Him, but until God opens their eyes, all your words won't change their thinking. All the love you offer can't change their hearts.

So why share your faith then? Isn't God saying the job is impossible?

Yes and no. Under our own power, the job *is* impossible. We can't reach places the Spirit does, and we can't know what barriers a person has thrown up against God. But God doesn't send us on fruitless missions. He isn't saying none can be saved. Our own lives are proof of the truth that He can and does save.

Our problem is that unbelievers don't go about with placards on them saying, "Don't bother with this one," or, "Almost ready, just talk to me." We never know if the resistant person is just a prayer away from faith. Some of us looked pretty hopeless on the day someone brought us the message and we believed.

So don't look on your neighbor or friend as an enemy just because he resists God. Pray for him. Tell him how God worked in your life. And maybe someday his eyes will open and his heart will be softened.

Lord, help me faithfully bear Your message
to all who need to hear.

For it is not possible that
the blood of bulls and of goats should take away sins.
HEBREWS 10:4

Once a year, on Yom Kippur, the Jewish priests made sacrifices for all the people to atone for their sins. In a nationwide holiday, the people mourned their sins and obeyed God's commandment concerning how they should get right with Him.

Any thinking person had to wonder just how the blood of bulls and goats affected sin. After all, the innocent animals had nothing to do with the human wrongdoing. It hardly seems fair that they should end their lives for it. But God was painting a picture for His people of just how awful sin is. It's so horrible that without the shedding of blood, Hebrews 9:22 tells us, it could not be forgiven. Perhaps the death of an innocent animal could show the people what terrible offenses they'd made against God.

Ultimately, the picture God painted of wrongdoing and forgiveness would be shown on the cross. All the bulls and goats were just stand-ins for Jesus, God's Son, who could really take away those sins. The sinless man could do what no animal's death could—remove sin from all who believe in Him.

Has your sin been removed? You can answer yes if you're trusting in Jesus.

Lord, thank You for making a way for me to be forgiven.

Blessed is the nation whose God is the LORD;
and the people whom he hath chosen for his own inheritance.
PSALM 33:12

Recently a lot of people have been saying "God bless America." Of course we'd like God's blessing on our nation, but people seem to say it so lightly, almost as if we deserve an extra blessing. *Do* we deserve it?

America may be a powerful nation, but have we really chosen the Lord as our God? He has to compete with so many other things that tempt people's hearts—money, "tolerance," and the desire to be broad-minded instead of faithful. While you see all these concepts in the news, God seems pretty much in the background.

Not that there aren't people who are faithful, but the ones He's chosen for His inheritance seem few and far between. When they lift up their voices, they're often ignored in Congress and their communities. "One nation under God" may be our motto, but it's hard to see it in action.

Do we want God's blessing again? This verse makes it clear what we must do. We have to return Him to a place of importance in our lives and our national life. Instead of mentioning Him in a crisis, we should honor Him daily. Then we'll be a nation truly blessed.

Lord, turn our nation to You.
We need Your blessing today.

The LORD did not set his love upon you, nor choose you,
because ye were more in number than any people;
for ye were the fewest of all people:
but because the LORD loved you, and because he would keep the oath
which he had sworn unto your fathers, hath the LORD...
redeemed you out of the house of bondmen,
from the hand of Pharaoh king of Egypt.

DEUTERONOMY 7:7–8

If any verse in Scripture proves that God has His own reasons for loving people, this is it. Even His favored nation, Israel, had nothing about it that was so special that God couldn't resist them. Indeed, if you look at Israel's history, it's more notable for the stubbornness of the people's unbelief than anything. Yet God chose to love His people and will never abandon them.

Whether or not we're Jewish, that's good news for us. Because we can be just as stubborn, just as faithless, just as irritating as Israel. In our honest moments, we're glad God doesn't have to see something wonderful in us before He chooses to love us—He might have passed us over in favor of someone better.

One of the most amazing things about God is the way He loves those who give Him no reason to love. He chooses the small nation, the outcast, the one who's unloved in his own family. Aren't we glad?

Thank You, Lord, for loving me
even when I have nothing to offer You.

"No man shall be able to stand before you all the days of your life;
as I was with Moses, so I will be with you.
I will not leave you nor forsake you."

JOSHUA 1:5 NKJV

When I'm feeling blue, one of my pets usually understands that and cuddles up to me. It feels good to have the comfort of a warm, furry body next to you when you hurt. It's the same when life is being challenging and you could use a hug.

But no matter what I'm going through, even when I don't feel as if He's as close to me as a cat or dog, God is right beside me. He may not offer a hug, but He's there, helping in many other ways. He's working out problems I can't solve but have prayed about. He's dealing with difficult relationships, work problems, and a thousand other things. Whether or not I feel His closeness, I can trust He's there. Even if I've sinned, He's calling me back to Him again.

If you believe in Jesus, you aren't standing alone, either. As he was with Moses and every other believer, God is close to you. You may not feel Him the way you feel a pet or the hug of a loved one, but He's there just the same. Didn't He say He'd never leave you?

Lord, thank You for being with me
even when I don't feel Your touch on my shoulder.

Having many things to write unto you,
I would not write with paper and ink:
but I trust to come unto you, and speak face to face,
that our joy may be full.
2 JOHN 12

Some people have had a powerful impact on your career. A mentor has shown you the ropes, but you've moved on from that first job, and you hardly keep in touch anymore. It's not that you don't care, but life gets in the way. Or perhaps one of you moved miles away, and keeping in touch is difficult.

John knew what separation from loved ones was like. He'd probably taught this "elect lady" (v. 1) whom he wrote to, and she and her family had won a place in his heart. Being apart made communication difficult, and perhaps John was nervous about putting his thoughts on paper, since this letter was likely to be read publicly and word would be passed on to the deceivers who were undoubtedly impacting the lady's church (v. 7).

John had to travel many miles to see the lady again. Though you might like to visit your friend, travel is not your only option. Drop her an E-mail. Pick up a phone and give him a call. You may not speak face to face, but the communion you have can still make your joy full.

Lord, thank You for my work friend.
Bless my friend and help us keep in touch.

If we are faithless, He remains faithful;
He cannot deny Himself.
2 TIMOTHY 2:13 NKJV

If you fail God, do you fear that He will give up on you? It's not a worry you need to spend any time on. According to this verse, not even our worst failures of faith can make God that unfaithful to us.

It isn't a matter of what we've done that keeps God faithful. Clearly, it's God's nature that makes Him faithful even when we seem to forget the meaning of that word. It just isn't like God to become unfaithful and give up on us. To do so would be to deny all that He is and everything He stands for.

God's faithfulness doesn't give us an excuse to stop being constant in our belief. God calls us to become more and more like Him. As we do, we remain faithful to our spouses when they fail us, stick by our children even when they make mistakes, and stand by our friends and help them right wrongs.

Lord, thank You for Your faithfulness.
Make me more and more like You.

*Beloved, you do faithfully whatever you do
for the brethren and for strangers.*

3 JOHN 5 NKJV

Do you greet visiting pastors or missionaries warmly in your church, or can't you wait to show them the door? When a family visits your church, do you treat them with suspicion or introduce them to your friends and pastor?

You don't know everyone who enters your church door, but if that person is a brother or sister in Christ, you act faithfully when you welcome and even house, feed, or clothe that sibling in Christ.

John commended his friend Gaius for taking in traveling preachers whom he'd never met. Because they preached Christ, Gaius cared for them, though Diotrephes, another influential church leader, discouraged people from taking in John's messengers and even put some members who supported the travelers out of the church.

Chances are, helping out a visitor isn't dangerous for you, as it was for Gaius, though it may cost you a meal or some time. So remember the faithful Gaius and emulate him however much you need to. You'll probably be blessed beyond your expectations.

*Lord, let me treat my siblings in Christ
and other strangers with Your love.*

I know thy works, and tribulation, and poverty,
(but thou art rich)
and I know the blasphemy of them which say they are Jews,
and are not, but are the synagogue of Satan.
REVELATION 2:9

The first-century church had some huge disagreements. It took a few hundred years for churchmen to hammer out what true faith really was and what teachings did not follow the gospel Jesus established during His ministry. The process was part of a natural growth process that occurs in individual churches and larger church bodies.

From the words of Jesus that John recorded, it's obvious that some Jews in the church at Smyrna had caused division in the church. Though they claimed to be believers, Jesus condemns their so-called faith. The poor, persecuted people of Smyrna might not have had money or status, but He commended their real, rich faith.

Though centuries have passed, the situation hasn't changed much. There are faithful and unfaithful people within the church, just as there were in John's day. Some wealthy congregations are poor in spirit, while a financially struggling one may be rich in Jesus' eyes. The amount of money they have is of less importance to Him than the state of their belief.

Today, even if it's having trouble paying the bills, are you attending a rich congregation?

Lord, make my church rich in faith.

Then it [wood] shall be for a man to burn,
for he will take some of it and warm himself;
yes, he kindles it and bakes bread;
indeed he makes a god and worships it;
he makes it a carved image, and falls down to it.

ISAIAH 44:15 NKJV

People have an incredible ability to manufacture their own idols. The Romans not only imagined the well-known grain goddess Demeter, but horticultural gods like Messor, the god of mowing, and Sterculius, god of manure. Such beings quickly become ridiculous. Can you conceive of having a god of manure?

Centuries before the Romans imagined these idols, Isaiah pointed out any god's foolishness. The same tree, he told the Israelites, that creates an idol makes a firewood that bakes bread. Just as you wouldn't expect your hearth fire to save you from sin, you can't expect a wooden idol to help you. And it doesn't make any difference if you make your idol from metal or stone. No created material saves you from sin.

Today, we think of ourselves as sophisticated. We wouldn't bow down to metal, stone, or wood. But idols don't have to be formed from physical materials. A job that keeps you from worship or family time can be as much an idol as anything the Romans forged or carved.

Anything that separates us from God is an idol. Is there one in your life?

Lord, rid my life of idolatry. I want to serve You alone.

You trample the poor and steal what little
they have through taxes and unfair rent.
Therefore, you will never live in
the beautiful stone houses you are building.
You will never drink wine from
the lush vineyards you are planting.

AMOS 5:11 NLT

The wealthy, privileged Israelites were looking out for themselves, building their private fortunes through taxes and rent. They also took bribes and won court cases against the impoverished (v. 12). It must have seemed God didn't care about their harshness to their fellow Israelites. They evidently never expected to answer for their deeds.

Then one day the prophet Amos called them to account with a warning. Though these wealthy folks had started some new building projects, they'd never see them completed. Their new vineyards would make wine for someone else. God had finally decided to take up the cause of all His people.

If you're a landlord or a boss, do you keep in mind that God sees your actions? Do you charge a fair rent and pay your workers honestly? Or do you figure that as long as things are going well for you, God approves of your actions?

To enjoy your money, gain it honestly, unless you want to hear an unpleasant warning.

Lord, I want to treat everyone rightly.
Help me do just that.

For the creation was subjected to frustration,
not by its own choice,
but by the will of the one who subjected it, in hope.
ROMANS 8:20 NIV

Today I experienced frustration—my computer went down three times in about fifteen minutes because of brief power outages. They took just a second each, and fortunately I had no unsaved copy on my screen, but it was still very irritating. Meeting a deadline becomes difficult when you can't use your computer. Instead I ended up writing longhand.

This world has frustration—sometimes lots of it—and it's hard to imagine that God had a purpose for putting us through all this. But Paul says God brings frustration into our lives in hope that it will turn us back to Him. When we get to the end of our ropes and have nowhere else to go, we may turn to Jesus. Then He can free us from sin's bondage (v. 21). That's true for the non-Christian who accepts Jesus' salvation and for the Christian, as continuing sin is uncovered.

Why did my computer go down? I can't tell you. But I know God can work some benefit from it. All I have to do is look to Him.

Lord, I turn my frustrations over to You.
Use them to free me from sin.

We are confident that as you share in suffering,
you will also share God's comfort.

2 CORINTHIANS 1:7 NLT

Taking on the job description of *apostle* might have spelled centuries of fame for Paul, but it also meant a lifetime of suffering for Christ. Though people down through the ages would know of him and his mission, no one would admire Paul for his fortune or cushy lifestyle. Earthly rewards didn't mean much to the early church leaders, and it's a good thing, because they didn't get many.

There's a big gulf between those early people of faith and today's leaders—outside the church and sometimes even in it. Unlike other parts of the world, Western Christians don't suffer a lot. Perhaps people mock our faith or look down on us, and we may have to fight to be able to mention our Jesus in the workplace, but we don't get maimed or killed for our faith. We suffer more emotional damage than physical harm.

But whether we suffer physical or emotional harm, Paul promises suffering also has a comfort—God's comfort. And Paul knew what he spoke of, for he'd both suffered and been powerfully comforted by God. When others failed him or harmed the apostle, God strengthened him.

Without suffering, we would never get to feel God's strength. Have you felt His power today?

Lord, no matter how I suffer, I need Your strength.
Thank You for Your comfort.

Dead flies putrefy the perfumer's ointment,
and cause it to give off a foul odor;
so does a little folly to one respected for wisdom and honor.
ECCLESIASTES 10:1 NKJV

Flies were just a way of life in ancient Israel. No refrigeration, few preservatives—you had to expect something like this to happen. Stinky things were a nasty part of life. Sometimes even in modern life we have to put up with powerful, nasty smells.

But do our lives stink? Whether or not they do depends on how we act. It doesn't take much to have a foul smell emanate from our lives. A little dishonesty or selfishness, and actions that once smelled like perfume instead smell like dead flies.

Some of today's corporate leaders have begun to smell like defunct flies. Their greed has impacted the lives of hundreds—even thousands—of employees and investors. While they've lied about their companies' bottom line, they've impacted the lives of thousands who have lost their jobs and money.

Not only do actions like that stink to us, they stink to God. Those who are found out lose the respect of others and pay a price. It may not consist of jail or unemployment, but it will certainly contain God's disapproval and punishment. Imagine smelling like putrefying flies to God's nose! What could be worse?

Lord, I want wisdom and honor to be in my path, not folly.
Help me follow You.

In those days you were living apart from Christ.
You were excluded from God's people, Israel,
and you did not know the promises God had made to them.
You lived in this world without God and without hope.

EPHESIANS 2:12 NLT

Remember a time when you did not know Jesus? Unless you were very young when you came to Him, you probably recollect the emptiness in your soul and the wrong attitudes and actions that came with it. Even those who become Christians as children sometimes fall away for a time, until they rediscover the joy of faith. When they return to Him, they appreciate how awful being without Jesus is.

Looking back on the days when you did not walk close to Jesus shouldn't be part of a "can you top this?" wickedness contest. That isn't what Paul wanted the Ephesians to get caught up in. Don't rejoice in how bad you were before Jesus.

But remembering what being without Christ was like can help you appreciate what God has done for you. In that hopeless time, life seemed worthless, harsh, and hard. Now you are no longer excluded from God's people and His promises, and life seems valuable and sweet. Nothing else causes such a powerful change in a life.

Don't live without hope; live with Jesus!

Lord, thank You for all You've done for me in Christ.
Life is worth living because of You.

You have wearied the LORD with your words;
yet you say, "In what way have we wearied Him?"
In that you say,
"Everyone who does evil is good in the sight of the LORD,
and He delights in them," or, "Where is the God of justice?"

MALACHI 2:17 NKJV

Imagine that—God gets tired of people's idle chatter. When they say obviously untrue things, He probably wants to stop His ears with His fingers or just walk away. But being God, He doesn't do that. He still lends an ear to His chosen ones.

Even people who believe they know God can go off in the wrong direction and start to think that what's right is wrong. Just as Judah claimed to be God's people yet acted unfaithfully, many folks who attend church talk a good Christian line yet allow the cynicism of the world to impact their faith.

But even when His people disobey, God tries to get their attention. He sends modern-day missionaries to them in the guise of friends. The pastor in their church or on the radio may tell them the truth. And God works in their hearts and lives to get their attention. He'll woo them with the truths they've missed until they come to Him. With repentance, they'll learn a new way to speak that recognizes God's justice and the wrongdoing of evil people.

Then God will be happy to listen again!

Lord, keep me from cynical doubts.

If a ruler's anger rises against you, do not leave your post;
calmness can lay great errors to rest.
ECCLESIASTES 10:4 NIV

Has your boss become angry at you? Don't quiver in fear or become angry. Though your manager may have more experience or expertise, you're working for a human. Misunderstandings happen, but they can also be corrected.

So face an angry leader with calmness and a willingness to make things right. Instead of fixing blame, take aim at the problem. People who become angry or fearful don't do anyone a favor. The problem's still at hand. But often one calm head who's willing to take the heat off others can change a conversation's direction. What began in anger can end in peace.

Solomon knew the truth of this because he ruled over people. He probably had his mad days, when no one seemed to serve him properly. But obviously he'd also experienced the peace brought on by a faithful servant who showed calmness under pressure.

So if another is angry, keep the peace with a few calm words.

Lord, keep me peaceful when others' dander is up.

But godliness with contentment is great gain.
1 TIMOTHY 6:6

Are you content with your job? Does it pay you enough to live on and maybe a little extra? Do you enjoy the work? Then don't give it up for a job that pays better but won't bring you much satisfaction and may put you at odds with God. Money isn't the only reason you work.

Godliness and contentment should go hand in hand. If you don't like your job, God doesn't say you can't change to a new field or get some more education so you can move on in the field you're already in. That may be a way of finding contentment. If you can't care for your family or pay your rent or mortgage, such a change might be a wise choice.

But looking only for money isn't the only reason to find more work. Unlike many business people, God doesn't make money the greatest reason for doing anything. Instead, He warns against the desire to get rich and says it may become a trap leading to destruction. Some jobs pay well but force you to do things that aren't good for your spiritual life. There's no way any Christian should take on such work.

So do all you can to be successful and happy in your work, but don't only work for the cash. It's a sure way to lose your contentment.

Lord, help me find contentment and godliness in my work.

In a year and some days you will be troubled,
you complacent women;
for the vintage will fail, the gathering will not come.
ISAIAH 32:10 NKJV

When my husband and I were first married, we knew there was a chance he could get laid off. I was working freelance in an area that didn't have a lot of publishing jobs. He was our major breadwinner. So we did what we could to conserve money. We didn't rent an expensive place, though we might have liked one better.

When he was laid off along with a lot of other good workers, it was still a shock. Much as we knew it could happen, we'd hoped it wouldn't. If his company had just gotten one major contract, it could have made a big difference. But like the women in this verse, we saw our harvest fail.

If you've been through unemployment, you've probably seen God provide, as we did—the job that comes up just in time, though it isn't one you'd like to spend a lifetime in or the bill that's less than it should have been and can only be described as an answer to prayer.

Even when the gathering doesn't come, God remains faithful to the righteous one (v. 17). When we're trusting in Him, we cannot fail.

Lord, help me trust in You,
even when my harvest fails.

Woe to them that go down to Egypt for help;
and stay on horses, and trust in chariots, because they are many;
and in horsemen, because they are very strong;
but they look not unto the Holy One of Israel,
neither seek the LORD!

ISAIAH 31:1

It's easy in the business world to trust in the wrong things. A huge corporation becomes your client, and everything seems great. But when you send out the billing, that company refuses to pay for months, and suddenly your company is strapped for cash. Especially if you work for a small business, that kind of problem can make a big difference.

Wise leaders don't put all their emphasis on a single client, or even a couple of them, because if those companies fail, their clients can, too. Having a broader view is better, in the long run, for any business.

When times are good and a client seems strong, it's hard not to trust in what you have at hand and think it could never go away. But all things on earth can disappear—only God does not change. So even when the economy is booming and you're having a hard time finishing your work, don't forget to look to God, who always pays you on time and never fails.

Lord, keep me and my bosses trusting in You.

*And the Lord make you to increase
and abound in love one toward another,
and toward all men, even as we do toward you.*

1 THESSALONIANS 3:12

According to the stories told by Corrie ten Boom, most people wouldn't have called her father a prosperous businessman. Sometimes the family's supper consisted of a thinner soup than they would have liked, especially if they had guests that night. Though Casper ten Boom was a gifted watchmaker, to him, being a successful Christian was more important than running a successful shop, and that's where he put more of his effort.

Casper didn't get any awards for the businessman who made the most money. But he was loved in the community. And better than that, he raised a family who loved God and served Him throughout their lives. During World War II, because of their faith, the family hid Jews in their home. Though they suffered greatly for it, they were faithful to God's call to help His chosen people.

Truly, love abounded in Casper ten Boom's life; it increased in his family and through the mission to the Jews. From one tiny home in Holland, Corrie became a missionary sharing God's love with the world, telling the story of her family's life and faith. And love abounded toward all.

*Lord, I want to be a successful Christian.
Show me just how to be that.*

Rend your heart and not your garments.
Return to the LORD your God,
for he is gracious and compassionate,
slow to anger and abounding in love,
and he relents from sending calamity.

JOEL 2:13 NIV

Have you ever made a mistake that was so big, you figured you could never put it right? How could God ever forgive you for those words, actions, or attitudes? You felt embarrassed to even try to face Him. Your heart hurt so badly, you didn't even want to pray for awhile, though part of you still cried out to God.

While you were hurting so, God wasn't pushing you away. That pull on your heart was Him trying to draw you back. Because when we sin, realize it, and want forgiveness, God doesn't reject us. Broken hearts are treated tenderly by the Lord, who uses them as agents for change. Only those with soft hearts are ready to do His will.

Instead of beating yourself up for any wrong, large or small, do what God asks: Repent and ask His forgiveness, and He will not punish you. Instead, He'll lift you up with love and keep all harm at bay. Return to God, who is waiting for you.

Lord, forgive me for my sin.
My heart is broken and I need Your uplifting love.

Moreover [let us also be full of joy now!]
let us exult and triumph in our troubles
and rejoice in our sufferings,
knowing that pressure and affliction and hardship produce
patient and unswerving endurance.
And endurance (fortitude) develops maturity of character
(approved faith and tried integrity).
And character [of this sort] produces [the habit of]
joyful and confident hope of eternal salvation.
ROMANS 5:3–4 AMP

Last year I trimmed back some bushes in my yard so far, I felt concerned they might not make it. I need not have worried. This year they've shot up, much taller than they've ever been. I'll prune them again this year.

Gardeners know pruning is good for trees and bushes. It strengthens their growth by keeping them from becoming weedy. You might say it focuses their growth.

God doesn't prune bushes—He leaves that to us—but He does prune people to focus their growth in faith. As one kind of suffering follows another, we grow in faith. We learn to endure and find we've developed character. Because we have character, we trust more firmly in Jesus.

Growing Christians suffer, but growing Christians also hope in Jesus. It's the only assurance that lasts.

Whether or not I hurt, Lord, I
want my eyes to be focused on You.

"Thus says the Lord God: 'Behold, I am against the shepherds,
and I will require My flock at their hand;
I will cause them to cease feeding the sheep,
and the shepherds shall feed themselves no more;
for I will deliver My flock from their mouths,
that they may no longer be food for them.' "

EZEKIEL 34:10 NKJV

Do you have Christians working for you if you're in management? Chances are good you do, even if you've never discussed the subject. Deal with them well and fairly because God requires it. Even though you're not within the walls of a church, remember that God looks out for His people 24/7. When you hurt them in the office, you are just as likely to be held accountable as if you took advantage of members of your own congregation. This verse was not only aimed at the religious leaders of Ezekiel's day.

Leadership is an important role, one God intends to be used carefully to the benefit of others and to bring glory to Him. If He's given you authority, He expects you to use it well, as if you were working for Him.

Take your position for granted and misuse it, and God may even take that place from you, just as He took leadership from the shepherds who misused His people in Ezekiel's time. He doesn't have to leave in power anyone who makes His people hurt.

Lord, I want to lead well
and follow Your leadership example.

> *"As a shepherd seeks out his flock on the day*
> *he is among his scattered sheep,*
> *so will I seek out My sheep and deliver them from all*
> *the places where they were scattered on a cloudy and dark day."*
>
> EZEKIEL 34:12 NKJV

Lost and scattered people covered Israel, just like sheep. On a dark day, when selfish leaders controlled the people, God suddenly acted. He gathered the people together and began leading them Himself.

God is always the ultimate leader of His people. If you're a follower, one of those cogs in the wheel that make a company work efficiently, remember that even when your bosses fail you, God has not. He is still the leader you follow, and if everything seems to be falling apart, He's still in charge. He can lead where no human can. He knows the future and what guidance you need.

When you feel lost and scattered, when life no longer makes sense, turn to Jesus. Ask for His leadership for yourself. Then ask that your boss will come to understand His leadership and begin to lead in a way that will glorify Him.

Then your future will be incredibly secure, no matter what happens to your job.

Lord, I want You to lead me wherever I need to go in life.
Help my boss follow You, too.

I will feed them in a good pasture,
and upon the high mountains of Israel shall their fold be:
there shall they lie in a good fold,
and in a fat pasture shall they feed upon the mountains of Israel.
EZEKIEL 34:14

Good sheep pens and fat pastures. God takes good care of His people, protecting and providing for them. A good shepherd looks out for the welfare of his animals.

Notice that in all this talk of sheep and shepherds in Ezekiel 34, you only hear about the shepherd's care for the sheep. Surely he also got hungry, needed to do laundry, or wanted some time with his friends. Fighting off wild animals and tracking down lost sheep was tiring work; yet despite these needs, the good shepherd places a priority on his valuable animals making it to the fold at night and grazing in good fields by day.

If you're in charge, are you being a good shepherd, taking good care of your company and its people? Or are you so busy building a name for yourself or covering yourself, in case you get in trouble, that you never have time to care for others?

If your people and company are valuable to you, do your best to give them fat green fields and keep them in a good fold (or office). Do that, and when the Good Shepherd reviews your work, He'll be pleased.

Lord, show me how to be Your good shepherd.

Therefore thus saith the Lord God unto them;
Behold, I, even I,
will judge between the fat cattle and between the lean cattle.
Because ye have thrust with side and with shoulder,
and pushed all the diseased with your horns,
till ye have scattered them abroad.

EZEKIEL 34:20–21

The fat animals took advantage of the weak ones—that's God's way of describing how the powerful people took advantage of the poor but faithful. They pushed them aside and got their own way. But was it the right way?

You've probably seen such things going on in the office and even in church life. Some people seem able to sway others to their opinions, even if they aren't right. While an average worker may have a point, it may not be heard when a manager overwhelms it with inaccurate statistics. Or leaders who look only at the financial balance and ignore ethics may be heard more often than the softer voice of right.

Right doesn't always make might in the workplace; in fact it often seems just the opposite. But just as it took God awhile to correct Israel's wrongdoing, it may take Him time to bring down the wrongs in a corporate environment. That doesn't mean it won't happen or that you want to be a fat sheep when the Good Shepherd comes to the aid of the weak ones.

Lord, keep me from becoming fat on weaker sheep.

I am the good shepherd:
the good shepherd giveth his life for the sheep.
JOHN 10:11

Martin Luther rocked the church when he began teaching from the Scripture instead of deferring to church tradition and the other ideas imposed on the church by its less-than-holy leaders. The pope didn't take the German monk's position seriously. He only wanted this fellow silenced. By the time he did take Luther seriously, many others had been won to the monk's teaching and the truths he expressed to the high-born and lowly alike.

Had Luther just been a rebellious monk or the drunkard the pope assumed him to be (German monks were stereotyped that way in Italy), his words would have died out quickly. But Luther had a godly message to preach, and the spiritually thirsty people of Germany drank in all he could offer. His advantage over the church hierarchy? He was a good shepherd who shared God's truths with all who heard him, from his students in Wittenberg University to the crowds before whom he preached.

Though he never quite lost his life for God's truth, Luther lost his church and began Protestantism's first denomination as a result. He often went in fear for his life and spent much time debating those who disagreed with him. It wasn't an easy life, but being a good shepherd sometimes isn't easy. It's just the only way for a faithful Christian to live.

Lord, whenever I lead others, let me be Your good shepherd.

As far as the east is from the west,
so far hath he removed our transgressions from us.
PSALM 103:12

Sally accepted Christ, then committed what she described as a terrible sin. It took awhile, but finally she came to God, confessed her wrongdoing, and began to put it behind her. But thoughts of that sin and the guilt attached to it kept popping up in her mind. Sally began to wonder if she was really forgiven. If she was, why did this sin continue to bother her?

Sometimes sin seems to have a life of its own. Even when we've been burned by it, hurt so badly we don't dare do it again, guilt for the past can grab ahold of us. Letting go of that forgiven sin can still be a challenge.

But God doesn't prompt guilt for forgiven sin. He says that when He forgives, it's done completely. Just as you can't identify a place where east and west meet, you can't find a common spot for forgiveness and sin. When God forgives, the sin is erased, gone, nothing.

If guilt bothers you, confess anything you haven't entirely given to God before. Then leave it all in His hands, trusting that you and it are separated, just like the east and west.

Lord, I ask Your forgiveness.
Separate me from unnecessary guilt.

But Jesus said, Suffer little children, and forbid them not,
to come unto me: for of such is the kingdom of heaven.
MATTHEW 19:14

There probably isn't a verse in the King James Bible that fewer people understand than this one. I've heard even biblically literate Christians use it as an explanation for why children sometimes suffer. That isn't what Jesus was talking about at all.

To understand this verse as talking about suffering, you cannot read it carefully. Read it in context with the verse before, and it becomes even clearer that it means something much different. Compare it to other Bible translations, and the problem clears itself up.

In seventeenth-century English, when the King James Bible was translated, *suffer* also meant *allow*. Jesus was commanding His disciples to allow children to see Him, not giving some sort of blessing to their anguish. No doubt some children do suffer, through illness, abuse, and other awful things. But God doesn't commend it. If our hard hearts ache at the sight of a suffering child, how much more the eternal Father's heart pains Him.

As you study the Word, remember how important right knowledge is. It touches you and those you share with. Come to a clear understanding as you read. You never know how important one verse could be.

Lord, help me understand Your Word.
I don't want to pass along a wrong message.

Samuel said, When you were small in your own sight,
were you not made the head of the tribes of Israel,
and the Lord anointed you king over Israel?
1 SAMUEL 15:17 AMP

God says he doesn't use big things to do His work, and Saul's story proves that. God took a humble man and made him king!

Too bad Saul didn't stay small in his own opinion. As his authority grew, the king got a swelled head; his theme song became "My Way." He forgot that God gave him power and could take it away. Although Saul attacked the Amalekites as God commanded, the king did not also kill all the people and destroy all they owned, as God had told him to. Saul kept the pagan king alive, along with all his best livestock. As a result, God removed His blessing from Saul, and the king's story begins to become a tragedy.

Perhaps being small in our own sight isn't such a bad thing. Pride and arrogance are not Christian virtues; and when they become the hallmarks of our careers, we may quickly follow in Saul's path. Instead of success, trouble marks our footsteps. Things never go as smoothly when we walk without God.

Authority without God isn't worth much.

Lord, any authority I have comes from You.
Help me use it wisely.

And Samuel said unto Jesse, Are here all thy children?
And he said, There remaineth yet the youngest,
and, behold, he keepeth the sheep.
And Samuel said unto Jesse, Send and fetch him:
for we will not sit down till he come hither.

1 SAMUEL 16:11

None of us likes to be forgotten or thought of as unimportant. Even though we may deny it and like to be thought of as independent, others' opinions count to us. We want people to respect our ideas and even seek them out. When there's an honor to be handed out, we'd like to be considered for it, whether it's a promotion or an award.

But even King David had a time when he was forgotten. Out watching sheep—a lowly job—David was out of the way. When the prophet Samuel asked Jesse to see his sons, the father forgot his youngest son. Who would imagine this boy as a king? No one in the family saw the promise in the youth who became a successful warrior and ruler.

Just because others don't see your promise, don't give up. God sees when others are blinded by their humanity. His wonderful, promise-filled future does not rely on human ideas of your value.

Even if the whole world forgets or ignores you, Jesus doesn't.

Lord, thank You for remembering me when the world forgets.

Give not that which is holy unto the dogs,
neither cast ye your pearls before swine,
lest they trample them under their feet,
and turn again and rend you.

MATTHEW 7:6

Did you know there are times when sharing your faith might not be the right thing to do? God wants you to let others know about Him, but He doesn't say you have to keep battering at people who show no response to His good news. Beating away at people whom the Spirit has not begun to work at is perfectly valueless.

If you work with antagonistic people who mock you for believing in Jesus, your best response might be to keep your mouth shut for awhile. That doesn't mean you can't pray for coworkers, but becoming a public mockery will not get you or God anywhere.

When you do get around to sharing your faith with an open heart, be certain you do it on a break or lunchtime, not on company time. Don't cut into the work your boss expects of you in order to witness and think God will still bless it. Though He wants people to hear the good news, He also wants you to give your boss a full day.

Witnessing to faith needs to be done with wisdom as well as fervor. Without both, you're going nowhere fast.

Lord, let my heart know when You want me to
open my mouth and when I need to quietly pray for another.

*"There are many rooms in my Father's home,
and I am going to prepare a place for you.
If this were not so, I would tell you plainly."*

JOHN 14:2 NLT

Cubicles are a way of life in the working world, and though they make concentration a real challenge, I have to wonder if God isn't using them to give us a preview of what heaven will be like. Maybe, when we receive our eternal reward, we'll all be living together so closely that we're right near all our loved ones.

Perhaps cubicles are one way God shows us how to get along well with others. If you work in cubicle space, you know that an inconsiderate conversation just outside your walls, as you're trying to concentrate, can become very irritating. If one offender has an office just around the corner, you may wish the speakers would do their talking in private.

Though offices are better for privacy than cubicles, cubicles can teach a lot of lessons about patience, consideration, and caring for others. God can use them to show us how to live well with others—even those who aren't wise or considerate.

Someday, in heaven, we'll have our own space. Will we be willing to share it or selfishly hoard it for our own good?

*Lord, let me learn a cubicle lesson here on earth
so I will readily share in heaven.*

And David reigned over all Israel;
and David executed judgment and justice unto all his people.
2 SAMUEL 8:15

Dropped in a seemingly unimportant spot, this verse is not as minor as its placement might make it seem. In fact, it sets the tone for David's rule of Israel. In the next chapter, the writer tells a tale that proves David's concern for ruling well. After Saul and Jonathan's death, the new king asked after their households. In a surprising moment, he offered a high honor to Jonathan's only surviving son, Mephibosheth. Though most rulers would hesitate at dealing with a possible contender for the throne with anything but a sword, David showed compassionate justice toward his enemy's grandson.

Though he had his faults, David is a good example— and a good warning—for leaders. At moments like this, David is a wonderful example, and God blesses him for his right acts.

God does bless good leaders. As long as they follow Him, they and their followers receive many benefits. Business leaders can benefit from that truth as much as leaders of a nation.

Whether you lead a large staff or are only a small part of it, are you concerned about justice and right judgment? If so, you're a real leader.

Lord, make me a real leader
who wants to be just and judge rightly.

They have set up kings, but not by me:
they have made princes, and I knew it not.
HOSEA 8:4

Election time is over, and for better or worse, we have officials ready to take up office. Some of them may be the people we voted for, and others we may wish were not in office. But there's no way around it; for some years we'll have to live with these leaders.

We need to support people who have biblical values because they can give us an honest, moral government. Those are the ones God desires to place in office. But when public opinion goes against God, He lets a nation have what they want. They get self-serving, greedy leaders until they see the wrong in them and turn again to their real Ruler, the Lord.

If you have leaders who do not recognize God's call on their lives, don't give up. Pray regularly that He will touch their hard hearts. Just because an elected official is in office doesn't mean he or she cannot change. Ask God to work within that person's heart, and God may make surprising alterations.

Lord, I pray for my elected officials.
May they come to know You, if they do not,
and may they do Your will in all their work.

> *But I do not think I am*
> *in the least inferior to those "super-apostles."*
> 2 CORINTHIANS 11:5 NIV

Imagine, the Corinthians didn't think Paul was much of an apostle! They preferred other men, whom the apostle sarcastically refers to as "super-apostles." The problem was these guys weren't really super, nor were they apostles—they were heretics, spreading lies instead of the gospel.

Could the Corinthians have been more misled? Paul's ministry brought the gospel to the Western world, while we don't even know the names of those not-so-super-apostles. It's hard to imagine why the Corinthians were so blind.

People don't always make right judgments about another's abilities. Perhaps a boss doesn't like an effective worker's personality or his irritating habit rubs her the wrong way. A lot can get in the way of a clear judgment.

But the final decision on who is really a good worker and who fails to make the grade isn't a boss—it's God. Though you might not be a good public speaker (neither was Paul, by his own account [v. 6]), you may tell your bosses a truth others wouldn't dare share. You may encourage doing good things others avoid.

To God, obedience to Him creates a good worker.

Lord, I'm no apostle, but I always want to work for You.
Show me what to do.

But by the grace of God I am what I am,
and His grace toward me was not in vain;
but I labored more abundantly than they all, yet not I,
but the grace of God which was with me.
1 CORINTHIANS 15:10 NKJV

Why do kids get sick enough to need a doctor's care only on days when we have to be in the office? If the kids are okay, the hot-water heater or dishwasher goes, and the repairman can only come on a crazy-hectic day.

These are times when God's grace needs to work over-time in our lives. If it doesn't, we're crabby to the (already grumpy) kids, we race around like mad, and nothing much gets done.

But once we recognize our need for help on an out-of-control day and trust in God to control things, the day goes better. It may be hectic—we'll work hard and travel too many places—but by the end of the day we'll discover we've accomplished a lot.

Paul, who thought of himself as the least of the apostles (v. 9), understood the part grace has in our lives. It fills those empty, weak spots and makes us able to take on large tasks for God. Paul needed grace to fulfill his ministry, and we need it to do God's will in our lives.

Lord, I need Your grace every day,
but especially on the busy ones. Please fill me now.

"We wish to inform you that we went to the construction site
of the Temple of the great God in the province of Judah.
It is being rebuilt with specially prepared stones,
and timber is being laid in its walls.
The work is going forward with great energy and success."

EZRA 5:8 NLT

When God wants something done and the people doing the work are dedicated to Him, no matter what troubles arise along the way, the work is successful. The Jews rebuilding the temple learned this. Even though they had to guard against their enemies, who resented the rebuilding, the work went on. So the enemies resorted to sending this report to the king.

It's the same with your work, whatever you do. If it honors God and He's in the work, you may offend some people. They may try to stop you with petty problems or bad attitudes. But if you're working for God, He will support you. You may be slowed down on occasion, but you won't be stopped. Every day, if you ask, He'll give you strength to go on and complete more than you expected.

That doesn't mean it will be an easy time. It doesn't mean you won't have troubles. But you can go forward, with energy and success.

Have a successful day today.

Lord, I want to be a success for You and through Your power.
Show me how.

*"Do not disturb the construction of the Temple of God.
Let it be rebuilt on its former site,
and do not hinder the governor of Judah
and the leaders of the Jews in their work."*

EZRA 6:7 NLT

Not only was God supporting the building of the temple, the complainer's objections to the building project were denied in this command from the king. Support can come from surprising places! Darius hadn't given the Jews the original command to rebuild the temple, but he went back in the court records and found that Cyrus had. Being an honest man, he ordered that the previous ruler's command be obeyed.

When God works this way, it's always a surprise. People you wouldn't have expected to come in on your side do. The project moves forward smoothly, despite objections.

Don't be afraid to thank your supporters. No matter why they came to your aid, they were a gift from God. Let them know that you don't take them for granted.

And don't forget to say a thank-you prayer to your Lord, either. After all, without Him, you never could have accomplished this.

*Thank You, Lord, for supporting
the work You've given me to do.
I could never have done it alone.*

And the king said, Divide the living child in two,
and give half to the one, and half to the other.
Then spake the woman whose the living child was unto the king...
O my lord, give her the living child, and in no wise slay it.
But the other said, Let it be neither mine nor thine, but divide it.

1 KINGS 3:25–26

Solomon asked God for wisdom, and God gave it to him. The Scriptures illustrate this with an amazing example of how the king used his gift from God.

Two women came to him, each claiming that a child was hers. The king, with no real knowledge of the situation, had to choose a mother for the boy. In a flash of inspiration, the king demanded that the boy be cut in half. Naturally the real mother refused, offering to give up the child so he could live. So the king knew to choose this woman.

Don't you wish you had such wisdom? Remember, Solomon didn't inherit it, wise as his father, David, was. Solomon got it from God when he asked to be wise so he could rule well.

Today, as you face questions and decisions, you, too, can ask God for wisdom. He'll be pleased to give it to you so you can benefit others.

Lord, please give me wisdom
so I can serve You better.

For it came to pass, when Solomon was old,
that his wives turned away his heart after other gods:
and his heart was not perfect with the LORD his God,
as was the heart of David his father.

1 KINGS 11:4

Solomon is a disturbing biblical character. He begins his reign wisely, blessed by God with an incredible wisdom. God allows him to build a glorious temple. Wealth and wisdom are his; what more could a man want?

But instead of obeying God's commands, Solomon marries many women from many pagan nations. Before long, the wise king unwisely begins to worship their gods. Before long, the man who built the temple has strayed far from his God. How could he do such a thing?

One-time wisdom doesn't last forever. The king did not realize that since his wisdom lay in God, he had to constantly keep up the connection. God could not combine wisdom and disobedience, so when Solomon failed to obey, his wisdom lessened. Soon troubles followed, and his life lost the peace and joy of his early years.

We, too, can lose out on wisdom by going our own way. But to continue to enjoy God's touch on our minds and hearts, we need only remain in Him.

Lord, I want to remain in You throughout my life.
Let me never stray.

"First here, then there—
you flit from one ally to another asking for help.
But your new friends in Egypt will let you down,
just as Assyria did before."
JEREMIAH 2:36 NLT

When trouble comes, to whom do you go? Jeremiah saw
God's people running all over the ancient Near East, looking for help from a powerful nation. As an unstable politi-
cal situation threatened Judah, it searched for security—in
all the wrong places. Eventually, Jeremiah prophesied, the
nation would be led into exile, because instead of looking to
God, it looked to other people (v. 37).

Getting some support from others is a good thing. We
all need help at home, on the job, and in the community. And
offering help to others is the right thing to do. But there are
things no human can help us with—solutions no person can
come up with. Ultimately, if we trust our lives to anyone but
God, we're looking for safety in the wrong place.

No matter what challenges you face today, have you
asked God for help? Whether it's tutoring one of the kids
in math or painting the house, have you placed your day in
His hands?

If so, you need never despair: He will help you today.

Thank You, Lord, for always being willing to come to my aid.
Help me accomplish all I really need to do today.

For in the multitude of dreams
and many words there is also vanity.
But fear God.
ECCLESIASTES 5:7 NKJV

You've met people like this in church and out. They talk a good line, but when you ask them to help out, they disappear. For some, a dream is more in their minds than the reality of this world. Christians often call this being so heavenly minded, you're no earthly good.

God doesn't say spirituality means having your head in the clouds. That kind of person is of no more benefit to Him than he or she is to a church leader trying to start a new ministry or encourage spiritual growth. God made this world and put us in it, and He gave us goals to reach here. We don't just get to sit around on a cloud now, and we won't in heaven, either. God is more active than that and expects us to be so, too.

So whether you visit shut-ins, write the church newsletter, take part in a witnessing program, or teach Sunday school, make use of your time here on earth, instead of wasting it in vain imaginings and wishes. Take God and His commandments seriously, and work at carrying them out. Then He'll know you're a Christian who's heavenly minded and earthly good.

Lord, keep my head in Your will, not in the clouds.
I want to do the spiritual work You have for me, too.

"Woe to him who builds a city with bloodshed
and establishes a town by crime!"
HABAKKUK 2:12 NIV

As I've been writing this book, Enron Corporation has filled the news. The seemingly expanding company was teetering on the edge of bankruptcy, then fell over the edge. Suddenly, the truth about the corporation's management finally came out: Executives had been bleeding the company dry while using illicit bookkeeping practices to create a fairy-tale kingdom of success. Over forty-five hundred people ended up losing their jobs, while the corporation and its accounting firm landed in the courts.

It's hard to imagine those leaders couldn't have figured out that the fairy tale wasn't going to last. Eventually, their wrongdoing had to damage the company—and it did, along with a lot of reputations.

God warns us that wrongdoing will not build a healthy city—and it can't build a strong company, either. Wrong finally becomes apparent and ruins any structure that's founded on it.

Is your company headed toward crime? Don't be part of it. Not only will you end up losing your job and reputation, if you take part, you'll be disobeying your heavenly Father, who would rather help you than judge you.

Instead, ask for His help today.

Lord, keep my company from wrongdoing,
and if I do face it on the job,
help me sound a warning.

Though thou exalt thyself as the eagle,
and though thou set thy nest among the stars,
thence will I bring thee down, saith the LORD.
OBADIAH 4

The accounting firm of Arthur Andersen was one of the most successful in the business when some sheets of shredded paper changed the whole company's future. Not only that, the wrongdoing of one employee became the basis of the damaging lawsuit that named the entire company liable and forced it to reorganize on a smaller scale. One choice to shred papers that would have shown Enron's real financial status and uncovered the criminal acts within the company lost thousands of people their jobs in both companies.

The next time you think your actions won't reflect on the company as a whole, think again. You probably aren't doing something illegal, but are you representing your company as being proud, uncaring, or rude? Don't let current success make you think nothing can change. Though you're flying like an eagle today, God can bring you down if you slide into evil.

Let God's Spirit be the wind that lifts your career on high, and He will never bring you down. Be exalted in Him, not in a company's profit sheet or positive reputation.

Lord, lift my career up so it will glorify You.

And Zacchaeus stood, and said unto the Lord;
Behold, Lord, the half of my goods I give to the poor;
and if I have taken any thing from any man by false accusation,
I restore him fourfold. And Jesus said unto him,
This day is salvation come to this house,
forsomuch as he also is a son of Abraham.

LUKE 19:8–9

Zacchaeus was what you might call the equivalent of a first-century Enron: He'd grown rich on the poverty of others. A tax collector who worked for the hated Roman government, he wasn't very popular with his fellow Jews, from whom he extorted as much money as possible. He wasn't on many people's list of favorite party guests, so no one could understand why Jesus even bothered with the man.

But Zacchaeus was ready for a change. Perhaps that's why he went to see Jesus when He came to Jericho. Shortly after their meeting, the tax collector decided to make things right. By the time he gave away all this money, he probably wouldn't be that wealthy anymore, but he'd have a peaceful heart.

Have you become caught up in wrongdoing? Zacchaeus shows the way out. Forgiveness from God is wonderful, but it isn't real until it's lived out. Making the situation right, as far as possible, is a critical part of real repentance.

Jesus commended the tax collector. Do right, and He'll commend you, too.

Lord, when I do wrong,
give me the courage to make things right.

*"Has not the LORD Almighty determined that
the people's labor is only fuel for the fire,
that the nations exhaust themselves for nothing?"*

HABAKKUK 2:13 NIV

What are you really working for? Money, fame, power? Then in the end, you'll be left with empty hands. God describes your work as fuel for the fire, efforts that lead nowhere because all they gain is burned up in the end. Or if you're a fine craftsman who builds materials to be proud of, you'll still end up with nothing, because the things of this earth do not translate to heaven. As the old saying goes, "You can't take it with you."

So why work at all? Because one day, the earth will be filled with the knowledge of God's glory (see v. 14). One day, everyone, believer or not, will be able to understand that God was all He claimed to be. They'll also be able to see that the witness you gave to His power and love were true.

So as you work at the office or building whatever widgets you make, do your best. But don't do it because money, paperwork, or widgets are important. Do it because through you, someone might learn how wonderful Jesus is. That's the work that won't be burned by fire or exhaust you for nothing.

*Lord, I always want to work for You.
No matter what my job, show me how to serve You best.*

Better it is to be of an humble spirit with the lowly,
than to divide the spoil with the proud.
PROVERBS 16:19

Do you recognize that a lot of "humble" people make your work possible? Like the cleaning people who come in at night to dust and polish or the person who carts away the garbage. Though you may never see these people, you know they exist because you don't have a thick layer of dust on your desk or a garbage pail that's overflowing.

In many companies, the humble people don't get much recognition or pay, but they're still important. Wait until your clean-up staff goes on strike or a key worker is out ill, and you'll know just how much they mean.

People in humble jobs can indeed be humble—or they may be very proud people, involved in a lot of wrongdoing. If you have honest people who work for low pay in your office, recognize how important their attitude is, and if you can, thank them for it.

Then take their example, and instead of getting in on all the goodies the proud folks in your office offer, side with the lowly—and God.

Lord, being humble isn't always attractive,
but I know it's what You want me to be.
Help me be willing to side with the lowly,
if that's where You are.

But you desire honesty from the heart,
so you can teach me to be wise in my inmost being.
PSALM 51:6 NLT

Being honest from deep inside the heart: It's a wonderful idea, but how many of us think we've completely achieved that? We may have our good and bad days, but entirely honest, from the center of the heart out? That's a tough order.

Maybe we're honest most days, but some little thing creeps in and topples us from our honesty pedestal. We don't necessarily have to open our lips—often we're being dishonest with ourselves, thinking we're better than we are or even that we're worse than we really are. We find a thousand dishonesties inside our own beings.

Part of the problem is that we know so little about ourselves. People are incredibly complex, and even the best of us hide some truths from ourselves. As we peel away layers of sin, those hidden dishonesties appear and make us feel awful. We wonder what to do with them.

God wants us to be honest, but He also shows us how to be. His Spirit pricks those deep places of hidden sin and brings them to the surface. As we confess them to God, He teaches us wisdom, deep down inside, where we've hardly ever been before. Suddenly a new, clean feeling fills our souls.

Lord, forgive my sin and make me clean inside.
I need Your wisdom!

The silver-haired head is a crown of glory,
if it is found in the way of righteousness.
PROVERBS 16:31 NKJV

When I was in high school, I remember looking at the back of the head of a student sitting in front of me. Though this boy was only about eighteen, his dark hair already had traces of gray in it. He probably went fully gray before he hit forty.

When you go gray doesn't really matter—it's related to genetics, not how wise you are. But most people go gray as they get older. So the Bible uses this hair color as an example of someone who's been around the block and has learned many important lessons.

God tells us not to get upset over a little gray hair—or even a head covered with it. What's important is that we've lived enough years to draw closer to Him, to learn more of His ways. That's a good thing, no matter what color our hair is.

But one thing God never recommends, with the hair-color change, it that we become fuddy-duddies. He doesn't give us carte blanche to criticize, condemn, or complain. The carte blanche we do get is to be more like Him, caring, sharing His love, and supporting those who struggle.

Is your head—no matter what its color—covered with righteousness or fuddy-duddyism?

Lord, help me grow in righteousness,
not just get stuck in my ways.

A friend loveth at all times,
and a brother is born for adversity.
PROVERBS 17:17

If your boss is also your friend, count yourself blessed. But also accept that at times she's going to make decisions you'll wish she hadn't made. Though you agree in many things, there will be some choices you would have made differently, for whatever reason. Those differences of opinion could destroy your friendship, if you let it.

But if you recognize that she has the position of authority and accept that, your friendship can stand firm. After all, if you were the boss, you'd get to make the decisions, but if you were wrong, you'd also get the flak. She makes her own choices and stands firm in them. If she makes a mistake, it's her responsibility, not yours.

If you truly are your boss's friend, you'll recognize that even people who disagree on some things can remain friends. You'll give her the kind of leeway you'd give a friend whose taste in clothes you didn't always agree on or who doesn't make the wisest choices in her romantic life. Though you might offer a suggestion on occasion, you won't take every different decision as a personal affront.

Love your friend faithfully, no matter what her position.

Lord, I'm glad my boss is my friend.
Let me always use that friendship wisely.

God wants you to be holy,
so you should keep clear of all sexual sin. . . .
Anyone who refuses to live by these rules is not
disobeying human rules but is rejecting God,
who gives his Holy Spirit to you
1 THESSALONIANS 4:3, 8 NLT

You've heard the excuses and explanations for romantic relationships outside of wedlock. Almost undoubtedly you've worked with someone who lived with a girlfriend or became romantically involved with someone who wasn't her husband.

Just because your coworkers do it doesn't mean that avenue is open to you. If you accepted Jesus, He wants you to be holy, set apart from the rest of the world, and that set-apartness includes your romantic life.

God's rule may seem kind of strict. You may wish you could join the crowd without offending Him. But the apostle makes it perfectly clear: Those who fall into sexual sin aren't just rejecting a rule, they're rejecting God.

Today you may feel as if God's way is difficult or even unnecessary, but you won't feel that way if you see a marriage fall apart from unfaithfulness or a romance of many years hit the rocks, leaving one partner heartbroken and financially insecure.

God's demand for holiness isn't just for His benefit, it's for ours, too. So live in a holy way and enjoy His Spirit daily.

Lord, thank You for letting me live in Your Spirit
instead of sin. Give me grace to be holy for You.

*"Come, let's get him drunk with wine,
and then we will sleep with him.
That way we will preserve our family line through our father."*
GENESIS 19:32 NLT

The Bible can be awfully honest about families. There are some, especially in the Old Testament, we're happy we don't have for our own. Lot's daughters are good examples of the kind of unwise kids most of us would be happy not to have.

As holiday time rolls around again, you're probably getting together with your family or at least making a phone call or two. Maybe there are some family members you'd be happy not to see or hear from, but because they're family, you hold your tongue at the table or say a few kind words on the phone.

No one chooses a family. You might say God picks that for you—even the family you marry into. It's not perfect, even if you really like it. But remember, even when you disagree, that some of those most difficult family members may never get this close to another Christian, no matter how many years they live. So love every person—even the irritating ones—for Jesus. You just never know how He may work in their lives.

*Lord, help me love my family for You,
even when they don't act kindly or lovingly in return.
Help me remember how hard I was to love
before I came into Your kingdom.*

Give thanks unto the Lord, call upon his name,
make known his deeds among the people.
Sing unto him, sing psalms unto him,
talk ye of all his wondrous works.
1 CHRONICLES 16:8–9

Is Thanksgiving a joyful time for you? It can be, if you're focused on the One who deserves thanks. But so often we become wrapped up in a large turkey dinner, a family get-together, and other holiday celebrations that we lose our joy.

Though the Pilgrims have been stereotyped as sour-faced folks, that image is wrong. When they had a successful harvest in 1621, they just had to rejoice. Some men went out to shoot game for their harvest celebration table, and the Pilgrims invited the Wampanoag Indians. Their celebration lasted three days. Though no formal religious service was part of the first celebration, Edward Winslow, who wrote a letter to England about it, reported that it was by God's goodness that the small band of Christians was far from want. They knew who to thank.

So make today a day of joy when you remember the blessings of God. He's been with you this whole year, no matter what it's included. Whether you're joining a large family or celebrating alone, it's a time to remember the love that's brought you to this point in your life.

Say one big "thanks" to God.

Thank You, Lord, for the blessing of Your love.
Keep me faithful in thanks all year long.

*"I call heaven and earth as witnesses today against you,
that I have set before you life and death, blessing and cursing;
therefore choose life,
that both you and your descendants may live."*
DEUTERONOMY 30:19 NKJV

God offered life to His people, but He knew some would reject Him. The problem was, they could not accept life apart from the Life Giver. Though the rejecters probably wanted the benefits of life, they also wanted to worship the pagan gods who demanded so little—and could give so little, too, if they would only realize it.

Those who chose life discovered it was indeed no short-term benefit. God promised to pass it on to their descendants, too, and He did. The powerful blessing on their lives communicated itself to their children and even the children of some whose parents chose death. God worked powerfully in His people and made them a forceful testimony.

But God's offering of life did not stop with an ancient people. He offers the same blessing today. Therefore, choose life in Christ. If you do, you and your family will experience the same blessing of His love.

*Lord, in all I do, help me to choose life.
I want to live with You and for You.*

NOVEMBER 29

Glory to God in the highest,
and on earth peace, good will toward men.

LUKE 2:14

The Christmas season is just starting—that wonderful time when going to a mall means being pushed and shoved or beaten out for a parking space that six months ago would have been yours with no questions asked.

Shopping at this time of year can bring the worst out in anyone. There's so much to do and so little time. And each of us wants the best for our loved ones. Aren't we just trying to show that love to the people dearest to us? Does it really matter if we cut off the driver who had her eye on our spot or grab the last red sweater out from under another shopper's nose?

If you're shopping for Santa, maybe it doesn't matter. But if you're shopping for Jesus—if you're a Christian who wants to share his faith during this blessed season—it could make a big difference. How will anyone know about good will if all she sees are selfish, greedy people who claim to be Christians? Maybe all she really needs to see is one person living out that faith—even when he's Christmas shopping.

Lord, help me live out my faith at this season
and trust that I'll be giving the best gift of all—You.

Jumping up, they mobbed him
and took him to the edge of the hill on which the city was built.
They intended to push him over the cliff,
but he slipped away through the crowd and left them.
LUKE 4:29–30 NLT

The people in Jesus' hometown of Nazareth were so angry at Him, they wanted to kill Him. In fact, they took Him to a cliff to throw Him over. A few more minutes, and if He hadn't been God's Son, He would have been history.

But did you miss the most important part of those verses? Jesus just slips away. An irate mob, and He just walks through it as if it were water. No one stops Him. No one questions Him. In a few minutes, He's on His way. Jesus' whole life—and death—was under God's control. Nothing could touch Him until the Father okayed it. No one could harm Him without God's permission.

To a lesser degree, that's true of God's children, too. When trouble comes our way, God hasn't lost control. He's in that situation with us, guiding our steps and sharing our sorrow. Don't forget the many times you've slipped through the crowd, as God has smoothed the way and made life simpler. He's saved you from harm because He had another plan, and a cliff wasn't in it. He's in control, no matter what happens.

Lord, whatever happens to me,
I'm glad You're in control.

And when they had received it,
they murmured against the goodman of the house, saying,
These last have wrought but one hour,
and thou hast made them equal unto us,
which have borne the burden and heat of the day.
MATTHEW 20:11–12

In this work-dispute parable, the workers complained to the man who hired them: They'd worked all day for the same wages as men who came later in the day; it wasn't fair. The employer objected that the early morning workers were greedy; they didn't want anyone to have it better than they did.

Jesus wasn't saying employers should treat their workers unfairly. But if a worker has a sick child, and your boss helps him out by giving him some time off with pay, don't become jealous. Be thankful, instead, that if it were you in his shoes, you might get help, too.

But Jesus wasn't even really talking about the workplace when He told this story. He wanted believers to realize that the things they thought "earned" them a good place in heaven didn't. God determines heavenly value, and He may place unlikely people in high places.

So if you start feeling jealous about another worker, remember this parable, and be thankful that God saved you and will give you a place in heaven, even if it's barely inside the gate.

Lord, I don't want to be jealous of the benefits You give others.
I just want to thank You for saving me.

*Behold, the hire of the labourers who have reaped down your fields,
which is of you kept back by fraud, crieth:
and the cries of them which have reaped are entered
into the ears of the Lord of sabaoth.*

JAMES 5:4

If your company shortchanges you come raise time, do you feel as if God doesn't care or is ignoring a great wrong? It's not so, according to this verse. God knows every wrongdoing in every corporation in the world. Even if the laborers haven't said a word, the wrong has reached God's ears. The Lord of sabaoth, the Lord of hosts, has not missed out on a penny.

God promises that the rich one who defrauds the poor will howl with miseries (v. 1). It may not be today, but eventually God will make all even.

Does that mean you should start watching out for the howling? Should you react in a way that will make your boss miserable? Is God finally saying revenge is right? No, God leaves revenge to Himself, and when He uses it, He uses it wisely. But the Christian who has been wronged should respond graciously, leaving everything in God's hands. Perhaps this wrong will become an opportunity for God to make things right in a big way. Those pennies you missed today could be a key to tomorrow's success if you leave it all in His hands.

*Lord keep me from vengeful thoughts,
and help me trust in You alone.*

And Mary said, My soul doth magnify the Lord,
and my spirit hath rejoiced in God my Saviour.
For he hath regarded the low estate of his handmaiden:
for, behold, from henceforth all generations shall call me blessed.

LUKE 1:46–48

Mary had the most unusual, important job in the universe—for nine months she carried God's Son, and for thirty-three years she loved Him with a tender maternal love.

God entrusted this important job to a young woman probably not yet out of her teens. She wasn't wealthy, well-born, or even important—except in God's eyes. Her qualifications would have seemed slim to most people. She hadn't had much education, lived in a "hick" town, and couldn't write much on her résumé—if she could write at all.

But the job God called her to didn't require extensive education, sophistication, or work background. It demanded one thing only: a heart completely devoted to Him, and that Mary had.

As we look at her, are we awed by Mary's faithfulness? She completely made her body a temple for God by willingly bearing His Son. She accepted the loss of respect that came with the perception she was an unwed mother. She bore the pain of loving her Son as He completed His difficult ministry with death on the cross.

Could we have taken on her job? Would we have wanted to?

Lord, help me be faithful like Mary.

[Add] to godliness brotherly kindness,
and to brotherly kindness love.
2 PETER 1:7 NKJV

As a part-time temporary worker, I often feel I never quite know what's going on. That truth was brought home to me powerfully one day when I tried to get into the building and my card wouldn't work. It seems that every temp employee who worked on a computer had been told about the need to get a new security card, but since I don't use a computer to proofread, I was never notified.

It turned into a funny adventure once I found out what was going on. But for that one moment, when I wondered if this was someone's odd way of firing me, it wasn't amusing at all. Fortunately, I work for a very kind boss, whom I could not imagine doing such a thing. Usually she keeps me up on all the important details, and it was probably just the shock of the situation that made me even think that way. As it turned out, it wasn't her fault.

Do you have a temporary worker in your office? If it's someone new to the job, recognize that feeling a little confused is part of the job description. Even temps who have worked a long time may occasionally feel that way. Be kind to your fellow workers and share some office news, important information, or just a cheerful hello!

Lord, help me treat my coworkers with kindness,
especially those who aren't always here.

But ye, brethren, be not weary in well doing.
2 THESSALONIANS 3:13

Christmas is coming up, with its parties and other enter-tainments. This is the season when the church really shines with all kinds of concerts, services, and special events. Chil-dren have special programs in school and church. Life be-comes incredibly busy.

With all those excitements going on, it can become hard to concentrate on work, especially if the labor you're doing isn't all that interesting. It would be easy to relax, take it easy, and forget to make the most of your work hours. Some may also feel tempted to do their online shopping on office hours, to take the pressure off home life.

But acting that way would go against all the truths of the Scriptures. Christmas isn't a time to take advantage of the boss, because that attitude would bring God no glory in His most glorious season. Giving non-Christians a reason to call Christians nasty names is not part of the season jollies.

So while you're shopping, going to parties, and so on, keep up the good work. Don't be weary of also doing all the good you can from nine to five.

Lord, keep me faithful in doing my work because it, too,
shows the truth about Your Son's birth.

Behold, I shew you a mystery;
We shall not all sleep, but we shall all be changed.

1 CORINTHIANS 15:51

Even the best love relationships contain mysteries—things you don't know or simply can't understand about the beloved. One of my current mysteries with my husband is why he always turns his socks inside out when he takes them off. I wash them and turn them right side out, but I wonder: If I left them the wrong way, would he turn them right side out when he removed them? Would he always have it right at least half the time?

If I asked my husband, I could clear up this simple mystery. But both of us also have some deeply mysterious parts to us—habits and attitudes we don't even understand about ourselves and can hardly explain to each other.

Similarly, our love relationship with God has mysteries. He makes decisions we cannot understand. To love Him, we don't have to comprehend all His actions; but we must trust Him, even more than we trust our mates.

Whether, like this verse, the Bible speaks of our mysterious rapture to heaven or a more mundane passage tells us how to act on earth, we need to trust the One who gave it to us. Remember, too, that if there were no mystery to our relationship with God, He would be even smaller than a human.

Thank You, Lord, that I can trust You
even when I don't understand You.

But let all who take refuge in you be glad;
let them ever sing for joy.
Spread your protection over them,
that those who love your name may rejoice in you.

PSALM 5:11 NIV

When I knocked several boxes off the table, I learned all over again why I wrap my Christmas ornaments in layers of paper. Stunned, in slow motion I watched the cartons head for the floor, but I could do nothing until they'd fallen.

When I picked up the cartons and carefully unwrapped a few ornaments, I felt as if I'd been given a gift. One object was broken again, along the same line it had broken before. A little glue fixed the problem. Most of the rest of the decorations came through the fall fine because they'd been well packaged.

Spiritually, we can also have a lot of wrapping during the hard times. God offers those of us who love Him a profound protection. When the road of life gets bumpy, if we're walking close to Jesus, He helps us over them. Like the padding on my Christmas ornaments, our faith protects us from breaking when situations hurt deeply. Though we struggle just like others, we don't fall apart.

So in this joyous season, rejoice in God's protection. Take refuge in the One who keeps you whole.

Lord, thank You for Your protection that
makes me rejoice in You.

*"All your life you will sweat to produce food, until your dying day.
Then you will return to the ground from which you came.
For you were made from dust, and to the dust you will return."*

GENESIS 3:19 NLT

If Adam had known how hard work would become after he sinned, he might have thought twice about disobeying God. Pulling all those weeds and tilling hard soil took a lot more effort than caring for the garden had before the Fall.

Even if we don't have agricultural jobs, we can relate. Perhaps because sin infiltrated everything, all work became chores after Adam fell. Even when we enjoy the kind of work we do, we have days when we struggle to keep going. We may not have physical weeds to pull, but the weeds of discouragement, doubt, and irritation creep into our work environment. Tasks that should have been no big problem can become full-time irritants.

Are we destined only to be dust? Will our work fall to pieces when we leave our offices and head into eternity?

Work shows us the harshness of sin and the harm it causes even those forgiven in Christ. Though Christians return to dust, just like everyone else, we serve Jesus from 9:00 to 5:00, as well as from 5:01 to 8:59. Work may be hard, but it has results if we do it for Jesus. We're also earning that eternal reward.

*Lord, even when work's hard,
may it be a blessing from You.*

In every thing give thanks:
for this is the will of God in Christ Jesus concerning you.
1 THESSALONIANS 5:18

Busy days are best organized by God. Over and over, that truth becomes apparent when you offer up your day to God and suddenly the irritation is eased or a light appears at the end of the tunnel for that "insoluble" problem. By the end of the day, you've accomplished a lot.

But when the day works out because you've prayed briefly (though perhaps frequently), do you take the credit for yourself, thinking, *I'm glad I worked it all out,* or do you recognize why it worked out in the end and thank the One who smoothed the way for you?

Not thanking God is a terrible oversight—and one that may be terribly easy to do. Remembering to thank God in an impossible situation, as when a friend or loved one is so ill the doctors can't help, isn't hard. We recognize our limitations and quickly thank Him when we hear the good news of healing. But a heart that's open to Him and seeks to serve Him day by day gradually recognizes His hand in everything, even the small things He encouraged us to have a part in.

So when your day goes better than expected, thank Him. He's always glad to hear words from a grateful heart.

Lord, thank You for making every day a better one.
Just knowing You eases my entire life.

She watches for bargains;
her lights burn late into the night.
PROVERBS 31:18 NLT

The woman in Proverbs 31 could be so easy to dislike. She's so perfect, it's hard to imagine being anything like her—at least it is about two weeks before Christmas, when there's so much to be done for the holiday. On top of that, the pace at the office is at its fastest.

As you read this description, you may realize you'll be blessed if you finish all your shopping on time, much less find bargains on everything! Is this Proverbs 31 woman too good to be real?

Don't resent her or her phenomenal organizational ability. This woman's an example—maybe one you won't live up to every day, especially at Christmastime—but she focuses every woman on the important household issues that need to be addressed.

The Bible doesn't say she did everything in one day. She only had twenty-four hours in a day, too. You don't have to do everything today, either—there are two weeks more until Christmas. Just make a plan that will get you ready by December 24 or even early on December 25, and others may see you as being as organized as she was.

Lord, help me plan out my time so that
I can share a blessed holiday with others.

Two are better than one,
because they have a good reward for their labor.
ECCLESIASTES 4:9 NKJV

Overwhelmed with seasonal work? Then take this biblical advice and get some help. It might seem incredibly obvious, but two people work faster than one.

Working together as a team may be something of a challenge. First you have to decide how to break up the work. You may be able to take a stack of papers and split them. "You do this, I'll do the other pile." That makes life easy. But a more complex job means you have to decide who does what and how to make decisions in both parts that will even out in the end. Communication suddenly becomes very important.

But God's all in favor of people working together. When their differences challenge them, they can learn to love each other in new ways. Deciding how to break up work and who's responsible for what makes two people move in the same direction. A shared job also has a shared goal and shared benefits. Both workers get to look forward to the same reward. If both do well, both get credit. If one does badly, both suffer. But according to God, two are still better than one.

Lord, help me work well with others
when I have to share a job.
Let my work improve both our reputations.

And it came to pass, that in the morning, behold, it was Leah:
and he said to Laban,
What is this thou hast done unto me?
did not I serve with thee for Rachel?
wherefore then hast thou beguiled me?
GENESIS 29:25

Jacob loved Rachel; but the morning after his wedding night, he discovered his father-in-law had given him her sister, Leah, as his wife instead of the beloved Rachel. No wonder he was angry: He'd served Laban for seven years in order to gain the right to marry his younger daughter. Replacing her with her sister just wasn't right.

So beguiling Laban made a deal with his son-in-law: Serve me another seven years, and I'll give you Rachel, too. Seemed to solve all the problems, right?

Not really. The sisters began a competition that destroyed their family and made their children vie for position, too.

You can't help but wonder how different things would have been if Jacob had looked to God, not Laban, for a solution. Yes, he'd been conned, but God could have brought justice. He asks people to look to Him in just this kind of tight spot.

Has someone done you wrong? Don't use Jacob as your example. Turn to God instead, and look for the solution He has prepared.

Lord, when someone does me wrong,
I want to turn to You, not wrong choices.

And I saw the dead, small and great, standing before God,
and books were opened.
And another book was opened, which is the Book of Life.
And the dead were judged according to their works,
by the things which were written in the books.

REVELATION 20:12 NKJV

One day all our works will have a final outcome whether or not we believe in Jesus. Imagine standing before everyone and having God tell you whether you got a passing grade or failed entirely, based on your entire life.

Maybe this is the passage that gave some folks the idea that all they have to do is have more good deeds than bad ones, and they'll be able to slide into heaven. But that's not what this means. In a number of places, Scripture talks about the Book of Life, where believers' names are inscribed. There's no grading on the curve, tallying up points, or good time off for good behavior. Those who accepted Jesus in this life will enter heaven, and those who never did that work will go to hell, based on their own actions.

Have you done the one work that will save? If not, tell Jesus you know you've sinned, are sorry, and need His help, and He'll come in and remake everything. In a second, your name will appear in that book, and you'll be with Him forever.

Lord, I want to spend eternity with You.
Take my life and make it good in You.

These people are grumblers and complainers,
doing whatever evil they feel like.
They are loudmouthed braggarts,
and they flatter others to get favors in return.
JUDE 16 NLT

As you near Christmastime, you may go to a service at a friend or relative's church. Dropped down in the middle of a congregation, you may wonder about this place. Does it teach the right things? Can you listen to the pastor and receive God's Word or a confusing substitute?

Jude warned some young Christians to take a look at the actions of teachers as well as their sermons. People came in to lead a congregation, but their mouths gave them away as false teachers. Every time they talked, they got themselves into trouble by grumbling and complaining, bragging about themselves and flattering influential people. They just didn't talk like mature Christians.

So listen carefully to what's said in the pulpit, but also listen after the end of the service and watch a leader's actions. That could help you decide if you really want to follow this leader's sermon advice.

Lord, help me hear a leader's words and see his actions, too.
I only want to follow those who love You.

The voice of one crying in the wilderness:
"Prepare the way of the LORD;
make straight in the desert a highway for our God."
ISAIAH 40:3 NKJV

The Lord is coming! Are you ready?

So many people in first-century Israel weren't ready for Jesus when He came to Bethlehem, though the Scriptures prophesied His coming. Their hearts were off somewhere else, not expecting their King. Though they'd heard of Him, they were not standing by to greet Him.

Today, Jesus' first coming is crystal clear—it's history. The long trip Joseph and Mary made, the tiny baby in the manger, the kings and shepherds are all familiar to us, perhaps too familiar. Though we accept it as true, it may not seem to mean much to us today, in the twenty-first century.

Have we forgotten that Christmas only celebrates Jesus' first coming? Like the first-century Israelites, we, too, are waiting. The King is coming again, and He has given us the signs to look for. Many have already come to pass. Is the road to our hearts ready to receive Him?

If our hearts are ready to celebrate Jesus' first coming, they should be prepared for His second coming, too. If not, we must offer every bump in our spiritual road to Him today. Jesus deserves a smooth path into our hearts.

Jesus, I'm glad you came to Bethlehem.
Make my heart ready for You to come to earth again.

"All the earth shall worship You and sing praises to You;
they shall sing praises to Your name."
Come and see the works of God;
He is awesome in His doing toward the sons of men.

PSALM 66:4–5 NKJV

You're working to please God, but did you know He's also been working for you? He gave you a beautiful world to live in, friends and family to love, and many other blessings. He also used His power to save you; He's freed you from sin and rules over your life.

But He didn't stop there. Every day, when you get up, you can count on God's protection, guidance, and the work of His Spirit to make you increasingly like His Son. He's doing a great work in you as well as working for you. Hasn't your life been changed from top to bottom? You're a new creature entirely. And He continues to work on you every day of your life, making you better and better.

When the psalmist thought of all God had done for him, he became so impressed that he just had to start praising his Lord.

Is praise rising to your lips, too?

I praise You, Lord,
for all the work You've done for me and in me.

And I will say to my soul, Soul,
thou hast much goods laid up for many years;
take thine ease, eat, drink, and be merry.
But God said unto him,
Thou fool, this night thy soul shall be required of thee.
LUKE 12:19–20

It's that party season—office parties, family celebrations, and all other kinds of get-togethers. And you're likely to hear all kinds of philosophies about life. Sooner or later, someone may even tell you to "eat, drink, and be merry." But they probably won't quote the verse next to it. People who follow this idea don't want to consider the state of their souls.

Enjoy your parties—eat (but don't overeat), drink (you know what you should and shouldn't have), and have some fun. But remember not to do anything you wouldn't do if Jesus were standing right next to you. That way, the next day you won't feel you need to avoid God because of all the wrong you've done.

And while you're enjoying all the blessings of life in food, drink, and good friends, you might want to think about how you could help someone who lacks some of these. Is this the time to support a child in a Third World country, help out at a local soup kitchen, or visit someone in a nursing home? As we're heading into this season of cheer, why not spread some?

Lord, help me not to think
only of my own pleasures this Christmas.

Unless the LORD builds a house,
the work of the builders is useless.
PSALM 127:1 NLT

We've all worked really hard and felt as if we were getting nowhere. Not every labor turns out well, even if we're committed to the job and do our best. Sometimes it's simply a matter of things that don't fit together because someone else on the job hasn't pulled his or her weight.

But at other times, we've started building a house without checking our ideas with the Master Architect. He would have told us we weren't using the right building materials, were planning on building in the wrong location, or should scrap the project before we started, but we never asked. So we spend all that money and effort, only to find ourselves in trouble.

If we want to build strong houses in every area of our lives, we need to check in regularly with God about both our spiritual and "secular" houses, because we can't separate one from the other. Really, for a Christian, nothing is secular. It's all committed to our Lord. If our whole lives are entrusted to Him, we won't "forget" to ask His help, whatever we're building.

Lord, remind me to check with You
before I build anything into my life.

He is the Rock; his work is perfect.
Everything he does is just and fair.
He is a faithful God who does no wrong;
how just and upright he is!
DEUTERONOMY 32:4 NLT

Did you learn your job from someone who was really skilled at it? Maybe it was challenging at first to see how easily your mentor could do things you struggled through. But after awhile, you gained skill and it became second nature to do the work. Though you may still have hard days, you've developed competence.

No matter how effective we become at our jobs, few of us would claim we're perfect at them (and those who do claim it should probably be reading a devotion on lying today). But there is One who never makes a mistake in His work, always treats everyone fairly, and faithfully never does wrong.

Before you start feeling threatened, recognize that He's working for you and in you, to make you like Him. He's not condemning your work, but coming alongside you to help you do better.

Believers in Jesus are standing on this perfect Rock. What better foundation could there be?

Lord, I want to become more like You,
on the job and off.
Please bless my work.

And she spake out with a loud voice, and said,
Blessed art thou among women, and blessed is the fruit of thy womb.
And whence is this to me, that the mother of my Lord
should come to me?

LUKE 1:42–43

How tuned in to God Elizabeth must have been. No sooner did Mary step foot over her doorstep than Elizabeth spoke these words. Immediately she knew God had done something wonderful in Mary's life. What comfort Mary must have found in the fact that someone comprehended her unusual situation. Cousin Elizabeth would not accuse or condemn her. Instead, she understood just what happened without Mary's saying a word. God gave His Son's mother a nearby wise heart and sympathetic ear just when she needed them most.

Like Elizabeth, we can tune in to God's truths. He may want to show us something we need to recognize about ourselves, a truth we need to learn about Him, or a fact we need to share with a non-Christian or new believer. And we can use those as blessings to ourselves and others. But we won't hear any of them unless, like Elizabeth, we're listening very carefully.

Are your ears open today?

Lord, keep my ears listening keenly for Your truths.
I want Your wisdom and encouragement
to flow from my life.

*Then Joseph being raised from sleep
did as the angel of the Lord had bidden him,
and took unto him his wife.*

MATTHEW 1:24

Joseph had just had the most amazing dream. Before he fell asleep, he'd been thinking about quietly divorcing Mary because she was carrying another man's child. But in his dreams, an angel came to the carpenter and told him this child didn't belong to a man, but to God. What a shock that must have been! Perhaps for a moment Joseph wondered if it was all his imagination, but he went ahead and obeyed the message from God and married Mary anyway.

They weren't married when Joseph got the news, but in first-century Israel, a betrothal was just as binding as a marriage and required a divorce. The legal action would have brought shame on Mary, even though she'd done no wrong. But because she was engaged to a godly man who could hear a strange message and trust it was from God, none of that happened to her.

God gives us some strange messages in His Word, too. His commandments don't agree with the popular views around us, and when we obey them, we often look odd. Are we willing to follow in Joseph's footsteps and stand out for Him? If we do, we might be caught in a moment of obedience, just like Jesus' earthly father.

*Lord, I want to obey You even when I don't understand.
Help me be faithful like Joseph.*

"At the end of every third year bring the tithe of all your crops
and store it in the nearest town. . . .
Then the LORD your God will bless you in all your work."
DEUTERONOMY 14:28–29 NLT

Did you know God's blessing on your work doesn't only depend on what you do during the week from nine to five? The money you place in the offering plate on Sunday may have an impact on how He blesses you the rest of the week.

If you thought you could separate your church giving from the rest of your life, think again. God doesn't say that. The way you treat Him on Sunday carries over to the rest of the week. Shortchange Him on the weekend, and He won't bypass it on a Monday. After all, if you stole from a friend on Sunday, you wouldn't expect him to welcome you with open arms on Monday, would you? When you steal from God by withholding from the offering plate, He still feels the pain on Monday morning.

Give generously to God's work—He says at least a tenth is His—and you can expect all your work to be blessed. That's a benefit you couldn't receive from this world, even if you gave every penny of your income and everything else you own.

Lord, I give control of my money to You.
Show me how to give it to Your glory.

> *"If you then, being evil,*
> *know how to give good gifts to your children,*
> *how much more will your Father who is in heaven*
> *give good things to those who ask Him!"*
>
> MATTHEW 7:11 NKJV

Is the gift you'd most like for Christmas a new job or a promotion? Maybe that's something you'd like deep down inside but feel afraid to go for.

Have you asked God if this is His will for you? Have you shown your willingness to take on new tasks and perform well on the job? Or is it just all wishful thinking?

God likes to give good gifts to His children, but He won't give them to children who would make bad use of them. Just as you wouldn't give a breakable object to a toddler who might hurt herself with it, God won't give you a job that would lead to the destruction of your career.

But if you've performed well on the job and you'd like a new job or promotion, do what you need to do. Make up a résumé or put your name in for a job that's been posted, but first make sure you also speak to God about it. He may just have been waiting for you to ask.

Lord, I know You give good gifts, and I'd like some,
but I only want the ones You say would be good for me.

Looking for that blessed hope,
and the glorious appearing of the great God
and our Saviour Jesus Christ.

TITUS 2:13

If you have young children, they've probably been ready for Christmas for weeks. All that time, you've heard what they'd like to have on the special day. Even people whose faith is only nominal can become excited by the expectation in these young hearts.

As adults, our expectation has cooled a bit, though we still may enjoy buying and receiving presents. We look at things differently from a child who can dream so big because nothing seems impossible.

But there's still one event we can expect with all a child's excitement—the second coming of Jesus. It's a big event, larger even than Jesus' first, quiet coming. Suddenly, He will appear so that the entire world, even unbelievers, will see and be unable to deny Him.

Like children eyeing a Christmas tree, we can get excited at the idea of Jesus' return. On that day, we'll be swept away from a sinful world and into eternity. What other gift could we desire?

When I think of Your second coming,
I get as excited as a child.
I want to meet You face-to-face, Lord.

For in Him all the fullness of Deity dwells in bodily form.
COLOSSIANS 2:9 NASB

"Very God of Very God" is the way the Nicene Creed expresses this description of Jesus' divine nature. But whether it's spoken of in a creed or Scripture, this concept of one person being both God and man goes way beyond our understanding. Hard as we try, we always seem to see either His human or His divine side. Putting them together is incredibly difficult.

God understood how hard it is for humans to understand Him. For centuries He'd communicated through the prophets, yet humanity didn't quite understand. So He sent His Son to graphically represent everything He wanted people to know.

Yet we can still be confused. When it comes down to it, we have to admit that God is so much larger than we, and only by His mercy can we begin to connect. But that's just why God sent a baby boy to earth—to touch us, fingertip to fingertip, and begin to give us an inkling of the fullness of the divine mercy.

It all started with one baby boy, but it will end when we see Him again in eternal heavenly glory.

Thank You, Jesus,
for coming to earth and communicating Your love.
Thank You for touching my life.

He is the kind of high priest we need because
he is holy and blameless, unstained by sin.
He has now been set apart from sinners,
and he has been given the highest place of honor in heaven.

HEBREWS 7:26 NLT

Jesus, who is "Very God of Very God," is so different from us. No wonder we find Him hard to understand.

The writer to the Hebrews describes our Lord as being set apart from us. In fact, this verse says, it's a good thing He is. That's so because we could never save ourselves. We need Someone bigger than ourselves to release us from our sin predicament. These words that describe Jesus, "holy" and "blameless" and "unstained by sin," don't describe the human race. They only describe what we'd like to be but can never become under our own steam.

But when we accept Jesus, He starts to describe us with those words. At first we're embarrassed. "Who, me?" we ask, recognizing our own weakness. But as we grow in Christ, we start seeing changes. We become set apart, different, horrified by sin—our own and others'.

As that happens, we're becoming more like the One who came to earth to save us, and that's what He'd intended all along.

Mission accomplished, Jesus!

Thank You, Jesus,
for being all the things I couldn't be
and bringing me to share some of Your nature.

Come unto me, all ye that labour and are heavy laden,
and I will give you rest.
MATTHEW 11:28

Christmas is over, the gift wrap is tossed out or put away. We're in the lull between Christmas and New Year's. It's a brief rest between two holidays, yet life can remain busy.

What holiday is this we just celebrated? Could it be the birth of the One who gave us today's message? Where is the "rest" in Christmas? Certainly not in the gift buying or returning, in the special services and all the extra work they entail. It's not in the entertaining or family dinners.

Our lives may have been blessed by all these things. We've enjoyed family time, chats with other church members, we may even have enjoyed shopping—especially if we did it online and didn't have to fight the crowds. But when we've done so much, we look forward to a time of rest.

The only place we'll really find rest is in Jesus. This could be a good day to take time, grab a Bible, and settle down to serious prayer and Bible reading. Get together with the One whose season you're celebrating, and the world will begin to relax.

Lord, I need Your rest.
Let's spend time together now.

After the wise men were gone,
an angel of the Lord appeared to Joseph in a dream.
"Get up and flee to Egypt with the child
and his mother," the angel said.
"Stay there until I tell you to return,
because Herod is going to try to kill the child."
That night Joseph left for Egypt with
the child and Mary, his mother.

MATTHEW 2:13–14 NLT

Perhaps because the message was so stark, God didn't have to tell Joseph twice. It was time to get Jesus out of Israel, to safety in Egypt, where no one would know the holy family. Immediately the couple gathered their things and headed out.

But if you've looked at the few images we have of Joseph in Scripture, you're probably not surprised he'd act that way. Joseph receives some amazing messages, yet he never stops to question them, goes for another opinion, or does anything but obey immediately. What God said, Joseph wanted to do.

As the New Year is approaching, can you say you obey with Joseph-like swiftness, or have you been doubting, questioning, and putting off something you know God wants? Maybe it's time to read over the story of Joseph and learn from him. Then saddle your donkey and start down the road God pointed out.

Lord, I don't want You to have to tell me twice.
I want to instantly obey Your every command.

Blessed are the peacemakers:
for they shall be called the children of God.
MATTHEW 5:9

In this season of peace, are you suddenly caught in a less than peaceful place between two coworkers? Though the holiday can bring out the best in people, the stress that comes with it can also bring out the worst. As a Christian, you want to live in peace, and you want those around you to be happy, too, as much as possible. Is there a solution?

Getting in between two coworkers is a dangerous thing. Both sides may end up hating you. But God does say that people who make peace will be blessed, so how do you sensibly handle the situation?

First, try not to get caught in the middle. Advise both parties, if you can, giving them tools to create a solution. But don't make a choice for them or force anything on them. That's a good way to open the door to more trouble.

Don't take sides in the disagreement, or your peace treaty is sure to fail. Present ideas in as unbiased a way as possible and create an atmosphere of give and take that can foster peace.

And most of all, pray. Peacemakers are God's children who seek to bring spiritual peace wherever they can. His peace is the only kind that lasts, in hearts and companies.

Lord, help me bring peace,
whether it's to a coworker or the world.

Thou shalt guide me with thy counsel,
and afterward receive me to glory.
PSALM 73:24

The New Year may have a lot of changes. How will you make decisions, and where will you look for guidance when a choice is beyond your own knowledge? Plenty of folks out there are willing to offer you "wisdom"—some for free and others at a price.

Sometimes the free advice is worth just what it cost; other times, it's incredibly valuable. But when you need real expert advice, it might be wise to pay for someone's expertise.

In the end, no matter who advises you, you'll need to make your own choices and take the responsibility for them. So how do you know who to listen to or what to do? Maybe you've had more than one opinion, and you need to choose between them.

You have another source of counsel—God. You may wonder if you should hire a staff member or someone to work in your home. How can you know whom to choose? Turn to the One who knows hearts and minds. He'll never misdirect you.

Lord, in all I do I need Your guidance.
Show me the way You want me to walk.

Truly God is good to Israel,
to those whose hearts are pure.
PSALM 73:1 NLT

What would make a good year for you? A new job? A huge raise? Good health?

The psalmist Asaph had been living for God, doing what was right, when he noticed that those who did wrong and ignored God had it better than he did. Why, Asaph wondered, did they have prosperity and health while the faithful often struggled? Wouldn't it be better to be wicked and wealthy and healthy?

Then Asaph visited the temple and was reminded where all that wealth and health would lead—straight to hell, unless they recognized the God who had given it all. Suddenly the psalmist recognized that even if he never had a large house or extra cash, his life would be better than the wealthy wicked man's. Better to live near God for eternity, Asaph said, than to own all the goods he could use in this life and have to give up God.

What would really make a good year? A year in which God is good to you. Make your heart pure by obeying Him each day, and you can count on having all the good you need.

Lord, I want to be pure before You.
If I do what You say is good,
I know I can't help but be blessed.

Scripture Index

Inspirational Library

Beautiful purse/pocket-size editions of Christian classics bound in flexible leatherette. These books make thoughtful gifts for everyone on your list, including yourself!

When I'm on My Knees　　　The highly popular collection of devotional thoughts on prayer, especially for women.
　　Flexible Leatherette. $4.97

The Bible Promise Book　　　Over 1,000 promises from God's Word arranged by topic. What does God promise about matters like: Anger, Illness, Jealousy, Love, Money, Old Age, and Mercy? Find out in this book!
　　Flexible Leatherette. $3.97

Daily Wisdom for Women　　　A daily devotional for women seeking biblical wisdom to apply to their lives. Scripture taken from the New American Standard Version of the Bible.
　　Flexible Leatherette. $5.97

A Gentle Spirit　　　With an emphasis on personal spiritual development, this daily devotional for women draws from the best writings of Christian female authors.
　　Flexible Leatherette. $5.97

Available wherever books are sold.
Or order from:

Barbour Publishing, Inc.
P.O. Box 719
Uhrichsville, OH 44683
www.barbourbooks.com

If you order by mail, add $2.00 to your order for shipping.
Prices are subject to change without notice.

Published by Barbour Publishing, Inc., P.O. Box 719, Uhrichsville, Ohio 44683, www.barbourbooks.com

Our mission is to publish and distribute inspirational products offering exceptional value and biblical encouragement to the masses.

Member of the
Evangelical Christian
Publishers Association

Printed in the United States of America.

DAILY WISDOM
FOR THE
WORKPLACE

Practical On-the-Job Insight
from Scripture

PAMELA MCQUADE

BARBOUR
PUBLISHING